The Younger Speaker

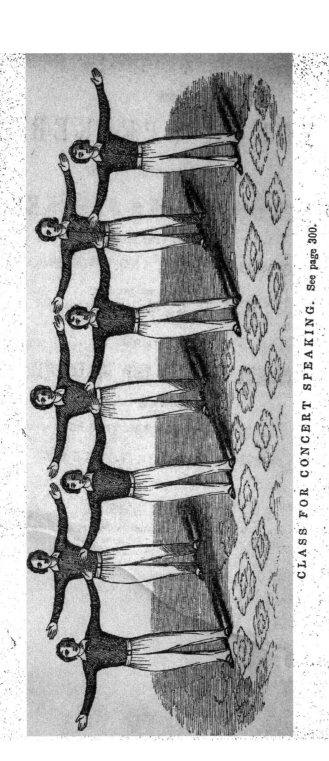

CLASS FOR CONCERT SPEAKING. See page 300.

THE

YOUNG SPEAKER:

AN INTRODUCTION TO THE

UNITED STATES SPEAKER;

DESIGNED TO FURNISH EXERCISES

IN BOTH READING AND SPEAKING,

FOR PUPILS BETWEEN THE AGES

OF SIX AND FOURTEEN;

COMPRISING SELECTIONS IN

PROSE, POETRY, AND DIALOGUE,

AND A VARIETY OF FIGURES

ILLUSTRATING PRINCIPLES OF

POSITION AND GESTURE.

BY JOHN E. LOVELL,

FORMERLY INSTRUCTOR OF ELOCUTION IN THE MOUNT PLEASANT
CLASSICAL INSTITUTION, AMHERST, MASS.; AND AUTHOR
OF THE U. S. SPEAKER, RHETORICAL DIALOGUES,
THE YOUNG PUPIL'S FIRST BOOK, AND YOUNG
PUPIL'S SECOND BOOK, IN READING.

NEW HAVEN:
PUBLISHED BY DURRIE & PECK.

1845.

Printed by J. H. BENHAM,
New Haven, Conn,

PREFACE.

THIS little work has been prepared for young students. It is divided into *five parts.*

PART FIRST is designed to accomplish these objects: 1. To guard the pupil against errors in Pronunciation, which occur, not unfrequently, in the conversation and reading of persons respectably educated. 2. To make him acquainted with the *names* and *uses* of the grammatical and rhetorical Pauses. 3. To teach him the nature of Inflection, and the application of the *simple slides* to the most obvious and useful cases. 4. To acquaint him with the nature and importance of Emphasis. 5. To instruct him as to the management of the Voice, and its adaptation to different kinds of composition. These lessons are brief and simple, so that few pupils who have reached their *tenth* year will find it difficult either to understand or apply them, while some even under that age may, it is believed, study them with advantage.

PART SECOND comprises a set of lessons intended *exclusively* for Reading. They are of an instructive and interesting character; well suited to cultivate a correct and graceful style of Elocution, and at the same time to improve the heart and enlighten the mind. Being chiefly in *prose*, they will, with the lessons in *part fourth*, balance any excess of *poetry* which may appear in the selections arranged for Recitation.

PART THIRD. This division of the book constitutes its chief distinctive feature. The lessons consist of *short* and *interesting* extracts in *prose* and *poetry*. They are designed as *single pieces* for Recitation. Not one of the whole number—*more than one hundred and fifty*—has been adopted without a careful examination as to its *fitness* for this object. The mere *brevity* of these selections gives them great value as exercises for beginners. The teacher who has been much engaged in instructing young persons to speak, will appreciate them for this peculiarity alone. But they possess other characteristics which entitle them to favor. They are, for the most part, on *subjects* interesting

1*

to the youthful mind, and expressed in *language*, plain, beautiful and
easily understood. They are such, withal, as seem to prompt a necessary and *natural* style of gesticulation. They have elicited a
preference, in this respect, from among hundreds of other excellent
pieces. It is in Gesture, that school-boys generally cut such a sorry
figure. There is no propriety, no meaning, no elegance in their un-
tutored action. It is almost uniformly a senseless, awkward, motonous
"sawing of the air."

With a desire to promote improvement, therefore, in this beautiful
and important branch of the art of Speaking, a number of Figures,
each exhibiting some appropriate gesture, have been introduced into
this division of the Young Speaker. Each is applied to a particular
passage and accompanied with an explanation. Next to the example
of an accomplished instructor—who is not often to be obtained, for
this subject has been most singularly neglected—no doubt, good *pictures* are the best medium of instruction. The idea is, that the pupil
will be benefited thus ;—the gestures presented in these pictures will
be impressed upon his imagination, and that he will address them to
other similar passages, as occasion shall require, and ability direct.
The plan is at least *original*; how far it shall prove *serviceable*, must
depend upon the fairness of experiment, and the intelligent judgment
of others.

PART FOURTH comprises a set of Reading lessons in *prose*, corresponding to those of *part third* ; differing only in the advanced
style of the composition.

PART FIFTH consists of Dialogues, with a few pieces arranged in
that form, for *alternate* Speaking. They are, chiefly, *short, interesting*,
and of a *juvenile* character. Teachers will please to *keep in mind*,
that these lessons and those of *part third*, though selected with special
reference to Recitation, are equally well adapted to the cultivation of
a spirited, correct, and manly style of Reading.

The work has been prepared for the use of a very interesting class
of students, and with the hope, that it may inspire many a young mind
with the love of moral and intellectual excellence, it is submitted to
a candid public.

                                                    J. E. L.

NEW HAVEN, Nov. 5, 1844.

CONTENTS.

PART FIRST.

DIRECTIONS FOR READING.

PART SECOND.

LESSONS EXCLUSIVELY FOR READING.

PART THIRD

LESSONS FOR SPEAKING OR READING.

CONTENTS.

x   CONTENTS.

CONTENTS. xi

PART FOURTH.

LESSONS EXCLUSIVELY FOR READING.

CONTENTS.

PART FIFTH.

DIALOGUES FOR SPEAKING OR READING.

THE

YOUNG SPEAKER.

PART FIRST.

DIRECTIONS FOR READING.

NOTE. TEACHERS may, perhaps, think it sufficient to require their younger pupils to *read* to them, occasionally, the lessons of this part; but the older ones would, no doubt, find it profitable to *commit to memory* those on Pause, Inflection, and Emphasis.

LESSON I.

PRONUNCIATION.

1. GIVE to every letter its proper sound.

2. In particular give a full sound to the vowels *a, e, i, o, u.*

3. Be careful not to drop the *g,* in words ending in *ing;* if you drop that letter, you will be found saying *mornin* for *morning; puddin* for *pudding; flyin* for *flying,* and the like. This is a very common fault.

4. Another fault equally common is to sound *ow,* like *ur:* thus many say *windur* instead of *window; pillur* instead of *pillow; feller* instead of *fellow,* and so on.

5. It is likewise very incorrect to give the sound of *r* at the end of words where the letter itself is not found. Some persons say *sawr* for *saw; lawr* for *law; idear* for *idea,* and thus in other words of the same class.

6. There are other words in which the sound of *r* is as improperly changed; thus we often hear *waw* for *war; stah* for *star; haus* for *horse,* and so on.

2

7. Do not omit to sound any letter which should be sounded. In this way injury is often done to such words as *every, several, vessel, memory,* and numerous others ; being improperly pronounced *ev'ry, sev'ral, vess'l, mem'ry,* and so forth.

8. Do not drop the *d* in the word *and,* nor say *git* for *get; yit* for *yet; fust* for *first; bust* for *burst; bile* for *boil; hoss* for *horse; idee* for *idea; ile* for *oil; jest* for *just; jine* for *join; ketch* for *catch; kittle* for *kettle; line* for *loin; pint* for *point; sich* for *such; yunder* for *yonder; shet* for *shut; fur* for *far; ben* for *been,* pronounced *bin; doos* for *does,* pronounced *duz; agin* for *again,* pronounced *agen; ware* for *were,* pronounced *wur,* and the like. Of many frequent faults in pronunciation, those mentioned above are some of the least excusable, and I hope all my young readers and speakers will be careful to avoid them.

LESSON II.

PAUSE.

1. PAY particular attention to the grammatical stops and other pauses. No person can read well without observing this rule.

2. At the *comma* printed thus **,** you may stop till you can pronounce *one.*

3. At the *semicolon* printed thus **;** you may stop till you can pronounce *one two.*

4. At the *colon* printed thus **:** you may stop till you can pronounce *one two three.*

5. At the *period* printed thus **.** you may stop till you can pronounce *one two three four.*

6. At the *interrogation* printed thus **?** and at the *exclamation* printed thus **!** you may stop about as long as at a *colon.*

7. The *parenthesis* printed thus **( )** requires a stop at its *beginning* and *end* about as long as at a *comma.*

8. At the *dash* printed thus **—** you should generally stop about as long as at a *semicolon,* and sometimes even as long as at a *period.* When it is added to either of the other stops, it increases the length of that stop.

9. The pause at the end of a *paragraph* should be longer than at the end of an ordinary sentence.

NOTE. The foregoing rules are as good, perhaps, as can be given: but the time occupied in pausing at each of the stops, will *sometimes* vary, no doubt, from that which has been directed. It must depend upon the nature of what is read.

10. It is frequently proper to pause where none of the grammatical stops are inserted: In the examples which follow, the *places* of pause will be marked by the *dash.* These are called *rhetorical* pauses.

11. After the *nominative case,* when it consists of more than one word, or of *one* important word, a pause is necessary ; thus

The price of improvement——is labor.
Washington——was a great and good man.

12. When *other words* come *between* the *nominative case* and the *verb,* they should be separated from *both* by a short pause ; thus

Trials——in this state of being——are the lot of man.
That course——if persevered in——will secure the prize.

13. Before the prepositions *in, of, with, from, to, beyond,* and the like, a short pause is often proper ; thus

Remember thy Creator——in the days——of thy youth.
We found him——with his faithful dog——in the wood.

14. Before the relatives *who, which, what,* and *that,* the adverb *how,* and *that* used as a conjunction, a short pause generally occurs ; thus

Honor thy father and thy mother——that thy days may be long upon the land——which the Lord——who is thy God, hath given thee.
Tell me——how did the accident happen.

15. The *infinitive mood* generally requires a short pause before it ; thus

He left the room——to see whether all was secured.
His highest enjoyment was——to relieve the distressed.

16. Words placed in *opposition* to each other should be distinguished by a short pause ; thus

Some——place the bliss in action, some——in ease ;
Those——call it pleasure, and contentment——these.

LESSON III.

INFLECTION.

1. If you will pronounce the following question with interest you will readily perceive that the voice slides upward in sounding the word rain: *Does it rain?* And in the answer *No*, you will as readily perceive that it slides downward. This is called *inflection.* Inflection is heard in the note of a bird when it seems to cry "*sweet.*"

2. Inflection then is that *sliding up* or *sliding down* of the voice which is heard in *finishing* the *pronunciation* of a word.

3. There are two simple inflections of the voice, the upward called the *rising* inflection, and the downward called the *falling* inflection.

4. The mark for the *rising* inflection is printed thus;

Does it ráin?

5. The mark for the *falling* inflection is printed thus;

Nò.

6. Other examples.

Was he obédient, or disobèdient?

He was obèdient, not disobédient.

Did he act polítely, or impolìtely?

He acted polìtely, not impolítely.

Was he treated kíndly, or unkìndly?

He was treated kìndly, not unkíndly.

7. All questions may be divided into two kinds, called the *direct* and *indirect.*

8. The *direct* question is that which *can* be answered by *yes* or *no :* this question is read with the *rising* slide ; thus

Were you treated kíndly? We wère.

9. The *indirect* question is that which *cannot* be answered by *yes* or *no :* this question is read with the *falling* slide ; thus

Who treated you kìndly? Our teàcher.

10. The *answers* to all questions are read with the *falling* slide.

11. In *affirmative* sentences, at the semicolon, colon, and period, the *falling* slide generally occurs ; thus

God is in every place ; he speaks in every sound we hear; he is seen in all that our eyes behold.

12. At the *comma* before either of these stops, the rising slide commonly takes place ; thus

As for man, his days are as grass : as a flower of the field, so he flourisheth.

13. In *negative* sentences the thing *denied* generally takes the *rising* slide ; thus

I cannot help it ; the fault is not mine.

I can accept of no excuse for profanity and falsehood.

14. The following examples contain both *affirmation* and *negation ;* thus

I came to bury Cæsar, not to praise him.

You were paid to fight against Alexander, not to rail at him.

15. In affirmative sentences expressing *opposition,* the first part takes the *falling* slide, and the latter the *rising ;* thus

If we have no regard for our own character, we ought to have some regard for the character of others.

Write them together ; yours is as fair a name ;

Sound them ; it doth become the mouth as well.

16. Words denoting an *address*, generally take the *rising* slide ; thus

John, fetch me your new book.

Friends, Romans, countrymen, lend me your ears.

17. The language of *grief, pity, affection,* and the like, inclines the voice to the *rising* slide ; thus

And he said, God be gracious unto thee, my son.

2*

Poor youth! the cares of the world have come early upon him, observed the father.

18. At the *rhetorical pause*, the rising slide generally occurs; thus

Lancaster—was the friend of youth.

That boy's desire is—to succeed in his studies.

19. When the word *or* expresses *uncertainty*, it takes the *rising* slide before and the *falling* after it; thus

Was John a good or a bad boy?

It was either Thursday or Friday.

20. The language of *command, reproof, threat,* and the like, requires the *falling* slide; thus

Go; study; and deserve my good opinion.

His lord answered, and said unto him, thou wicked and slothful servant.

21. When a word is *repeated* with stress, it generally takes the *falling* slide; thus

John, John, bring me the prize composition.

It is unjust, I say it is unjust to treat him so.

22. The *exclamation*, in general, denotes the *falling* slide, except where much *feeling* is expressed, or when it implies a *question* or the repetition of one; thus

How blessed is that man who puts his trust in God!

A liar! oh, what a fault is that my children!

Will you forever Athenians, do nothing but walk up and down the city, asking one another, "what news?"—what news!

23. The *parenthesis* receives the same inflection at its *close* as that which immediately *precedes* it, whether rising or falling. It should also be read in a lower tone of voice, and somewhat quicker than the rest of the sentence; thus

Industry—(however good may be his talents)—will be necessary to complete success.

Then went the captain with the officers, and brought them without violence—(for they feared the people lest they should have been stoned)—and when they had brought them they set them before the council.

24. When several nouns, alone or connected with other words, *begin* a sentence and do *not end* it, each takes the *falling* slide except the *last;* thus

Dependence and obedience belong to youth.

The young, the healthy, and the prosperous, should not presume on their advantages.

25. When several nouns, alone or connected with other words, *end* a sentence, each takes the *rising* slide except the *last;* thus

The spirit of true religion breathes gentleness and affability.

Industry is the law of our being; it is the demand of nature, of reason, and of God.

LESSON IV.

EMPHASIS.

1. *Emphasis* is a certain stress of voice given to a particular word or words in a sentence to *bring out their meaning in the best manner.*

2. The words which receive the emphasis are generally in *opposition* to other words expressed or implied.

3. This sentence—*Shall you ride to town to-day ?*—will show the *nature* and *importance* of emphasis.

4. It is capable of being taken in *four different senses,* according as the emphasis is laid. The emphatic word is marked in *italics ;* thus

Shall *you* ride to town to-day?
Shall you *ride* to town to-day?
Shall you ride to *town* to-day?
Shall you ride to town *to-day ?*

5. Wherever there is inflection there is always *some degree* of emphasis, but the amount of it must depend upon the importance of the words upon which it occurs; thus

It was James not John who told the falsehood.

LESSON V.

THE VOICE.

1. EVERY person has three *pitches* in his voice, the *high*, the *middle*, and the *low* one.

2. The *high* is that which he uses in calling aloud to some person at a distance.

3. The *low* is that which he uses when he speaks almost in a whisper.

4. The *middle* is that which he employs in common discourse, and which he should use in *reading*.

5. The voice in reading should be the same as it would be in *speaking* on the same subject.

6. In order to be well heard, observe a due degree of slowness; pronounce every word and *syllable* distinctly; a *distinct* manner will do more than mere *loudness* of sound.

7. No person can read well if he read in a *hurry*.

8. Nor on the other hand must the words drop from the lips in a *faint* and *feeble* manner.

9. At the beginning of a paragraph, pitch the voice *low*, that it may be allowed gradually to *swell*; and increase rather than diminish the sound at the *end* of each period.

10. Let the voice be smooth and gentle, and not too noisy.

11. A round mellow voice is pleasing both in speaking and reading.

12. The voice in all cases should be made to *suit* the subject.

13. Whether it be serious, familiar, gay or humorous, the voice should at all times *correspond*.

14. It would be wrong to read a *familiar* piece in a *mournful* strain, or a *serious* one in a *gay* and *lively* manner.

15. In particular—the sublime language of the sacred *Scriptures* should be read with a *care* and *deliberation*, befitting their solemn dignity and importance, and not in the familiar style of common conversation.

16. Study to *understand* what you read, and you will probably read with taste and propriety.

THE YOUNG SPEAKER.

PART SECOND.

LESSONS EXCLUSIVELY FOR READING.

THIS Figure is intended to show the *younger* pupils the manner in which they may hold the book. It should be kept at a distance of from four to six inches from the breast, and in such a position that the *whole face* may always be seen. The little finger of each hand touches the edge of the back of the book *nearly*, while the other fingers are spread easily on the lids; the corners of the book rest between the lower parts of the thumb and fore finger, and the thumbs themselves touch the inside of the book at about the middle of the bottom of the page. The *older* pupils will find a better mode for holding *their* books described on the first page of Part Fourth.

LESSON I.

CLOUDS.—Anonymous.

How beautiful are the clouds at morn; they look like ruby gems set round with gold; and the lark mounts toward them, and sings as if he were at heaven's gate.

How bright are the clouds at mid-day, when high in the sky they hang, and show their pearly whiteness in the azure sky.

At sunset they again are beautiful, and in the far west they take all hues and forms. Sometimes they look like towers and castles, high thrones and lofty palaces, of topaz and of gold.

At night, when the moon shines on them, they look fair and white, and pure, and when all is hushed and still, seem like a flock of little lambs asleep.

Yet what are clouds but vapors? soon they pass away, soon they change: now they become dark with tempest; now they swell in storm; but then the bow of mercy is seen, and nature, in the midst of showers, is cheered.

Life is like a cloud, fleeting and changeable: to-day it is gay and bright, to-morrow it is dark and full of gloom; yet again the sun shines upon it, and it sinks to its rest in peace.

What gives to the clouds their brightness and their beauty? it is the sun that lights them, gilds them with his beams, and paints them with his smiles.

What gives to life its glory? it is the smile of Him who formed the clouds to water the earth with rain, and to refresh all plants and herbs.

It is He who gives to life's morning its bright joys; who in manhood's prime, exalts us and sustains; who in the storm and darkness, like the rainbow, smiles upon us; and who at even time, when death would draw his curtains round us, brightens the soul with hope.

LESSON II.

EARLY RISING.—Mechelen.

I beg you will accustom yourself to early rising, all your life time. This habit has many great advantages: in the first place, it is necessary for our health; and in the next place, it gives us more time for our occupations. One hour more employed in a day, makes a great deal of time at the end of a single year; it is snatched as it were from death. Yes, my children, think that sleep is a kind of death; and the time that we can deprive ourselves of it, is a time really acquired. You will understand this better by a supposition, which may afford you pleasure.

Let us suppose that Peter and Paul both died at the age of sixty. Peter has, however, found means to live a much longer time than Paul, and this is the method he pursued: Paul never rose till nine in the morning; Peter, on the contrary, was up every day at five. These two men went to bed every night at ten, therefore Peter's day was seventeen hours long, and Paul's was only thirteen; this made a difference of four hours in a day. Four hours in a day, make at the end of a year, fourteen hundred and sixty hours, which is a hundred and twelve days, at the rate of thirteen hours each, which was the length of the day Paul enjoyed. You clearly perceive, my children, this is nearly the third of a year more for Peter. But let us continue, and you will be surprised at the time Paul lost. At the end of sixty years, Peter had by his diligence, gained six thousand seven hundred and twenty days, which make eighteen years and eight months.

Observe that these eigtheen years and eight months, are taken from the time that Paul was increasing in years. I do not, in this calculation, comprehend the time which nature requires us to allot to sleep. In order to shake off the remains of a sleep likely to be troublesome, get up immediately. Reflect, and endeavor to appreciate the value of time, and I am certain you will never allow yourselves to lose much of a life so short.

LESSON III.

A DROP OF DEW —Anonymous.

Behold yon drop of crystal dew, which hangs pendent from a blade of grass. How it sparkles in the sun! it looks like a little star in the green mead.

"Whence comest thou, little diamond drop? and why comest thou? I have seen thee as a pure gem on buds and leaves, and flowers, making all bright and cheerful about thee.

"Sometimes thou liest like a deep fond tear, in the snow-drop's bell, and one would almost think the flowers did weep, were you not so bright and they so gay."

"I came from the sea, my child; from the place of pearls and shells, and gems; from dark rocks and whirling sands; from coral caves and diamond mines,—but I had no light from them.

"The sun called me from the deep sea, that I might rejoice in his light. I arose at his call, and leaving the salt and bitter ocean, became pure and clear; and then *he* threw his beams upon me to make me *bright*.

"I came not for my own good, but that I might do good to others. I moisten the blighted plant, and it springs up again. I restore the withered flower. I call the dying unto life.

"So hast thou been called from the dust, my child, by the God who made thee. So must thou rise to welcome His light and love. So must thou shed blessings and comfort around thee, sweet child.

Look at me again, do you not see that while I sparkle, the whole image of the sun is reflected in me.

"So beameth the spirit of God in thine own soul; so will his light illumine thy heart, and so will his image be reflected from thee, if thou art His child.

"So wilt thou give new life, and joy, and peace, to all around; comfort the stricken heart, brighten the darksome breast, and be a solace to those that droop and mourn."

LESSON IV.

DIVINE EXCELLENCE.—BARBAULD.

COME, and I will show you what is *beautiful*. It is a Rose fully blown. See how she sits upon her mossy stem, like the queen of all the flowers! Her leaves glow like fire; the air is filled with her sweet odor; she is the delight of every eye.

She is beautiful; but there is a *fairer* than she. He that made the rose is more beautiful than the rose: he is all lovely; he is the delight of angels and of men.

I will show you what is *strong*. The Lion is strong; when he raises himself up from his lair, when he shakes his mane, when the voice of his roaring is heard, the cattle of the field fly, and the wild beasts of the desert hide themselves, for he is very terrible.

The lion is strong; but he that made the lion is *stronger* than he. His anger is terrible; he could make us die in a moment, and no one could save us out of his hand.

I will show you what is *glorious*. The Sun is glorious. When he shines in the sky,—when he sits on his bright throne in the heavens, and looks abroad over all the earth, he is the most excellent and glorious creature the eye can behold.

The sun is glorious; but he that made the sun is *more glorious* than he. The eye beholds him not; for his brightness is more dazzling than we could bear. He sees in all dark places, by night as well as by day; and the light of his countenance is over all his works.

Who is this great Being, and what is his name?—The name of this great Being, is God. He made all things, but he is himself more excellent than all which he has made. They are beautiful, but He is *beauty;* they are strong, but He is *strength;* they are perfect, but He is *perfection*

LESSON V.

THE HUNDRED AND THIRD PSALM.—Bible.

Bless the Lord, O my soul! and all that is within me, bless his holy name. Bless the Lord, O my soul! and forget not all his benefits;—who forgiveth all thine iniquities; who healeth all thy diseases; who redeemeth thy life from destruction; who crowneth thee with loving kindness and tender mercies; who satisfieth thy mouth with good things, so that thy youth is renewed like the eagle's.

The Lord is merciful and gracious, slow to anger and plenteous in mercy. He will not always chide, neither will he keep his anger forever. He hath not dealt with us after our sins, nor rewarded us according our iniquities. For as the heaven is high above the earth, so great is his mercy toward them that fear him. As far as the east is from the west, so far hath he removed our transgressions from us. Like as a

3

father pitieth his children, so the Lord pitieth them that fear him; for he knoweth our frame, he remembereth that we are dust.

As for man, his days are as grass; as a flower of the field, so he flourisheth: for the wind passeth over it, and it is gone; and the place thereof shall know it no more. But the mercy of the Lord is from everlasting to everlasting upon them that fear him, and his righteousness unto children's children; to such as keep his covenant, and to those that remember his commandments to do them.

The Lord hath prepared his throne in the heavens; and his kingdom ruleth over all. Bless the Lord, ye his angels, that excel in strength, that do his commandments, hearkening unto the voice of his word. Bless the Lord, all his works, in all places of his dominion. Bless the Lord, O my soul!

LESSON VI.

THE COTTAGE ON FIRE.—Anonymous.

The flames spread rapidly,—they had nearly consumed the habitation, from which farmer Ashford had, however, removed every article of consequence; fortunately no lives were lost, and I was conversing with this good man, and listening to his grateful ejaculations on seeing his family safe, when the shouts of the surrounding laborers informed us, that a little cottage, adjacent to the farm, had taken fire.

I ran towards the spot.—I saw the flames bursting from the casements.—Poor Randal, the laborer, who inhabited it, rushed forward; he had borne his wife, and his boys through the flames, when a rafter, having fallen upon his arm, disabled him; his wife, the image of despair, clasped her children to her bosom. Her husband watched the progress of the flames in stupid horror, then suddenly he started, and exclaimed, "My mother!" "My grandmother!" cried a fine boy of about twelve, and dashing amidst the spreading flames and falling rafters, remained deaf to the entreaties of those who considered his endeavors as hopeless.

"My boy, my boy!" cried the father; the mother sunk, fainting amidst the crowd! But that Being, who animated this pure and generous-hearted little fellow, spread around him

his protecting shield. Edward appeared; his aged grandmother, supported on his arm, to which the occasion had given
supernatural strength; he cheered her, he sought to give her
courage, unmindful of aught but the sacred charge he was
preserving.

Every tongue was silent; the surrounding multitude scarcely dared to breathe, through agitation, dread, and awe.—They
reached the door; Edward supported her steps across the
threshold, when the whole fabric fell in. A shout of joy, a
murmur of applause, followed.—Edward was praised and
blessed as a little hero; while, with a countenance illumin-
ed with happiness, he exclaimed, "She is safe! dear father;
my beloved grandmother is safe!"

I cannot describe the scene that followed; Randal looked
around on his children,—their mother, and the dear partner of
his heart, the venerable and respected author of his days, all,
all were safe. "Oh no!" he cried, "merciless flames, I
will not repine at your devastations; myself and my Edward
will work to renew whatever ye may destroy!—and this
night, dreadful as it has been, is not without its blessings,
since it has proved the real worth of my Edward's heart."

LESSON VII.

CRUELTY TO INSECTS.—PERCIVAL.

A CERTAIN youth indulged himself in the cruel entertainment of torturing and killing flies. He tore off their wings
and legs, and then watched with pleasure their impotent at-
tempts to escape from him. Sometimes he collected a number
of them together, and crushed them at once to death; glorying,
like many a celebrated hero, in the devastation he committed.
Alexis remonstrated with him in vain on this barbarous conduct. He could not persuade him to believe that flies are
capable of pain, and have a right, no less than ourselves, to
life, liberty, and enjoyment. The signs of agony, which,
when tormented, they express by the quick and various con-
tortions of their bodies, he neither understood nor would attend to.—Alexis had a microscope, or glass, for enabling us
to see small objects; and he desired his companion one day
to examine a most beautiful and surprising animal. Mark,

said he, it is studded from head to tail with black and silver,
and its body all over beset with the most curious bristles!   The
head contains a pair of lively eyes, encircled with silver hairs:
and the trunk consists of two parts, which fold over each other.
The whole body is ornamented with plumes and decorations,
which surpass all the luxuries of dress in the courts of the
greatest princes.   Pleased and astonished with what he saw,
the youth was impatient to know the name and properties of
this wonderful animal.   It was withdrawn from the magnifier,
and, when offered to his naked eye, proved to be a poor fly,
which had been the victim of his wanton cruelty.

LESSON VIII.

WINTER.—Anonymous.

December has come! Winter is here! These are com-
mon-place words, but they mean more, perhaps, than we are
apt to consider.
   Winter, then, means that the myriad leaves of the forest
are shriveled and torn from the trees, and scattered in the valley: it means that the sap of the trees has ceased to flow, and
that these giants of the vegetable world, have passed into a
state of stupor, in which they must remain till spring again
returns.
   Winter means that the myriad races of annual weeds and
plants are dead, to revive again no more; that myriads of blossoms have faded forever from the view; that the verdure of
the forest has passed away; that the gemmed garment of the
meadow is exchanged for the thin brown mantle of leanness
and poverty; that the velvet of the lawn has given place to
the scanty covering of dried and faded grass.
   Winter means that the minstrelsy of the birds is gone, and
that the field and forest, so lately cheered by a thousand forms
and sounds of happy existence are now silent, or rendered
more dreary and desolate by the moaning winds. It means
that the birds are gone to their southern retreats; that the
myriad races of insects are dead; that the whole generation of
butterflies has perished; that the grasshoppers have sung their
last song; that even the pensive cricket has gone to his long
home. It means that death has breathed on our portion of the

world, and that nature herself, as if weary of her efforts, has fallen into a cold and fearful slumber.

Winter means all these melancholy things; but it also means something more. It means that the granary of the farmer is full; that his barn is supplied; that there is good and ample store for the beasts that look to man for support, and for man himself. It means, too, that the comfortable fire will be kindled, around which the family will assemble, and where, secure from the bitter blast without, there will still be peace, comfort and content. It means, too, that there is such a thing as poverty, shivering without fire, without food—perhaps, without sufficient shelter; and it means that charity should seek and save those who are suffering in such a condition.

And winter means something more than all this: it means, by its examples of decay and death, to teach us that we, too, must pass away; and that it is well for us to make preparation for the great event. Winter also brings us to the end of the year, and suggests a serious self-inquiry, and self-examination. It would ask us, if the last year has been one of profit or loss? Are we better, and wiser, than when it began? Are we more kind, more just, more patient, more faithful, more fond of truth? Summer is the season for the harvest of the field; winter is the season for the moral harvest of the heart. Let it not pass with any of us, as a barren and unproductive season, in which we neither sow nor reap the fruits of wisdom and peace.

LESSON IX.

APPLICATION.—Dodsley.

Since the days that are past are gone forever, and those that are to come may not come to thee, it behooveth thee, O man! to employ the present time, without regretting the loss of that which is past, or too much depending on that which is to come.

This instant is thine; the next is in the keeping of futurity, and thou knowest not what it may bring forth.

Whatsoever thou resolvest to do, do it quickly; defer not till the evening what the morning may accomplish.

3*

Idleness is the parent of want and of pain; but the labor of virtue bringeth forth pleasure.

The hand of diligence defeateth want; prosperity and success are the industrious man's attendants.

Who is he that hath acquired wealth, that hath risen to power, that hath clothed himself with honor, that is spoken of in the city with praise, and that standeth before the king in his counsel? Even he that hath shut out idleness from his house; and hath said unto sloth, Thou art mine enemy.

He riseth up early and lieth down late; he exerciseth his mind with contemplation, and his body with action; and preserveth the health of both.

The slothful man is a burden to himself; his hours hang heavy on his hand; he loitereth about, and knoweth not what he would do.

His days pass away like the shadow of a cloud; and he leaveth behind him no mark for remembrance.

His body is diseased for want of exercise; he wisheth for action, but hath not power to move. His mind is in darkness; his thoughts are confused; he longeth for knowledge, but hath no application. He would eat of the almond, but hateth the trouble of breaking its shell.

His house is in disorder; his servants are wasteful and riotous; and he runneth on towards ruin: he seeth it with his eyes; he heareth it with his ears; he shaketh his head and wisheth, but hath no resolution, till ruin cometh upon him like a whirlwind, and shame and repentance descend with him into the grave.

LESSON X.

THE SLOTH AND THE BEAVER.—PERCIVAL.

THE Sloth is an animal of South America; and is so ill-formed for motion, that a few paces are often the journey of a week; and so indisposed to move, that he never changes his place, but when impelled by the severest stings of hunger. He lives upon the leaves, fruit, and flowers of trees, and often on the bark itself, when nothing besides is left for his subsistence. As a large quantity of food is necessary for his support, he generally strips a tree of all its verdure in less than a fortnight; and, being then destitute of food, he drops down like a lifeless mass, from the branches to the ground. After remaining torpid for some time, from the shock received by the fall, he prepares for a journey to some neighboring tree, to which he crawls with a motion almost imperceptible. At length arrived, he ascends the trunk and devours with famished appetite whatever the branches afford. By consuming the bark, he soon destroys the life of the tree; and thus the source is lost, from which his sustenance is derived. Such is the miserable state of this slothful animal. How different are the comforts and enjoyments of the industrious Beaver! This creature is found in the northern parts of America, and is about two feet long and one foot high. The figure of it somewhat resembles that of a rat. In the months of June and July, the beavers assemble and form a society, which generally consists of more than two hundred. They always fix their abode by the side of a lake or river; and, in order to make a dead water above and below, they erect with incredible labor, a dam, or pier, perhaps fourscore or a hundred feet long, and ten or twelve feet thick at the base. When this dike is completed, they build their several apartments, which are divided into three stories. The first is beneath the level of the mole, and is for the most part full of water. The walls of their habitations are perpendicular, and about two feet thick. If any wood project from them, they cut it off with their teeth, which are more serviceable than saws; and by the help of their tails, they plaster all their works, with a kind of mortar, which they prepare of dry grass and clay mixed together. In August or September, they begin to lay up their stores of food; it consists of the wood of the birch, the plane, and of some other trees. Thus they pass the gloomy winter in ease and plenty.—These two American animals, contrasted with each other, afford a most striking picture of the blessings of industry, and the penury and wretchedness of sloth.

LESSON XI.

TRUTH ABOVE ALL THINGS.—Aikin.

"Truth is the highest thing that man can keep," says the good old English poet Geoffry Chaucer; and in all times and places there have been some excellent people who have shown that they were resolved to keep it, whatever it might cost them.

Abdool-Radir, a Persian boy, the son of a widow, desired leave of his mother to take a journey to Bagdat to seek his fortune; she wept at the thoughts of the parting; then, taking out forty of the gold coins called dinars, she gave them to him, telling him that was the whole of his inheritance. After this, she made him swear never to tell a lie; then she bade him farewell.

The boy set out upon his journey. On the road, the party with which he traveled was suddenly attacked by a great troop of robbers. One of them asked Abdool-Radir, what money he had got. "Forty dinars," he answered "are sewed up in my garments." The robber took this for a jest, and laughed. Another asked him the same question, and he made the same reply. When they began to divide the plunder among them, he was called to the chief, who was standing on an eminence, and he too asked him what he had got. "I have told two of your men already," said he, "that I have forty dinars carefully sewed up in my clothes." The chief immediatley ordered the clothes to be ripped up, and the gold was found. He was astonished. "How came you," said he, "to discover what had been so carefully hidden?" "Because," replied Abdool-Radir, "I will not be false to my mother, to whom I have promised never to tell a lie!" "What, child!" said the chief, "hast thou, at thy age, such a sense of thy duty to thy mother, and have I at mine, so little sense of my duty to my God, as to lead the life of a robber!" Give me thy hand, innocent boy, that I may swear upon it to forsake my evil ways." And he swore it; and his followers, all struck like him with sudden repentance, made the same vow; and as the first fruits of it, returned to the travelers whatever they had taken from them.

LESSON XII.

THE SEASONS.—BARBAULD.

Who is this beautiful virgin that approaches, clothed in a robe of light green? She has a garland of flowers on her head, and flowers spring up wherever she sets her foot. The

snow which covered the fields, and the ice which was on the
rivers, melt away when she breathes upon them. The young
lambs frisk about her, and the birds warble to welcome her
coming; when they see her, they begin to choose their mates,
and to build their nests. Youths and maidens, have ye seen
this beautiful virgin? If ye have, tell me who she is, and
what is her name.

Who is this that cometh from the south, thinly clad in a light
transparent garment. Her breath is hot and sultry; she
seeks the refreshment of the cool shade, she seeks the clear
streams, the crystal brooks, to bathe her languid limbs. The
brooks and rivulets fly from her, and are dried up at her approach. She cools her parched lips with berries and the
grateful acid of fruits. The tanned haymakers welcome her
coming; and the sheep-shearer, who clips the fleeces off his
flock with his sounding shears. When she cometh, let me lie
under the thick shade of a spreading beech-tree,—let me walk
with her in the early morning, when the dew is yet upon the
grass,—let me wander with her in the soft twilight, when the
shepherd shuts his fold, and the star of the evening appears.
Who is she that cometh from the south? Youths and maidens, tell me, if you know, who is she, and what is her
name.

Who is he that cometh with sober pace, stealing upon us
unawares? His garments are red with the blood of the grape,
and his temples are bound with a sheaf of ripe wheat. His
hair is thin, and begins to fall, and the auburn is mixed with
mournful gray. He shakes the brown nuts from the tree.
He winds the horn, and calls the hunters to their sport.
The gun sounds. The trembling partridge, and the beautiful pheasant flutter, bleeding in the air, and fall dead at the
sportsman's feet. Youths and maidens, tell me, if you know,
who is he, and what is his name.

Who is he that cometh from the north, in furs and warm
wool? He wraps his cloak close about him. His head is
bald; his beard is made of sharp icicles. He loves the bla-
zing fire high piled upon the hearth, and the wine sparkling
in the glass. He binds skates to his feet, and skims over the
frozen lakes. His breath is piercing and cold, and no little
flower dares to peep above the surface of the ground when he
is by. Whatever he touches turns to ice. Youths and maidens, do you see him? He is coming upon us, and soon will
be here. Tell me, if you know, who is he, and what is his
name.

LESSON XIII.

THE NESTS OF BIRDS.—Sturm.

How curious is the structure of the nest of the goldfinch or chaffinch! The inside of it is lined with cotton and fine silken threads; and the outside cannot be sufficiently admired, though it is composed only of various species of fine moss. The color of these mosses, resembling that of the bark of the tree on which the nest is built, proves that the bird intended it should not be easily discovered. In some nests, hair, wool, and rushes, are dexterously interwoven. In some, all the parts are firmly fastened by a thread, which the bird makes of hemp, wool, hair, or more commonly of spiders' webs.— Other birds, as for instance the blackbird and the lapwing, after they have constructed their nest, plaster the inside with mortar, which cements and binds the whole together; they then stick upon it, while quite wet, some wool or moss, to give it the necessary degree of warmth.—The nests of swallows are of a very different construction from those of other birds. They require neither wood, nor hay, nor cords; they make a kind of mortar, with which they form a neat, secure, and comfortable habitation for themselves and their family. To moisten the dust of which they build their nests, they dip their breasts in water, and shake the drops from their wet feathers upon it. But the nests most worthy of admiration are those of certain Indian birds, which suspend them with great art from the branches of trees, to secure them from the depredations of various animals and insects. In general, every species of birds has a peculiar mode of building: but it may be remarked of all alike, that they always construct their nests in the way that is best adapted to their security, and to the preservation and welfare of their species.

Such is the wonderful instinct of birds with respect to the structure of their nests. What skill and sagacity! what industry and patien ce do they display! And is it not apparent that all their labors tend towards certain ends? They construct their nests hollow and nearly round, that they may retain the heat so much the better. They line them with the most delicate substances, that the young may lie soft and warm. What is it that teaches the bird to place her nest in a situation sheltered from the rain, and secure against the attacks of other animals ? How did she learn that she should lay eggs,—that eggs would require a nest to prevent them from falling to the ground, and to keep them warm ? Whence does she know that the heat would not be maintained around the eggs if the nest were too large ; and that, on the other hand, the young would not have sufficient room if it were smaller ? By what rule does she determine the due proportions between the nest and the young, which are not yet in existence ? Who has taught her to calculate the time with such accuracy that she never makes a mistake, and produces her eggs before the nest is ready to receive them ? Admire in all these things the power, the wisdom, and the goodness of her Creator !

LESSON XIV.

PART OF CHRIST'S SERMON ON THE MOUNT.
TESTAMENT.

BLESSED are the poor in spirit : for theirs is the kingdom of heaven.

Blessed are they that mourn : for they shall be comforted.

Blessed are the meek : for they shall inherit the earth.

Blessed are they which do hunger and thirst after righteousness : for they shall be filled.

Blessed are the merciful : for they shall obtain mercy.

Blessed are the pure in heart : for they shall see God.

Blessed are the peace-makers : for they shall be called the children of God.

Blessed are they which are persecuted for righteousness' sake : for theirs is the kingdom of heaven.

Ye have heard that it was said by them of old time, Thou shalt not kill ; and whosoever shall kill shall be in danger of the judgment :

But I say unto you, That whosoever is angry with his brother without a cause, shall be in danger of the judgment ; and whosoever shall say to his brother, Raca, shall be in danger of the council ; but whosoever shall say, Thou fool, shall be in danger of hell-fire.

Therefore, if thou bring thy gift to the altar, and there rememberest that thy brother hath aught against thee ;

Leave there thy gift before the altar, and go thy way ; first be reconciled to thy brother, and then come and offer thy gift.

Again, ye have heard that it hath been said by them of old time, Thou shalt not forswear thyself, but shalt perform unto the Lord thine oaths :

But I say unto you, Swear not at all : neither by heaven ; for it is God's throne :

Nor by the earth ; for it is his footstool : neither by Jerusalem ; for it is the city of the great King :

Neither shalt thou swear by thy head ; because thou canst not make one hair white or black.

But let your communication be Yea, yea ; Nay, nay : for whatsoever is more than these cometh of evil.

Ye have heard that it hath been said, Thou shalt love thy neighbor, and hate thine enemy :

But I say unto you, Love your enemies, bless them that curse you, do good to them that hate you, and pray for them which despitefully use you, and persecute you ;

That ye may be the children of your Father which is in heaven : for he maketh the sun to rise on the evil and on the good, and sendeth rain on the just and on the unjust.

Judge not, that ye be not judged.

For with what judgment ye judge, ye shall be judged : and with what measure ye mete, it shall be measured to you again.

Therefore, whosoever heareth these sayings of mine, and doeth them, I will liken him unto a wise man, which built his house upon a rock :

And the rain descended, and the floods came, and the winds blew, and beat upon that house ; and it fell not : for it was founded upon a rock.

And every one that heareth these sayings of mine, and doeth them not, shall be likened unto a foolish man which built his house upon the sand :

And the rain descended, and the floods came, and the winds blew, and beat upon that house ; and it fell : and great was the fall of it.

LESSON XV.

FILIAL AFFECTION.—Anonymous.

Let the commands of your parents be ever sacred in your ears, and implicitly obeyed, where they do not contradict the commands of God. Pretend not to be wiser than they who have had so much more experience than you; and despise them not, if haply you should be so blest as to have gained a degree of knowledge or of fortune superior to theirs. Let your carriage toward them be always respectful, your words always affectionate; and especially beware of pert replies, and peevish looks. Never imagine, if they oppose your inclinations, that this arises from anything but love to you; but let the remembrance of what they have done, and suffered for you, preserve you from acts of disobedience, and from paining those good hearts which have already felt so much for you. Admire and imitate the following examples of *filial love* :—

Boleslaus the Fourth, king of Poland, had a picture of his father, which he carried about his neck, set in a plate of gold; and when he was going to say or do any thing of importance, he took this pleasing monitor in his hand, and kissing it, used to say, "My dear father! may I do nothing unworthy of thy name!"

During an eruption of Mount Etna, the inhabitants of the adjacent country were obliged for safety to abandon their houses, and retire to a great distance. Amidst the hurry and confusion of the scene, while every one was carrying away whatever he deemed most precious, two sons, in the height of their solicitude to preserve their wealth and goods, recollected their father and mother, who were both very old, were unable to save themselves by flight. Filial tenderness set aside every other consideration. "Where," cried the generous youths, "shall we find a more precious treasure than those who gave us being?" This said, the one took up his father on his shoulders, and the other his mother, and they thus made their way through the surrounding smoke and flames. The fact struck all beholders with admiration; and ever since, the path they took in their retreat has been called "the Field of the Pious," in memory of this pleasing incident.

While Octavius was at Samos, after the famous battle of Actium, which made him master of the world, he held a coun-

4

cil in order to try the prisoners who had been engaged in Antony's party. Among the rest was brought before him Metellus, an old man oppressed with infirmities and ill fortune, whose son sat as one of the judges. At first the son did not recognize the father. At length, however, having recollected his features, the generous youth, instead of being ashamed to own him, ran to embrace the old man, and cried bitterly. Then, returning toward the tribunal, "Cæsar," said he, " my father has been your enemy, and I your officer; he deserves to be punished, and I to be rewarded. The favor I desire of you is, either to save him on my account, or to order me to be put to death with him." As was to be expected, all the judges were touched with pity at this affecting scene ; and Octavius himself, relenting, granted to old Metellus his life and liberty.

The emperor Decimus, intending and desiring to place the crown on the head of Decius, his son, the young prince refused it in the most strenuous manner. "I am afraid," said he, "lest, being made an emperor, I should forget that I am a son. I had rather be no emperor and a dutiful son, than an emperor and a disobedient son. Let then my father bear the rule; and this only be my empire, to obey with all humility whatsoever he shall command me." Thus the solemnity was waived, and the young man was not crowned,—unless it be thought that this signal piety toward an indulgent parent was a more glorious diadem than the crown of an empire.

LESSON XVI.

TIRED OF PLAY.—WILLIS.

TIRED of play ! Tired of play !
What hast thou done this livelong day !
The birds are silent and so is the bee ;
The sun is creeping up steeple and tree ;
The doves have flown to the sheltering eaves,
And the nests are dark with the drooping leaves ;
Twilight gathers and day is done—
How hast thou spent it—restless one !

Playing ? But what hast thou done beside
To tell thy mother at eventide ?
What promise of morn is left unbroken ?
What kind word to thy playmate spoken ?
Whom hast thou pitied, and whom forgiven ?
How with thy faults has duty striven ?
What hast thou learned by field and hill,
By greenwood path, and by singing rill ?

There will come an eve to a longer day,
That will find thee tired—but not of play !
And thou wilt lean, as thou leanest now,
With drooping limbs and aching brow,
And wish the shadows would faster creep,
And long to go to thy quiet sleep.
Well were it then if thine aching brow
Were as free from sin and shame as now !
Well for thee if thy lip could tell
A tale like this, of a day spent well.
If thine open hand hath relieved distress—
If thy pity hath sprung to wretchedness—
If thou hast forgiven the sore offense,
And humbled thy heart with penitence—
If Nature's voices have spoken to thee
With her holy meanings eloquently—
If every creature hath won thy love—
From the creeping worm to the brooding dove—
If never a sad low-spoken word
Hath plead with thy human heart unheard :
Then when the night steals on, as now,
It will bring relief to thy aching brow,
And with joy and peace at the thought of rest,
Thou wilt sink to sleep on thy mother's breast.

LESSON XVII.

THE SHETLAND PONY.—Anonymous.

This diminutive breed of horses, many of which are not
larger than a Newfoundland dog, is common in Shetland, and
all the islands on the north and west of Scotland ; also in the

mountainous districts of the mainland along the coast. They are beautifully formed, and possess prodigious strength in proportion to their size. The heads are small, with a flowing mane and a long tail, reaching to the ground.

They are high-spirited and courageous little animals, but extremely tractable in their nature. Some of them run wild about the mountains, and there are various methods of catching them, according to the local situation of the district which they inhabit.

The shelties, as they are called, are generally so small, that a middling-sized man must ride with his knees raised to the animal's shoulders, to prevent his toes from touching the ground. It is surprising to see with what speed they will carry a heavy man over broken and zigzag roads in their native mountains.

When grazing, they will clamber up steep ascents, and to the extreme edge of precipices which overhang the most frightful abysses, and there they will gaze round with as much complacency as if on a plain.

These horses, small as they may be, are not to be considered a degenerate breed, for they are possessed of much greater physical strength, in proportion to their size, than larger horses. They are called garrons in the highlands of Scotland.

A gentleman, sometime ago, was presented with one of these handsome little animals, which was no less docile than elegant, and measured only seven hands, or twenty-eight inches, in height. He was anxious to convey his present home as speedily as possible, but being at a considerable distance, was at a loss how to do so most easily. The friend said, "can you not carry him in your chaise?" He made the experiment, and the shelty was lifted into it, covered up with the apron, and some bits of bread given him to keep him quiet. He lay quite peaceable till he reached his destination; thus exhibiting the novel spectacle of a horse riding in a gig.

A little girl, the daughter of a gentleman in Warwickshire, England, playing on the banks of a canal which runs through his grounds, had the misfortune to fall in, and would in all probability have been drowned, had not a little pony, which had long been kept in the family, plunged into the stream and brought the child safely ashore, without the slightest injury.

A gentleman had a white pony, which became extremely attached to a little dog that lived with him in the stable, and whenever the horse was rode out, the dog always ran by his side. One day, when the groom took out the pony for exercise, and accompanied, as usual, by his canine friend, they met a large dog, which attacked the diminutive cur, upon which the horse reared, and to the astonishment of the bystanders, so effectually fought his friend's battle with his fore feet, that the aggressor found it for his interest to scamper off at full speed, and never again ventured to assail the small dog.

Shelties sometimes attain a great age. There was, in the village of Haddington, England, a very small black pony, of this breed, which, at forty-seven years of age, looked remarkably fresh; trotted eight miles an hour for several miles together; had a very good set of teeth; eat corn and hay well; was able to go a long journey; and had not, to appearance, undergone the least alteration, either in galloping, trotting, or walking, for twenty years preceding.

LESSON XVIII.

TEST OF GOODNESS.—Anonymous.

The father of a family, being advanced in years, was desirous of settling his worldly affairs. Three sons remained living to inherit his estate. Having summoned them before him, he pointed out to each his allotted share,—reserving, however, a diamond of great value. "This," said he, "I have determined to bequeath to him who shall, within three months, give the most decided proof of his having performed an *act of goodness.*"

They departed accordingly, each in a different direction, to seek an opportunity of accomplishing an action, that might be deemed worthy of the proposed reward. At the time appointed, they all returned, and presented themselves again before their venerable parent.

"Father," said the oldest, "I found, during absence, a stranger so circumstanced, that he was under the necessity of intrusting me with the whole of his fortune. He had no written security from me, nor could he bring any proof of the deposite; yet I faithfully returned him every shilling of the

4*

money. Does there not appear something meritorious in such an action?" "Thou hast, indeed," said the father, "fulfilled a duty that was incumbent on thee. He who could act otherwise, would be unworthy to live; for honesty is an indispensable moral duty. Thine was an act of *justice*,—not of goodness."

On this the second advanced. "In the course of my travels," said he, "I came to the border of a lake, in which a child was on the point of drowning. I plunged into the water, and saved its life, in the presence of a number of the neighboring villagers, all of whom can attest the truth of my assertion." "It was well done," interrupted the father; "but thou hast only obeyed the dictates of *humanity*. A man may be humane, without being really good."

The youngest of the three now came forward. "I happened," said he, "to meet my mortal enemy. Bewildered by the darkness of the night, he had lost his way; and being overcome with fatigue, he sat down to rest on the brink of a precipice. Here, unconscious of his danger, he had fallen fast asleep; and he was lying in such a position, that the least involuntary motion would have plunged him headlong into the frightful abyss. I gently awoke him, removed him cautiously from his perilous situation, and led him safely home."

"Ah! my son," exclaimed the good old man, while he pressed him with transport to his heart, "to thee belongs the diamond, and thou hast well deserved it. He who thus repays injury with kindness, performs, indeed, an act of *goodness*. The principle that could promp to such a deed, far excels both justice and humanity."

LESSON XIX.

REMEMBRANCE OF GOD.—Wood.

REMEMBER thy Creator in the days of thy youth. Remember that every thing which thou seest, above, beneath, around thee—the sun, the moon, and stars, the lofty mountains, the wide abyss of the ocean, are all the workmanship of his Almighty, though invisible hand. At his command, day and night—the beauties of spring—the glories of sum-

mer—the rich profusion of harvest—and the dread desolation
of winter, succeed each other in regular progression. In him
all the countless tribes of living creatures, that every where
people this vast universe, live, and move, and have their being. When he sendeth forth his Spirit, they are created;
when he openeth his hand, they are filled with good; when
he hideth his face, they are troubled; when he taketh away
their breath, they die, and return to their dust. But, above
all, remember him as *thy* Creator—as the heavenly Father,
who called thee into being, and to whom thou art indebted for
every blessing which thou hast been permitted to enjoy.
Thy health, thy strength, thy reason; the air thou breathest:
the light which cheers, the food which nourishes, the raiment
which clothes, the dwelling which shelters thee; thy mother's
fostering care; thy father's sustaining arm; the kindness of
thy friends;—these, and all the other blessings of thy condition, flow from the liberal hand of him, who alone is the Giver
of all good. Remember that this kind Parent and bountiful
Benefactor is also the continual spectator of thy conduct, and
of the manner in which thou improvest the benefits he hath
so liberally bestowed upon thee; that each act thou dost,
each word thou utterest, each thought thou conceivest within
thy bosom, is known to him; and that for each he shall one
day require of thee an account. Let, then, his presence be
ever impressed upon thy mind. Let thy devotions ascend to
him, with every morning's dawn, and every evening's close;
accustom thyself to behold him in all his works; hallow his
holy name and word; and, above all, in every moment of thy
life, let it be thy first study to do his will. Sweet will be each
prayer that rises from thy youthful bosom; sweet each ac-
cent of gratitude and praise. Ever bear in mind that solemn
admonition of tried experience and paternal love, "Thou,
Solomon, my son, know thou the God of thy father, and serve
him with a perfect heart, and with a willing mind: if thou
seek him, he will be found of thee; but if thou forsake him,
he will cast thee off forever."

"Thou shalt love the Lord thy God with all thy heart, and
with all thy soul, and with all thy mind."

LESSON XX.

INFERENCE-MAKING.—Aikin.

MAKING an inference, is a way of finding out something which we do not know, from some other thing which we do know. This is a very curious and useful art, and it will be therefore worth while to give you a few examples, that you may understand clearly what it is.

A dog, it is said, can make an inference; for when he has lost sight of his master, and follows him by the scent; if he comes to a place where three roads part, he will smell at the first, and if the scent is not there, he will smell at the second, but if the scent is not there neither, he will run along the first road without smelling; thinking thus with himself: My master is not gone *this* way, nor yet *that* way, *therefore* he must be gone the third way, since there is no other.

I have heard of a more curious instance of a dog who had cunning enough to draw his master into a false inference. This dog, who was tied up in a yard at night, had found out that his collar was so loose that he could slip his neck in and out as he pleased; and he took advantage of this to go out in the dark and kill sheep. When he came back, after committing this offense, he always put his neck into the collar again, that his master might say, "My dog is safe tied up here, as I left him, *therefore* it could not have been he who killed the sheep." At last, however, the rogue was closely watched, and his trick found out.

Columbus, sailing along an undiscovered coast, came to the mouth of a river larger than he had ever seen, he inferred that the land must be a part of some mighty continent, and not an island; because all the springs which could rise, and all the rain which could fall in an island, could never, as he calculated, supply water enough to feed so prodigiously broad and deep a river. He was right: this was the first discovery of the great continent of America, and the river was the Orinoco.

There are some inferences which any body can make who will think, and pay attention to the common things which pass before his eyes; others it requires knowledge and book-learning of various kinds to be able to make.

When king Henry the Sixth of England, was a boy, and

his uncle, the duke of Gloucester, governed the country for
him, it is related, that a man was brought before the duke
who said that he was born blind, and had just received his
sight by a miracle. "Aye!" said the duke, "were you
born quite blind?" "Quite blind, my lord." "And you
see very clearly now?" "O yes!" "Well; what color is
that gown?" "Black as a crow, my lord." "Right. And
what color is this cloak?" "Red, my lord, red as blood."
"I will have you whipped," said the duke, "for a rogue and
a cheat; if you had been born blind, and had but just now
gained your eye-sight, you would be able to distinguish the
colors indeed, but how should you have known the *names* of
them?" This was an inference which any person might
make who had his wits about him; but not so the other
which I am going to mention.

Aristippus, a Grecian *philosopher*, which means a lover of
wisdom, in passing over from Corinth to Asia, was shipwreck-
ed on the isle of Rhodes. Observing, as they landed, some
mathematical figures, such as squares, circles and triangles,
drawn upon the sands, he said to his companions, "Take
courage! I see the footsteps of men!" inferring, not only
that the island must be inhabited by human creatures, but
that they could not be savages, since mathematics was known
among them. The same Aristippus, having no doubt observed how many inferences his own knowledge had enabled him
to make, more than others, said that it was better to be poor
than ignorant; for the poor man wanted only money, but the
ignorant man wanted what distinguishes men from brutes.

Thus you perceive, that the more knowledge people have,
and the more they work with their heads in thinking, the
greater number of useful and interesting inferences they can
make; and this ought to be an encouragement to you to take
pains to learn and consider things.

LESSON XXI.

THE GOLDFINCH.—Anonymous.

This is one of the most elegant of English birds; graceful
in form, and arrayed in much more brilliant colors than the
birds of that climate usually exhibit. It has also a sweet and

cheerful song, which is heard from the earliest days of spring;
but it is in the month of May that it gives out its sweetest and
fullest strains: perched on a tree it will pour forth its notes
from early morning till set of sun, and make the orchard re-
sound with its music. It continues to sing till the month of
August, except during the period at which it is rearing its
young; then all its time and attention are devoted to parental
duties. The male bird, though very attentive to his pretty
mate, does not assist her in building the nest; but he is constantly watching over her, either close by her side, or perched on the nearest tree; and this he does, both when she is
seeking her food, and while engaged in preparing the abode
for her future progeny. The nest is small and elegant; its
outside consists of fine moss curiously interwoven with other
soft materials; and the inside is lined with grass, horse-hair,
wool, feathers, and down. Here the hen bird deposits five or
six white eggs, spotted with brown toward the thick end.
While she is hatching, her companion never leaves her except to procure food; but sits on a neighboring tree and
cheers her with his song. If disturbed, he flies away; but it
is only as a feint to prevent the nest from being discovered,
and he soon returns. On her part, she devotes herself with
the utmost patience and constancy to her maternal cares.
As the time approaches when the young ones will make their
appearance, she is evidently increasingly interested in their
preservation, and will brave every thing to defend them from
injury: the stormiest gales of wind, the drenching rain, or
the pelting hail-storm, do not drive her from her nest; there
she remains, and her faithful mate continues in attendance
on her. At last the little birds pierce the shell, and faint cries
proclaim their wants to their parents; then there is full em-
ployment to procure food sufficient to supply five or six cra-
ving little creatures.

The goldfinch is easily tamed, and with no great trouble
may be taught to perform many curious tricks with surprising accuracy. It will draw up cups of water to its cage; it
will stand upon its head; it will imitate a soldier and mount
guard as a sentinel; it will light a match and fire a small
cannon; it will imitate death and suffer itself to be taken up
by its claws without the least sign of life; fire-works may
be exploded all around it, without frightening it. Many other surprising things are told of it. Mr. Albin mentions a lady
who had one which was even able to speak several words
with great distinctness. This beautiful bird, has been known

to live sometimes to the age of twenty years. It is said,
withal, to be extremely fond of the society of its own species
—even the resemblance of another goldfinch is sufficient to
console it in captivity. If a glass is placed near the cage, it
is evidently pleased to look at its own image reflected in it,
and is often seen to take its hemp-seed, grain by grain, and
go and eat before the mirror, thinking, no doubt, that it is
feeding in company. Poor little bird! how much more delightful to see it flying gaily among its feathered mates of the
field and the orchard, than thus cheated with the semblance
of society.

The song of the goldfinch has been fancifully supposed to
resemble the words, "*Take* me with you *if* you please," chanted in recitative, with a strong emphasis on the first and fifth
words in the sentence.

> *Take* me with you *if* you please,
>   I 'm a merry little bird;
> I love the orchard's sheltering trees,
>   And there my cheerful note is heard.
>   Softly blows the summer breeze;
>   *Take* me with you *if* you please.
>
> I love the woods and meadows too,
>   Where other small birds gaily sing;
> I sip with them the morning dew,
>   And with them prune my glossy wing;
>   Softly blows the summer breeze,
>   *Take* me with you *if* you please.

LESSON XXII.

WINTER.—BARBAULD.

It is now Winter, dead Winter. Desolation and silence
reign in the fields, no singing of birds is heard, no humming
of insects. The streams murmur no longer; they are locked up in frost.

The trees lift their naked boughs like withered arms into
the bleak sky; the green sap no longer rises in their veins;

the flowers and the sweet-smelling shrubs are decayed to their roots.

The sun himself looks cold and cheerless; he gives light only enough to show the universal desolation.

Nature, child of God, mourns for her children. A little while ago, and she rejoiced in her offspring; the rose shed its perfume upon the gales; the vine gave its fruit; her children were springing and blooming around her, on every lawn, and every green bank.

O Nature, beautiful Nature, beloved child of God, why dost thou sit mourning and desolate? Has thy father forsaken thee—has he left thee to perish? Art thou no longer the object of his care?

He has not forsaken thee, O Nature; thou art his beloved child, the eternal image of his perfections; his own beauty is spread over thee, the light of his countenance is shed upon thee.

Thy children shall live again—they shall spring up and bloom around thee; the rose shall again breathe its sweetness on the soft air, and from the bosom of the ground, verdure shall spring forth.

And dost thou not mourn, O nature, for thy human births; for thy sons and thy daughters that sleep under the sod; and shall they not also revive? Shall the rose and the myrtle bloom anew, and shall man perish? Shall goodness sleep in the ground, and the light of wisdom be quenched in the dust, and shall tears be shed over them in vain?

They also shall live; their winter shall pass away; they shall bloom again. The tears of thy children shall be dried up when the eternal year proceeds. O come that eternal year!

LESSON XXIII.

THE CORAL ISLAND.—Aikin.

A TALL ship from Europe, crossing the Indian Ocean to China or New Holland, will sometimes strike suddenly upon a sunken rock, that is, a rock which does not rise to sight above the water, in a place where, a few years before, no rock was to be found. What are these *new* rocks do you, suppose, or how are they produced? Wonderful to tell! they are the work of insects, formed by them out of matter collected in their own bodies, in the same manner as the spider forms its web, or the bee its comb, or the snail its shell. But the coral insects are more extraordinary creatures than these. They are of a great variety of shapes and sizes; the commonest is in the form of a star, with arms, or feelers, from four to six inches long, which it moves nimbly around in search of food. Others are sluggish creatures, of the size and shape of a finger, and of a dark color. Some are as fine as a thread, and several feet long, sometimes blue and sometimes yellow; others look like snails, others like very little lobsters. When they have built up any part of their sea-castle so high that it rises above the water at low tide, it appears, when dry, to be a firm and solid rock, very hard and rough; but as soon as ever the tide rises again, and the waves begin to wash over it, the insects are seen thrusting out their bodies from thousands of little holes which were before invisible, and in a short time the whole rock appears to be alive with their countless multitudes. And so the rock goes on, rising taller and taller in a shape like a cauliflower, till the water cannot reach its top, even at high tide. Then they can build it up no further, for they must be within reach of the water to get their food; and when the insects die, it becomes a bare, dead rock, with neither plant, nor any living thing upon it.

But presently the sea, in some great tempest, will throw over it some sea-weeds, and sand, and bones, and dead fishes, and perhaps the wreck of some lost ship, which its waters have overwhelmed; and some fruits, and berries, and seeds will be mixed in the heap. All these things decaying together, will make a thin covering of mould, in which some of the seeds will spring up. Then a cocoa-nut will float to it from some neighboring shore, and it will take root, and thrive, and multiply; for this plant loves to grow in reach of salt water. When the cocoa-palms begin to wave their heads invitingly, birds will stretch their wings thither: the parrot and the dove will perch there, and within their bodies they will convey the seeds of other plants on which they feed; and when these spring up, doves and parrots will build their nests, and make it their dwelling. Sea-birds will come there too, and lay their eggs; and insects will be wafted thither by tempestuous winds, and insect-eating birds will follow them; and thus it will become a little green islet, all alive and gay with beautiful winged creatures; but no beast can set his foot upon it, and even man, should he happen to discover it, will not take possession, for one thing it wants—a fountain of fresh water.

A little rain will lodge in the hollows of the rock, enough for the birds, but men and cattle must have a running spring.

LESSON XXIV.

INDIAN GRATITUDE.—Dwight.

Not many years after the county of Litchfield began to be settled by the English, a strange Indian came one day into an Inn, in the town of Litchfield, in the dusk of the evening, and requested the hostess to furnish him with some drink and a supper. At the same time, he observed, that he could pay for neither, as he had had no success in hunting; but promised payment as soon as he should meet with better fortune. The hostess refused him both the drink and the supper; called him a lazy, drunken, good-for-nothing fellow; and told him that she did not work so hard herself, to throw away her earnings upon such creatures as he was. A man who sat by, and observed that the Indian, then turning about to leave so inhospitable a place, showed by his countenance, that he was suffering very severely from want and weariness, directed the hostess to supply him with what he wished, and engaged to pay the bill himself. She did so.

When the Indian had finished his supper, he turned to his benefactor, thanked him, and assured him that he should remember his kindness, and whenever he was able would faithfully recompense it.

Some years after, the man who had befriended him, had occasion to go some distance into the wilderness between Litchfield, then a frontier settlement, and Albany, when he was taken prisoner by an Indian scout, and carried to Canada. When he arrived at the principal settlement of the tribe, on the southern border of the St. Lawrence, it was proposed by some of the captors that he should be put to death. During the consultation, an old Indian woman demanded that he should be given up to her, that she might adopt him in the place of a son, whom she had lost in the war. He was accordingly given to her, and lived through the succeeding winter in her family, experiencing the customary effects of savage hospitality.

The following summer, as he was at work in the forest alone, an unknown Indian came up to him, and asked him to meet him at a place which he pointed out, upon a given day. The prisoner agreed to the proposal, but not without some apprehensions that mischief was intended him. During the interval, these apprehensions increased to such a degree, as to dissuade him effectually from fulfilling his engagement. Soon after, the same Indian found him at his work again, and very gravely reproved him for not performing his promise. The man apologized awkwardly enough, but in the best manner in his power. The Indian told him that he should be satisfied, if he would meet him at the same place on a future day, which he named. The man promised to meet him, and fulfilled his promise.

When he arrived at the spot, he found the Indian provided with two muskets, ammunition for them, and two knapsacks. The Indian ordered him to take one of each and follow him. The direction of their march was to the south. The man followed, without the least knowledge of what he was to do, or whither he was going ; but concluded, that, if the Indian intended him harm, he would have despatched him at the beginning ; and that, at the worst, he was as safe where he was, as he could be any where else in the power of his Indian captors. Within a short time, therefore, his fears subsided ; although the Indian preserved a profound and mysterious silence concerning the object of the expedition. In the day time, they shot such game as came in their way, and at night kindled a fire, by which they slept. After a tedious journey of many days, they came, one morning, to the top of an eminence, presenting a prospect of a cultivated country, in which were a number of houses. The Indian asked his companion, whether he knew the ground. He replied eagerly, that it was Litchfield. His guide, then, after reminding him that he had, so many years before, relieved a famishing Indian at an Inn, in that town, subjoined, "I that Indian ; now I pay you ; go home." Having said this, he bade him adieu, and the man joyfully returned to his own home.

LESSON XXV.

INDUSTRY.—Bible.

Whatsoever thy hand findeth to do, do it with all thy might: for there is no work, nor device, nor knowledge, nor wisdom, in the grave, whither thou goest. Seest thou a man diligent in his business ?—he shall stand before kings ; he shall not stand before mean men.

A slothful man hideth his hand in his bosom, and will not so much as bring it to his mouth again. He coveteth greedily all the day long. The soul of the sluggard desireth, and hath nothing. An idle soul shall suffer hunger.

Slothfulness casteth into a deep sleep. Love not sleep, lest thou come to poverty. Drowsiness shall clothe a man with rags. He that is slothful in his work is brother to him that is a great waster. By much slothfulness the building decay-eth : and through idleness of the hands the house droppeth through.

Be thou diligent to know the state of thy flocks, and look well to thy herds. For riches are not forever ;—and doth the crown endure to every generation ? Wealth gotten by van-ity, shall be diminished ; but he that gathereth by labor shall increase.

If riches increase, set not your heart upon them. Wilt thou set thine eyes upon that which is not ?—for riches cer-tainly make themselves wings ; they fly away, as an eagle toward heaven.

He that trusteth in his riches shall fall. There is that maketh himself rich, yet hath nothing : there is that maketh himself poor, yet hath great riches. The blessing of the Lord,—it maketh rich ; and he addeth no sorrow with it. The labor of the righteous tendeth to life ; the fruit of the wicked to sin.

Labor not to be rich. He that hasteth to be rich hath an evil eye, and considereth not that poverty shall come upon him. There is that withholdeth more than is meet ; but it tendeth to poverty. He that oppresseth the poor to increase his riches, and he that giveth to the rich, shall surely come to want. Envy thou not the oppressor, and choose none of his ways. Whoso is partner with a thief, despiseth his own soul.

Better is the poor that walketh in his uprightness, than he

that is perverse in his ways, though he be rich. Better is a little, with the fear of the Lord, than great treasure, and trouble therewith. The sleep of a laboring man is sweet; but the abundance of the rich will not suffer him to sleep.

Remove far from me vanity and lies; give me neither poverty nor riches: feed me with food convenient for me; lest I be full, and deny thee, and say, "Who is the Lord?"—or lest I be poor, and steal, and take the name of my God in vain.

LESSON XXVI.

THE ANT.—Cobbin.

"Go to the ant, thou sluggard; consider her ways and be wise." Prov. vi. chapter and 6th verse.

There are many curious and industrious insects, such as the bee and the spider; but Solomon, the wise man, here calls our attention to the ant.

There are various sorts of ants, but all of them are examples of industry; they are masons, carpenters, miners, and carvers; and their work is skillful and curious. The earthen hillock of the mason-ant, contains within it, lodges, vaults, and galleries. Some hillocks have twenty stories above the ground, and as many below; these are for change of air; for when it is too hot above, from the burning rays of the sun, they all go below; and when it is too cold below, for want of the sun, they all go above. The carpenter-ants chisel out their stories, chambers, galleries, and colonnades, in the bodies or roots of growing trees. Another species builds its house upon the branches of trees, and glues the points of leaves together so as to form a purse: these nests differ in size, from a fist to a human head, and even a hogshead! But the white ants of the tropical climates, which are very hot, are more extraordinary still. Their houses are five hundred times higher than themselves. They are frequently twelve feet high; and some are even twenty feet high, and large enough to contain twelve men! Were our houses built according to the same proportions, they would be twelve or fifteen times higher than the London Monument, and four or five times higher than the Pyramids of Egypt, with a suita-

5*

ble base! Some of these ants, of a smaller kind, build their houses like a pillar, three feet high, whose shape resembles a mushroom, having an overhanging roof: In all, there are a number of apartments, galleries, and magazines. This ant will give some faint idea of the wonderful industry of these little insects, thousands of which may, at one tread, be crushed under our feet.

"Go," then "to the ant, thou sluggard; consider her ways, and be wise."

He is a sluggard that loves his ease, lives in idleness, minds no business, sticks to nothing, brings nothing to pass, and in a particular manner, is careless in the business of religion. Let such go to school to the ant, and the little busy insect will teach them industry. In particular, let them learn wisdom from the industry of the ant, in gathering "her meat in the summer." Childhood and youth are the summer time of life; and if we then do not lay up against old age, we shall be very poor, unless our fathers have laid up before us, and made us rich. We must also lay up for the mind as well as for the body; and if we have no treasure there to supply our wants, we shall be poor miserable old creatures, when pains come upon us, and we can enjoy no society, and are unable both to talk and to read. And we must lay up for the soul; for if we have no spiritual store, the poor soul will find itself starving just as it is going into eternity. Be wise then by times: " Seek the Lord while he is to be found ; call upon him while he is near!" "Lay up for yourselves treasures in heaven."

> "The little ants for one poor grain,
> Labor, and tug, and strive ;
> Yet we who have a heaven to obtain,
> How negligent we live."

LESSON XXVII.

LOKMAN.—Aikin.

LOKMAN, surnamed the Wise, lived in very early times, probably in the days of king David and king Solomon, and his name is still famous in the East as the inventor of many fables and parables ; and various stories are told of his wisdom. It was said that he was a native of Ethiopia, and either a tailor, a carpenter, or a shepherd, and that afterwards he was a slave in various countries, and was at last sold among the Israelites.

One day, as he was seated in the midst of a company who were all listening to him with great respect and attention, a Jew of high rank, looking earnestly at him, asked him whether he was not the same man whom he had seen keeping the sheep of one of his neighbors. Lokman said he was. "And how," said the other, "did you, a poor slave, come to be so famous as a wise man?" "By exactly observing these three rules," replied Lokman; "always speak the truth without disguise, strictly keep your promises, and do not meddle with what does not concern you." Another time he said that he had learned his wisdom from the blind, who will believe nothing but what they hold in their hands; meaning that he always examined things, and took great pains to find out the truth.

Being once sent with some other slaves to fetch fruit, his companions ate a great deal of it, and then said it was he who had eaten it; on which he drank warm water to make himself sick, and thus proved that he had no fruit in his stomach; and the other slaves, being obliged to do the same, were found out.

Another story of him is, that his master having given him a kind of melon called the coloquintida, which is one of the bitterest things in the world, Lokman immediately ate it all up without making faces or showing the least dislike. His master, quite surprised, said, "How was it possible for you to swallow so nauseous a fruit?" Lokman replied, "I have received so many sweets from you, that it is not wonderful that I should have swallowed the only bitter fruit you ever gave me." His master was so much struck by this generous and grateful answer, that he immediately rewarded him by giving him his liberty.

At this day, 'to teach Lokman,' is a common saying in the East to express a thing impossible: it is said too that he was as good as he was wise; and, indeed, it is the chief part of wisdom to be good. He was particularly remarkable for his love to God and his reverence of his holy name. He is reported to have lived to a good old age; and many centuries after, a tomb in the little town of Ramlah, not far from Jerusalem, was pointed as Lokman's.

LESSON XXVIII.

THE HUNDRED AND FOURTH PSALM.—BIBLE.

BLESS the Lord, O my soul! O Lord my God! thou art very great; thou art clothed with honor and majesty: who coverest thyself with light as with a garment; who stretchest out the heavens like a curtain; who layeth the beams of his chambers in the waters; who maketh the clouds his chariot, who walketh upon the wings of the wind; who laid the foundations of the earth, that it should not be removed for ever. Thou coverest it with the deep, as with a garment: the waters stood above the mountains. At thy rebuke they fled; at the voice of thy thunder they hasted away. They go up by the mountains; they go down by the valleys, unto the place which thou hast founded for them. Thou hast set a bound that they may not pass over; that they turn not again to cover the earth.

He sendeth the springs unto the valleys, which run among the hills. They give drink to every beast of the field: the wild asses quench their thirst. By them shall the fowls of the heaven have their habitation, which sing among the branches. He watereth the hills from his chambers: the earth is satisfied with the fruit of thy works. He causeth the grass to grow for the cattle, and herb for the service of man, that he may bring forth food out of the earth.

He appointed the moon for seasons; the sun knoweth his going down. Thou makest darkness, and it is night; wherein all the beasts of the forest do creep forth. The young lions roar after their prey, and seek their meat from God. The sun ariseth—they gather themselves together, and lay them down in their dens. Man goeth forth unto his work, and to his labor, until the evening.

O Lord, how manifold are thy works! in wisdom hast thou made them all: the earth is full of thy riches. So is this great and wide sea, wherein are things creeping innumerable, both small and great beasts. There go the ships: there is that leviathan, whom thou hast made to play therein.

These wait all upon thee, that thou mayest give them their meat in due season. That thou givest them, they gather; thou openest thy hand—they are filled with good. Thou hidest thy face—they are troubled; thou takest away their breath—they die, and return to their dust. Thou sendest forth thy spirit—they are created; and thou renewest the face of the earth.

The glory of the Lord shall endure forever: the Lord shall rejoice in his works. I will sing unto the Lord as long as I live; 1 will sing praise to my God, while I have my being. Praise ye the Lord!

LESSON XXIX.

THE BUTTERFLY'S BALL.—Roscoe.

Come, take up your hats, and away let us haste
To the butterfly's ball and the grasshopper's feast;
The trumpeter, gadfly, has summoned the crew,
And the revels are now only waiting for you.

On the smooth shaven grass by the side of the wood,
Beneath a broad oak that for ages has stood,
See the children of earth and the tenants of air,
For an evening's amusement together repair.

And there came the beetle so blind and so black,
Who carried the emmet his friend on his back;
And there was the gnat, and the dragonfly too,
With all their relations, green, orange, and blue.

And there came the moth in his plumage of down,
And the hornet with jacket of yellow and brown,
Who with him the wasp his companion did bring;
But they promised that evening to lay by their sting.

And the sly little dormouse crept out of his hole,
And led to the feast his blind brother the mole;
And the snail, with his horns peeping out from his shell,
Came from a great distance,—the length of an ell.

A mushroom their table, and on it was laid
A water-dock leaf, which a table-cloth made;
The viands were various, to each of their taste,
And the bee brought his honey to crown the repast.

There close on his haunches, so solemn and wise,
The frog from a corner looked up to the skies;
And the squirrel, well-pleased such diversion to see,
Sat cracking his nuts overhead in the tree.

Then out came the spider, with fingers so fine,
To show his dexterity on the tight line ;
From one branch to another his cobwebs he slung,
Then as quick as an arrow he darted along.

But just in the middle, oh ! shocking to tell !
From his rope in an instant poor Harlequin fell ;
Yet he touched not the ground, but with talons outspread,
Hung suspended in air at the end of a thread.

Then a grasshopper came with a jerk and a spring,
Very long was his leg, though but short was his wing :
He took but three leaps, and was soon out of sight,
Then chirped his own praises the rest of the night.

With step so majestic the snail did advance,
And promised the gazers a minute to dance ;
But they all laughed so loud that he pulled in his head,
And went to his own little chamber to bed.

Then as evening gave way to the shadows of night,
Their watchman, the glowworm, came out with his light ;
Then home let us hasten while yet we can see,
For no watchman is waiting for you and for me.

LESSON XXX.

HOPE AND MEMORY.—Mrs. Sigourney.

A BABE lay in its cradle. A being with bright hair, and a
clear eye, came and kissed it. Her name was Hope. Its
nurse denied it a cake, for which it cried; but Hope told it
of one in store for it to-morrow. Its little sister gave it a
flower, at which it clapped its hands joyfully, and Hope
promised it fairer ones, which it should gather for itself.

The babe grew to a boy. He was musing at the summer

twilight. Another being, with a sweet, serious face, came and sat by him. Her name was Memory. And she said, "Look behind thee, and tell me what thou seest."

The boy answered, "I see a short path, bordered with flowers. Butterflies spread out gay wings there, and birds sing among the shrubs. It seems to be the path where my feet have walked, for at the beginning of it is my own cradle."

"What art thou holding in thy hand?" asked Memory. And he answered, "a book which my mother gave me." "Come hither," said Memory, with a gentle voice, "and I will teach thee how to get honey out of it that shall be sweet when thy hair is gray."

The boy became a youth. Once, as he lay in his bed, Hope and Memory came to the pillow. Hope sang a merry song, like the lark when she rises from her nest to the skies. Afterward, she said, "Follow me, and thou shalt have music in thy heart, as sweet as the lay I sung thee."

But Memory said, "He shall be mine also. Hope, why need we contend? For as long as he keepeth Virtue in his heart, we will be to him as sisters, all his life long." So he embraced Hope and Memory, and was beloved of them both.

When he awoke, they blessed him, and he gave a hand to each. He became a man, and Hope girded him every morning for his labor, and every night he supped at the table of Memory, with Knowledge for their guest.

At length, age found the man, and turned his temples white. To his dim eye it seemed that the world was an altered place. But it was he himself who had changed, and the warm blood had grown cold in his veins.

Memory looked on him with grave and tender eyes, like a loving and long-tried friend. She sat down by his elbow-chair, and he said to her, "Thou hast not kept faithfully some jewels that I entrusted to thee. I fear that they are lost."

She answered mournfully and meekly, "It may be so. The lock of my casket is worn. Sometimes I am weary, and fall asleep. Then Time purloins my key. But the gems that thou gavest me when life was new, see! I have lost none of them. They are as brilliant as when they came into my hands."

Memory looked pitifully on him, as she ceased to speak, wishing to be forgiven. But Hope began to unfold a radiant wing which she had long worn concealed beneath her robe, and daily tried its strength in a heavenward flight.

The old man lay down to die. And as the soul went forth

from the body, the angels took it. Memory ascended by its
side, and went through the open gate of heaven. But Hope
paused at the threshold. There she expired, like a rose faintly
giving forth its last odors.

A glorious form bent over her. Her name was Immortal
Happiness. Hope commended to her the soul, which she had
followed through the world. "Religion," she said, "planted
in it such seeds as bear the fruit of heaven. It is thine forever."

Her dying words were like the music of some breaking
harp, mournful but sweet. And I heard the voices of angels
saying, "Hope that is born of the earth must die, but Memory
is eternal as the books from which men are judged."

LESSON XXXI.

SELF-DENIAL.—Taylor.

THE clock had just struck nine, and Harry recollected that
his mother had desired them not to set up a minute after the
clock struck. He reminded his elder brother of this order.
"Never mind," said Frank, "here is a famous fire, and I
shall stay and enjoy it." "Yes," said Harry, "here's a famous fire, and I should *like* to stay and enjoy it; but that
would not be self-denial, would it, Frank?" "Nonsense,"
said Frank, "I shall not stir yet, I promise you." "Then
good night to you," said Harry. Six o'clock was the time at
which the brothers were expected to rise. When it struck
six the next morning, Harry started up; but the air felt so
frosty that he had a strong inclination to lie down again.
"But no," thought he, "here is a fine opportunity for self-denial;" and up he jumped without farther hesitation. "Frank,
Frank," said he to his sleeping brother, "past six o'clock, and
a fine star-light morning." "Let me alone," cried Frank, in
a cross, drowsy voice. "Very well, then, a pleasant nap to
you," said Harry, and down he ran as gay as the lark. After
finishing his Latin exercise, he had time to take a pleasant
walk before breakfast; so that he came in fresh and rosy,
with a good appetite, and, what was still better, in a good
humor.

But poor Frank, who had just tumbled out of bed when the

bell rang for prayer, came down, looking pale, and cross, and cold, and discontented. Harry, who had some sly drollery of his own, was just beginning to rally him on his forlorn appearance, when he recollected his resolution. "Frank does not like to be laughed at, especially when he is cross," thought he, so he suppressed his joke; and it requires some *self-denial* even to suppress a joke.

During breakfast his father promised that if the weather continued fine, Harry should ride out with him before dinner on the gray pony. Harry was much delighted with this proposal; and the thought of it occurred to him very often during the business of the morning. The sun shone cheerily in at the parlor windows, and seemed to promise fair for a fine day. About noon, however, it became rather cloudy, and Harry was somewhat startled to perceive a few large drops upon the flag-stones in the court. He equipped himself, nevertheless, in his great coat, at the time appointed, and stood playing with his whip in the hall, waiting to see the horses led out. His mother now passing by, said, "My dear boy, I am afraid there can be no riding this morning: do you see that the stones are quite wet?" "Dear mother," said Harry, "you surely do not imagine that I am afraid of a few drops of rain; besides, it will be no more than a shower at any rate." Just then his father came in, who looked first at the clouds, then at the barometer, and then at Harry, and shook his head. "You intend to go, papa, don't you?" said Harry. "I must go, I have business to do; but I believe, Harry, it will be better for *you* to stay at home this moring," said his father. "But, sir," repeated Harry, "do you think it possible now, that this little sprinkling of rain should do me the least harm in the world, with my great coat and all?" "Yes, Harry," said his father, "I do think that even this sprinkling of rain may do you harm, as you have not been quite well: I think, too, that it will be more than a sprinkling. But you shall decide on this occasion for yourself; I know you have some self-command. I shall only tell you, that your going this morning would make your mother uneasy, and that we both think it improper;— now determine." Harry again looked at the clouds, at the stones, at his boots, and last of all at his kind mother; and then he recollected himself. "This," thought he, "is the best opportunity for *self-denial* that I have had to-day!" and he immediately ran out to tell Roger that he need not saddle the gray pony.

"I should like another, I think, mother," said Frank that

day at dinner, just as he had despatched a large hemisphere of mince pie. " Any more for you, my dear Harry ?" said his mother. " If you please ;—no, thank you, though," said Harry, withdrawing his plate, " for," thought he, " I have had enough, and more than enough, to satisfy my hunger; and now is the time for *self-denial.* " Brother Harry," said his little sister after dinner, " when will you show me how to do that pretty puzzle you said you would show me a long time ago ?" " I am busy now, child," said Harry, " don't tease me now ; that's a good girl." She said no more, but looked disappointed, and still hung upon her brother's chair. " Come, then," said he, suddenly recollecting himself, " bring me your puzzle," and laying down his book, he very good-naturedly showed his little sister how to place it.

That night, when the two boys were going to bed, Harry called to mind, with some complacency, the several instances in the course of the day in which he had exercised *self-denial,* and he was on the very point of communicating them to his brother Frank. " But no," thought he, " this is another opportunity still for *self-denial ;* I will not say a word about it ; besides, to boast of it would spoil all." So Harry lay down quietly, making the following sage reflections :—" This has been a pleasant day to me, although I have had one great disappointment, and done several things against my will. I find that *self-denial* is painful for a moment, but very agreeable in the end ; and, if I go on this plan every day, I shall stand a good chance of leading a happy life."

LESSON XXXII.

THE SHEPHERD-BOY AND HIS DOG SHAG.—ANONYMOUS.

ONE Saturday evening Halbert's mother was taken very ill ; the cottage they lived in was away among the mountains, far from any path. The snow fell in large, heavy flakes, and Malcolm—that was the shepherd's name—took down his long pole with the intention of setting out to the village to procure some medicine for his wife. " Father," said little Halbert, " I know the sheep-path through the dark glen better than you ; and, with Shag, who will walk before me, I am quite safe ; let me go for the doctor, and do you stay and comfort my mother." Malcolm consented. Halbert had been accustomed to the mountains from his earliest infancy; and Shag set out with his young master, wagging his tail, and making many jumps and grimaces. They went safely on—Halbert arrived at the village—saw the doctor—received some medicine for his mother—and then commenced his return with a cheerful heart.

Shag went on before to ascertain that all was right;—suddenly, however, he stopped, and began snuffing and smelling about. "Go on, Shag," said Halbert. Shag would not stir. "Shag, go on, sir," repeated the boy; "we are nearly at the top of the glen; look through the night, you can see the candle glimmer in our window." Shag appeared obstinate for the first time in his life; and at last Halbert advanced alone, heedless of the warning growl of his companion. He had proceeded but a few steps when he fell over a precipice, which had been concealed by a snow-wreath.

Malcolm repeatedly snuffed the little candle which he had affectionately placed so as to throw light over his boy's path—replenished the fire—and spoke to his wife that comfort in which his own anxious heart could not participate.

Often did he go to the door, but no footstep sounded on the crackling ice—no figure darkened the wide waste of snow. "Perhaps the doctor is not at home, and he is waiting for him," said his poor mother. She felt so uneasy at her child's absence. that she almost forgot her own pain. It was nearly midnight, when Malcolm heard the well-known bark of the faithful Shag. "My son! my son!" cried both parents at the same moment. The cottage-door opened, and Shag entered without his master! "My brave boy has perished in the snow!" exclaimed the mother; at the same moment the father saw a small packet round the dog's neck, who was lying panting on the floor. "Our boy lives," said the shepherd; "here is the medicine tied with his handkerchief; he has fallen into some of the pits; but he is safe. Trust in God! I will go out, and Shag will conduct me safely to the rescue of my child." In an instant, Shag was again on his feet, and testfied the most unbounded joy as they both issued from the cottage. You can imagine the misery and grief the poor mother suffered—alone in her mountain-dwelling—the snow and the wind beating round her solitary cot—the certainty of her son's danger, and the fear lest her husband also might perish. She felt that both their lives depended on the sagacity of a poor dog; but she knew that God could guide the dumb creature's steps to the saving of both; and she clasped her hands, and fervently prayed that God would not desert her in the most severe trial she had ever met.

Shag went on straight and steadily for some yards, and then suddenly turned down a path which led to the bottom of the crag over which Halbert had fallen. The descent was steep and dangerous, and Malcolm was frequently obliged to support himself by the frozen branches of the trees. Providentially, however, it had ceased snowing, and the clouds were drifting fast from the moon. At last Malcolm stood at the lower and opposite edge of the pit into which his son had fallen;—he hallooed—he strained his eyes, but could not see or hear anything. Shag was making his way down an almost perpendicular height, and Malcolm resolved at all hazards to follow him. After getting to the bottom, Shag scrambled to a projecting ledge of rock, which was nearly bedded in snow, and commenced whining and scratching in a violent manner. Malcolm followed, and after some search found what appeared to be the dead body of his son. He hastily tore off the jacket, which was soaked with blood and snow; and, wrapping Halbert in his plaid, strapped him across his shoulders, and with much toil and difficulty re-ascended. Halbert was placed in his mother's bed; and by using great exertion they aroused him from his dangerous sleep. He was much bruised, and his ankle dislocated; but he had no other hurt: and when he recovered his senses, he fixed his eyes on his mother, and his first words were, "Thank God! —but did you get the medicine, mother?" When he fell, Shag had descended after him, and the affectionate son used what little strength he had left to tie what he had received from the doctor round his neck, and directed him home with it.

It is many years since this happened, and Shag is now old and gray; but he still toddles about after his master, who is now one of the most handsome and trusty shepherds among the bonny Highlands of Scotland.

LESSON XXXIII.

THE BRIGHT FIRMAMENT.—BARBAULD.

THE golden orb of the sun is sunk behind the hills; the colors fade away from the Western sky; and the shades of evening fall fast around me.

Deeper and deeper they stretch over the plain; I look at the grass, it is no longer green; the flowers are no more tinted with various hues; the houses, the trees, the cattle, are all lost in the distance. The dark curtain of night is let down over the works of God; they are blotted out from the view, as if they were no longer there.

Child of little observation! canst thou see nothing because thou canst not see grass and flowers, trees and cattle? Lift up thine eyes from the ground, shaded with darkness, to the heavens that are stretched over thy head; see how the stars, one by one, appear and light up the vast concave.

There is the moon, bending her bright horns, like a silver bow, and shedding her mild light, like liquid silver, over the blue firmament.

There is Venus, the evening and the morning star; and the Pleiades, and the Bear that never sets, and the Pole star that guides the mariner over the deep.

Now the mantle of darkness is over the earth; the last little gleam of twilight is faded away; the lights are extinguished in the cottage windows, but the firmament burns with innumerable fires; every little star twinkles in its place. If you begin to count them they are more than you can number; they are like the sands of the sea-shore.

The telescope shows you far more; and there are thousands and ten thousands of stars which no telescope has ever reached.

Now, Orion heaves his bright shoulder above the horizon, and Sirius, the dog-star, follows him—the brightest of the train.

Look at the milky-way, it is a field of brightness; its pale light is composed of myriads of burning suns.

All these are God's families; he gives the sun to shine with a ray of his own glory; he marks the path of the planets; he guides their wanderings through the sky, and traces out their orbit with the finger of his power.

If you were to travel as swift as an arrow from a bow, and to travel on further and further still, for millions of years, you would not be out of the creation of God.

New suns in the depth of space would still be burning around you, and other planets fulfilling their appointed course.

Lift up thine eyes, child of earth, for God has given thee a glimpse of heaven.

The light of one sun is withdrawn that thou mayest see

6*

ten thousand. Darkness is spread over the earth, that thou mayest behold, at a distance, the regions of eternal day.

This earth has a variety of inhabitants; the sea, the air, the surface of the ground, swarm with creatures of different natures, sizes, and powers; to know a very little of them is to be wise among the sons of men.

What, then, thinkest thou, are the various forms, and natures, and senses, and occupations of the peopled universe?

Who can tell the birth and generations of so many worlds? who can relate their histories? who can describe their inhabitants?

Canst thou measure infinity with a line? canst thou grasp the circle of infinite space?

Yet these all depend upon God; they hang upon him as a child upon the breast of its mother; he tempereth the heat to the inhabitants of Mercury; he provideth resources against the cold in the frozen orb of Saturn. Doubt not that he provideth for all beings that he has made.

Look at the moon when it walketh in brightness; gaze at the stars when they are marshaled in the firmament, and adore the Maker of so many worlds.

The mountain hiding its snowy head in the clouds; the river rolling its irresistible current, swelled with all the waters of heaven; the boundless expanse of ocean; the raging agitations of the tempest—these are grand and sublime objects which affect the most stupid and unfeeling hearts. But what are these, in comparison of Him "who counteth the nations as the small dust of the balance; who taketh up the isles as a very little thing; who stretcheth out the north over the empty space, and hangeth the earth upon nothing?"

Reputation, of all possessions, is the most valuable, next to a good conscience; to which indeed it of right belongs, and from which it naturally springs. The root lies out of the reach of injury. Your innocence no one can take from you, without your own consent: but the fruit of a fair reputation, so beautiful and fragrant, and in all respects so precious, this, alas! hangs exposed to the assault of every passenger: the lowest, as he goes along, can fling a stone upwards, and laugh to see the prize fall, though he cannot gather it.

THE YOUNG SPEAKER.

PART THIRD.

LESSONS FOR SPEAKING OR READING.

THERE are *four principal positions of the feet*. The above Figure represents a boy standing in one of them. The pupil will perceive that the *right* foot is *advanced* and supports nearly all the *weight* of the body, while the *left* foot touches the floor but *lightly*. He will notice, also, that the toes are turned moderately outward, and that the *left heel*,—at a distance of about *half the length of the foot*,—falls directly behind the *right heel*. This is the *first right position*.

LESSON I.

OUR NATIVE LAND.—M. M. B.

WE come, a youthful, happy band,
 Rejoicing in our native land;
A rich inheritance we claim,
 Our fathers' deeds, our fathers' fame.

In other lands, we read in story,
 Are kings, and thrones, but 'tis our glory
That we are free;—no tyrant's frown
 We fear—no man who wears a crown!

In freedom's cause we'll bravely dare
 To climb the steeps of fame, and share
A nation's love—a priceless gem—
 Who wins it, wants no diadem!

LESSON II.

WHY YIELD TO GRIEF.—ANONYMOUS.

'TWAS when the seas with hideous roar
 A little bark assailed,
And potent fear, with awful power,
 O'er each on board prevailed—

Save one, the captain's darling child,
 Who fearless view'd the storm,
And playful with composure smiled,
 At danger's threatening form,—

"Why sporting thus?" a seaman cried,
 "When sorrows overwhelm?"—
"Why yield to grief," the boy replied—
 "My father's at the helm?"

LESSON III.

ETERNITY.—HENRY.

ARITHMETICIANS have figures to compute all the progressions of time. Astronomers have instruments to calculate the distances of the planets. But what numbers can state, what lines can guage, the lengths and breadths of eternity? "It is higher than heaven; what canst thou do? deeper than hell; what canst thou know? the measure thereof is longer than the earth, broader than the sea."

Mysterious, mighty existence! A sum not to be lessened by the largest *deductions!* an extent not to be contracted by all *possible diminutions!* Never can it be said, after the most prodigious waste of ages, "So much of eternity is gone." When millions of centuries are elapsed, it is but just commencing; and when millions more have run their ample round, it will be no nearer ending. Eternity, vast, boundless, amazing eternity!

LESSON IV.

THE SKATER'S SONG.—ANONYMOUS.

Away, away, with a curve and a dash,
    And a light and a bounding spring,
For the racing steed and the lightning's flash,
    Only vie with the skater's fling.

Then away o'er the plain of the glassy stream,
    Will I speed in my airy flight,
And I'll laugh at the car with its hissing steam,
    And spurn at its boasted might.

Now away do I skim o'er the slippery field
    Like a bird in the calm blue sky,
And declare to the winds that I never will yield,
    As I proudly go dashing by.

LESSON V.

CONTENT.—ANONYMOUS.

It is not youth can give content,
  Nor is it wealth's decree ;
It is a gift from Heaven sent,
  Though not to thee or me.

It is not in the Monarch's crown,
  Though he'd give millions for't :
It dwells not in his Lordship's frown,
  Or waits on him to court.

It is not in a coach and six,
  It is not in a garter ;
'Tis not in love or politics,
  But 'tis in *Hodge the carter*.

LESSON VI.

BRUTUS ON THE DEATH OF CÆSAR.—SHAKSPEARE.

ROMANS, countrymen, and friends ; hear me for my cause ;
and be silent that you may hear.   Believe me for mine hon-
or, and have respect to mine honor, that you may believe.
Censure me in your wisdom, and awake your senses that
you may the better judge.   If there be any in this assembly,
any dear friend of Cæsar's, to him I say, that Brutus's love to
Cæsar was no less than his.   If then that friend demand,
why Brutus rose against Cæsar, this is my answer : not that
I loved Cæsar less, but that I loved Rome more.   Had you
rather Cæsar were living and die all slaves, than that Cæsar
were dead, and live all freemen ?   As Cæsar loved me, I
weep for him ; as he was fortunate, I rejoice at it ; as he was
valiant, I honor him ; but as he was *ambitious, I slew* him !
There are *tears* for his *love, joy* for his *fortune, honor* for his
valor, and *death* for his *ambition !*

This figure represents a boy in the *second right position*. The arrangement of the feet is in all respects similar to the *first right* described on page 67; he pupil will notice this *difference*, however, that the *left* foot now supports the *weight* of the body, while the *right* foot touches the floor but lightly, and the *heel* is turned a little more *outward*.

LESSON VII.

FAINT NOT.—Anonymous.

Up and doing—be not faint
   Nor loiter by the way;
Waste no time in sad complaint
   If ye would gain the day.

Persevere, and you shall win—
   So doth the world declare;
Triumph o'er the hosts of sin,
   And palms of victory bear.

Onward—upward—be your aim,
   Unheeding curse or frown;
They who bear the Christian's name
   Must labor for the crown.

LESSON VIII.

A WORD IN KINDNESS.—ANONYMOUS.

A LITTLE word in kindness spoken,
    A motion or a tear,
Has often healed the heart that's broken,
    And made a friend sincere.

A word—a look—has crushed to earth
    Full many a budding flower,
Which, if a smile had owned its birth,
    Had blessed life's darkest hour.

Then deem it not an idle thing
    A pleasant word to speak;
The face you wear, the thoughts you bring,
    A heart may heal or break.

LESSON IX.

DEPEND NOT ON EARTHLY BLISS.—HERVEY.

You have seen, no doubt, a set of pretty painted birds perching on your trees, or sporting in your meadows. You were pleased with the lovely visitants, that brought beauty on their wings and melody in their throats. But could you ensure the continuance of this agreeable entertainment? No, truly. At the least disturbing noise, at the least terrifying appearance, they start from their seats; they mount the skies, and are gone in an instant—are gone forever.

Would you choose to have a happiness which bears date with their arrival, and expires at their departure? If you could not be content with a portion, enjoyable only through such a fortuitous term, not of years, but of moments, O! take up with nothing earthly; set your affections on things above; there alone is " no variableness or shadow of turning."

LESSON X.

THE ARAB STEED.—Anonymous.

O give me but my Arab steed, a shield and falchion bright,
And I will to the battle speed, to save him in the fight :
His noble crest I'll proudly wear, and gird his scarf around ;
But I must to the field repair, for hark ! the trumpets sound !
   Hark ! hark ! hark ! the trumpets sound !

Oh ! with my Arab steed I'll go, to brave the embattled plain,
Where warriors tried their valor show, and drain each noble
     vein :
His brow, that oft the battle braves, with fadeless laurels
     crown'd,
Shall guide me where his falchion waves,—but hark ! the
     trumpets sound !
   Hark ! hark ! hark ! the trumpets sound !

LESSON XI.

THE BATTLE CALL.—Percival.

Loud rings the battle trumpet,
Far resounding, far swelling !
Rouse, heroes, rouse to the conflict !
See, yonder the dark foe
Sweeps, like a winter storm !

On speeds the fierce invader,
Wild as ocean high heaving !
Strong nerve ye, boldly to meet him !
Back hurl him, as dashed wave
Rolls from the rock-bound shore !

Earth far has shook beneath him,
All invading, all subduing !
Yet fear not—country is sacred !
Who arms for his loved home,
Fights with the sword of heaven !

7

LESSON XII.

YOU CANNOT CONQUER AMERICA.—CHATHAM.

I KNOW the valor of your troops; I know the skill of your officers; I know the force of this country; but in such a cause, your success would be hazardous. America, if she fell, would fall like the strong man: she would embrace the pillars of the state, and pull down the constitution with her. Is this your boasted peace? Not to sheathe the sword in the scabbard, but to sheathe it in the hearts of your countrymen? The Americans have been wronged; they have been driven to madness by injustice. Will you punish them for the madness you have occasioned? No; let this country be the first to resume its prudence and temper. I will pledge myself for the colonies, that, on their part, animosity and resentment will cease. Let affection be the only bond of coercion. Upon the whole I will beg leave to tell the House in a few words what is really my opinion. It is, that the Stamp Act be repealed—ABSOLUTELY—TOTALLY—and IMMEDIATELY.

LESSON XIII.

CARE OF THE DEITY.—ANONYMOUS.

THE insect, that with puny wing,
　Just shoots along the summer ray:
The floweret, which the breath of spring
　Wakes into life for half a day;
The smallest mote, the slenderest hair—
　All feel our common Father's care.

E'en from the glories of his throne
　He bends to view this wandering ball;
Sees all, as if that all were one,
　Loves one, as if that one were all;
Rolls the swift planets in their spheres,
　And counts the sinner's lonely tears.

The *first left* position is just the *reverse* of the first right. The pupil will see by the Figure, that the *left* foot is advanced and supports the weight of the body, while the *right* foot touches the floor but lightly. In all other respects it is the same as the first *right*, described on the first page of Part Third.

LESSON XIV.

JOSEPH LANCASTER.—Mrs. Fitzgerald.

He has faded from earth, like a star from on high,
    In the evening of wearisome age,
But the glory which lingered, when dimmed was his sight,
Shall be told by the nations of earth with delight,
    And recorded on history's page.

For he lived not in vain—clad in simple attire,
    Benevolence writ on his face,—
He fixed his keen gaze,—like that bird of the sky,
Who looks on the sunbeam with firm, steady eye,—
    Determined to better his race.

'Twas accomplished, and Lancaster's name shall survive,
    And be graven in letters of love
On the hearts of the millions, his labors have blest,
When long he has passed from those labors to rest,
    And reached his bright mansion above.

LESSON XV.

THE RAINBOW.—HERVEY.

BEHOLD a *bow*, of no hostile intentions! a bow painted in variegated colors, on the disburdened cloud. How vast is the extent, how delicate the texture, of that *showery arch!* It compasseth the heavens with a glorious circle, and teaches us to forget the horrors of the storm. Elegant its form, and rich its tinctures; but more delightful its sacred significancy. While the violet and the rose blush in its beautiful aspect, the olive-branch smiles in its gracious import. It writes in radiant dyes, what the angel sung in harmonious strains; "Peace on earth, and good-will toward men." It is the stamp of *insurance*, for the continuance of seed-time and harvest; for the preservation and security of the visible world. It is the comfortable *token* of a better state, and a happier kingdom;—a kingdom where sin shall cease, and misery be abolished; where storms shall beat, and winter pierce no more; but holiness, happiness and joy, like one unbounded spring, for ever, *ever* bloom.

LESSON XVI.

THE CREATOR'S WORKS.—ANONYMOUS.

THERE's not a star whose twinkling light
    Illumes the distant earth,
And cheers the solemn gloom of night,
    But mercy gave it birth.

There's not a cloud whose dews distill
    Upon the parching clod,
And clothe with verdure, vale and hill,
    That is not sent by God.

There's not a place in earth's vast round,
    In ocean deep, or air,
Where skill and wisdom are not found;
    For God is every where.

Around, beneath, below, above,
  Wherever space extends,
There heaven displays its boundless love,
  And power with mercy blends.

LESSON XVII.

MEET THE FOE.—Percival.

Ye sons of sires, who fought and bled
  For liberty and glory,
Whose fame shall ever wider spread
  Till Time is bent and hoary—
Awake to meet the invading foe !
  Rouse at the call of danger !
Beat down again his standard low,
  And backward hurl the stranger !

They knew no fear, those sires of old—
  'Mid swords and bayonets clashing,
Still high they bore their banner's fold,
  Its stars, like lightnings flashing.
Be like those sires !—With freeborn might,
  Renew the deeds of story !
Who lives, shall win a wreath of light—
  Who falls, shall sleep in glory !

LESSON XVIII.

NATIONAL GREATNESS.—Harper.

Mr. Speaker,—There cannot be the least doubt, but that,
when France is at length convinced that we are firmly resolved to call forth all our resources, and to exert all our
strength to resist her encroachments and aggressions, she will
soon desist from them. She need not be told, sir, what these
resources are; she knows well their greatness and extent.
She will not, therefore, drive us to extremity, but desist as
soon as she finds us determined. If our means, sir, of repelling

the attacks of France, were less than they really are, they might be rendered all-sufficient, by resolution and courage. It is in these that the strength of nations consists, and not in fleets, nor armies, nor population, nor money : in the " unconquerable will ; the courage never to submit or yield."

These are the true sources of national greatness ; and to use the words of a celebrated writer, " where these means are not wanting, all others will be found or created." It was these that made Rome the mistress of the world, and Athens the protectress of Greece.

THE *second left* position is just the *reverse* of the second right. The pupil will see by the Figure that the *right* foot now supports the weight of the body, while the *left* foot touches the floor but lightly, and the right *heel* is turned a little more outward. A careful observance of the *four positions* described is important to a free, graceful and manly action.

LESSON XIX.

THE THREE DOVES.—Aldrich.

As a mother wan and weeping,
Sad and silent watch was keeping
O'er her faintly breathing child,
By too flattering hope beguiled,
A gentle slumber came to bless
Softening down her wretchedness,
When beheld she in her dreaming
On the sky a halo gleaming,

And with her strange vision blending
Saw two white doves thence descending,
A moment o'er the child they hovered,
When the mother well discovered
'Neath the keen stars brightly burning
Three white doves to heaven returning!
Woke she now from joy to weeping,
Her sweet babe in death was sleeping!

LESSON XX.

THE CAPTIVE CHIEF.—PALMER.

PALE was the hue of his faded cheek,
As it leaned on its cold damp pillow;
And deep the heave of its troubled breast,
As the lift of the ocean billow:
For the thought of the days when his restless foot
Through the pathless forest bounded,
And the festive throng by the hunting-fire,
Where the chase song joyously sounded.

He had stood in the deadly ambuscade,
While his warriors were falling around him;
He had stood unmoved at the torturing stake,
Where the foe in his wrath had bound him;
He had mocked at pain in every form—
Had joyed in the post of danger;
But his spirit was crushed by the dungeon's gloom,
And the chain of the ruthless stranger.

LESSON XXI.

SPEECH OF LOGAN.—ASHE.

I APPEAL to any white man to say, if ever he entered Logan's cabin hungry, and he gave him not meat; if ever he came cold and naked, and he clothed him not. During the course of the last long and bloody war, Logan remained idle in his cabin, and an advocate for peace! Such was my love

for the whites, that my countrymen pointed as they passed, and said, "*Logan is the friend of white men !*"   I had even
thought to have lived with you, but for the injuries of one
man.   Colonel Cresap, the last spring, in cold blood, and un-
provoked, murdered all the relations of Logan, not sparing
even my women and children.   There runs not a drop of my
blood in the veins of any living creature.   This called on me
for revenge.   I have sought it : I have killed many : I have
fully glutted my vengeance.   For my country, I rejoice at
the beams of peace.   But do not harbor a thought that mine
is the joy of fear !   Logan never felt fear !   He will not turn
on his heel to save his life !   Who is there to mourn for Logan ?   Not one !"

LESSON XXII.

A MOTHER'S LOVE.—Miss Taylor.

Hast thou sounded the depths of yonder sea,
And counted the sands that under it be ?
Hast thou measured the height of heaven above ?
Then mayst thou mete out a mother's love.

Hast thou talked with the blessed of leading on
To the throne of God some wandering son ?
Hast thou witnessed the angel's bright employ ?
Then may'st thou speak of a mother's joy.

There is not a grand, inspiring thought,
There is not a truth by wisdom taught,
There is not a feeling, pure and high,
That may not be read in a mother's eye.

There are teachings on earth, and sky, and air;
The heavens the glory of God declare ;
But louder than voice beneath, above,
He is heard to speak through a mother's love.

LESSON XXIII.

THE PATRIOT WARRIOR'S DIRGE.—Anonymous.

Waft, waft ye winds, your rending tale !
 Go, bid the nation weep ;
The chief, beloved, is lying bound
 In death's unconscious sleep.

The warrior-heart in days of dread
 That felt the startling thrill—
That bounded 'mid the battle's fires,
 Is pulseless now and still.

In war he won, in peace he *wore*
 Fame's rich undying wreath ;
But ah ! that brow is wearing now,
 The diadem of death !

Waft, waft ye winds, with mournful speed !
 Haste with your tale of gloom ;
Tell youthful hearts, a deathless name,
 Alone, survives the tomb.

It will sometimes be necessary to *change* the positions of the feet ; this the pupil should learn to do with freedom and simplicity. In changing from the *first right* to the second, the left foot slides back about *four* inches, and receives the weight of the body, while the right foot naturally follows it and rests lightly upon the floor, at the same distance from it, as before the position was changed. In changing from the *second* right to the *first*, the right foot slides forward and receives the weight of the body, while the left follows it and rests lightly behind it.

LESSON XXIV.

REFLECTIONS IN A VAULT.—Hervey.

Good Heavens! what a solemn scene! How dismal the *gloom!* Here is perpetual darkness and night even at noonday.—How doleful the *solitude!* Not one trace of cheerful society; but sorrow and terror seem to have made this their dreadful abode.—Hark! how the hollow dome resounds at every tread. The *echoes*, that long have slept, are awakened; and lament and sigh along the walls.—Hark again! what sound is *that!*—In such a situation, every noise alarms.—Solemn and slow, it breaks upon the silent air,—it is the *striking of the clock.* Designed, one would imagine to ratify all my serious meditations. Methinks, it says *Amen,* and sets a seal to every improving hint. It tells me that another portion of my appointed time is elapsed. It is the knell of my departed hours. O may the admonition sink deep into an attentive and obedient mind. May it teach me that *heavenly arithmetic,* "of numbering my days, and applying my heart unto wisdom."

LESSON XXV.

FREDERICK THE GREAT.—Haven.

Are these the dictates of eternal truth?
  These the glad news your boasted reason brings?
Can these control the restless fire of youth,
  The craft of statesmen, or the pride of kings?

Whence is the throb that swells my rising breast,
  What lofty hopes my beating heart inspire?
Why do I proudly spurn inglorious rest,
  The pomp of wealth, the tumult of desire?

Is it to swell the brazen trump of fame,
  To bind the laurel round an aching head,
To hear for once a people's loud acclaim,
  Then lie forever with the nameless dead?

Oh no! far nobler hopes my life control,
Presenting scenes of splendor, yet to be;—
Great God! thy word directs the lofty soul
To live for glory, not for man, but thee.

LESSON XXVI.

COLUMBIA.—Dwight.

Columbia, Columbia, to glory arise,
The queen of the world and the child of the skies!
Thy genius commands thee ; with rapture behold,
While ages on ages thy splendors unfold.
Thy reign is the last, and the noblest of time,
Most fruitful thy soil, most inviting thy clime,
Let the crimes of the east ne'er encrimson thy name,
Be freedom, and science, and virtue, thy fame.

To conquest and slaughter let Europe aspire ;
Whelm nations in blood, and wrap cities in fire ;
Thy heroes the rights of mankind shall defend,
And triumph pursue them, and glory attend.
A world is thy realm : for a world be thy laws,
Enlarged as thine empire, and just as thy cause ;
On freedom's broad basis, that empire shall rise,
Extend with the main, and dissolve with the skies.

LESSON XXVII.

ADDRESS TO THE YOUNG.—Logan.

Now is your golden age. The morning of life rejoices
over your head; every thing around you puts on a smiling
appearance. All nature wears a face of beauty, and is animated with a spirit of joy. You walk up and down in a new
world; you crop the unblown flower, and drink the untasted
spring. Full of spirit, and high in hope, you set out on the
journey of life : Visions of bliss present themselves to view :
Dreams of joy, with sweet delusion, amuse the vacant mind:
You listen and accord to the song of hope, " To-morrow shall

be as·this day, and much more abundant." But ah! my friends, the flattering scene will not last. The spell is quickly broken, and the enchantment soon over. God forbid, that I should anticipate the evil day, unless I could arm you against it now; then *remember* your Creator; consecrate to him the early period of your days, and the light of his countenance will shine upon you through life. *Then*, let the tempest beat and the floods descend, you are safe and happy under the shelter of the Rock of Ages.

LESSON XXVIII.

THE SLEEPER.—Anonymous.

My master traveled far away,
　And left me much to do;
Alas! I trifled all the day,
　Although my days were few.

Wandering and playing like a child,
　And moved by every wind,
The fleeting moments I beguiled,
　Forgetting that I sinned.

I went to sleep like all the rest,
　Whilst time seemed still and dumb;
But soon he struck upon my breast,
　And cried, "Thy Master's come."

'Twas grass cut down by sudden mower,
　Or tree by lightning's stroke:—
"Oh! time, time, *time*, is this the hour?"
　And, trembling, I awoke.

LESSON XXIX.

THE SWISS COWHERD'S SONG.—Montgomery.

O, when shall I visit the land of my birth,
The loveliest land on the face of the earth:
When shall I those scenes of affection explore,

Our forests, our fountains,
Our hamlets, our mountains,
With the pride of our mountains the maid I adore?
O, when shall I dance on the daisy-white mead,
In the shade of an elm, to the sound of the reed?

When shall I return to that lovely retreat,
Where all my fond objects of tenderness meet,—
The lambs and the heifers that follow my call,
My father, my mother,
My sister, my brother,
And dear Isabella, the joy of them all?
O, when shall I visit the land of my birth?
'Tis the loveliest land on the face of the earth.

THE positions of the *left* foot
are changed in precisely the
same manner as those of the
right foot, described on page 81.

LESSON XXX.

INFLUENCE OF OUR COUNTRY.—BEMAN.

FAR be it from me to cherish, in any shape, a spirit of na-
ional prejudice, or to excite in others a disgusting national
vanity. But when I reflect upon the part which this country

8

is probably to act in the renovation of the world, I rejoice that I am a citizen of this great Republic. The character and institutions of our country have already produced a deep impression upon the world we inhabit. What but our example has stricken the chains of despotism from the provinces of South America—giving, by a single impulse, freedom to half a hemisphere? A Washington here, has created a Bolivar there. The flag of independence which has long waved from the summit of our Alleghany, has now been answered by a corresponding signal from the heights of the Andes. And the same spirit, too, that came across the Atlantic wave with the pilgrims, and made the rock of Plymouth the corner-stone of freedom and of this Republic, is traveling back to the East. It has already carried its influence into the cabinets of princes; and it is, at this moment, sung by the Grecian bard, and emulated by the Grecian hero.

LESSON XXXI.

ONE GOOD TURN DESERVES ANOTHER.—Mrs. Gilman.

Will Wag went to see Charley Quirk,
    More famed for his books than his knowledge,
In order to borrow a work
    He had sought for in vain over college.

But Charley replied, " My dear friend,
    You must know I have sworn and agreed,
My books from my room not to lend,—
    But you may *sit by my fire and read.*"

Now it happened, by chance, on the morrow,
    That Quirk, with a cold, quivering air,
Came his neighbor Will's bellows to borrow,
    For his own they were out of repair.

But Willy replied, " My dear friend,
    I have sworn and agreed, you must know,
That my bellows I never will lend,—
    But you may *sit by my fire and blow.*"

LESSON XXXII.

THE SAILOR'S DEPARTURE.—Miss Baillie.

Oh ! fresh blows the gale, o'er the wide mantling ocean,
  And proudly the frigate repels the white foam ;
And high beats my heart with tumultuous emotion,
  On leaving for fortune my dear native home.

Perhaps for the last time my father has blessed me ;
  I see his white locks, and the tears on his cheek ;
And my mother, how close to her bosom she pressed me,
  And kissed me and sobbed as her kind heart would break,

I may roam through the wide world, and friendship may
    court me,
  And love on my heart its soft characters trace ;
But ne'er shall affection lend aught to support me,
  So sacred, so pure, as that parting embrace.

Friends and protectors ! when dangers surround me,
  When pleasure, when wealth, spread their lures for my
    fame,
That moment's good angel shall hover around me,
  To chase every thought would dishonor your name.

LESSON XXXIII.

POWER OF DEATH.—Crafts.

Death has been among us, my friends, and has left a melancholy chasm. He has torn his victim from the heart of society, and from the altar of the living God. He has triumphed over the blushing honors of youth, the towering flight of genius, and the sacred ardor of devotion. Virtue, philanthropy, religion, are bereaved, and in tears. Death, terrible and insatiate, has been among us, and we are met to pay him tribute. O thou destroyer of human hope and happiness ! Was there no head, frosted by time, and bowed with cares, to which thy marble pillow could have yielded rest ? Was there no heart-broken sufferer to seek refuge from his

woes in thy cheerless habitation ? Was there no insulated
being, whose crimes or miseries would have made thee welcome ! who had lived without a friend, and could die without
a mourner. These, alas, could give no celebrity to thy conquests, for they fall, unheeded as the zephyr. Thy trophies
are the gathered glories of learning, the withered hopes of
usefulness, the tears of sorrowing innocence, the soul-appal-
ing cries of the widow and the orphan. Thou delightest to
break our happiness into fragments, and to tear our hearts
asunder.

To change from the *second right*
position to the *second left*, the head
is first turned, the eye resting on the
point to which the position is to be
directed, then, the *right* foot, with
the *heel* turned a little *outward* from
its former position, slides out in a
straight line to the right about *four
inches*, and receives the weight of
the body ; while the left foot, with
the heel turned a little more *inward*,
is drawn in about the same distance,
and touches the floor but lightly.
The change from the second left to
the second right is made in precisely
the same manner.

LESSON XXXIV.

THE DEATH BED.—Hood.

WE watched her breathing through the night,
  Her breathing soft and low,
As in her breast the wave of life
  Kept heaving to and fro !

So silently we seemed to speak—
  So slowly moved about !

As we had lent her half our powers,
    To eke her living out.

Our very hopes belied our fears,
    Our fears our hopes belied,—
We thought her dying when she slept,
    And sleeping when she died!

For when the morn came dim and sad—
    And chill with early showers,
Her quiet eyelids closed—she had
    Another morn than ours.

LESSON XXXV.

LIFE WITHOUT FREEDOM.—Moore.

From life without freedom, oh! who would not fly?
For one day of freedom, oh! who would not die?
Hark! hark! 'tis the trumpet! the call of the brave,
The death-song of tyrants and dirge of the slave.
Our country lies bleeding—oh! fly to her aid;
One arm that defends is worth hosts that invade.
From life without freedom, oh! who would not fly?
For one day of freedom, oh! who would not die?

In death's kindly bosom our last hope remains—
The dead fear no tyrants, the grave has no chains!
On, on to the combat! the heroes that bleed
For virtue and mankind are heroes indeed.
And oh! even if Freedom from this world be driven,
Despair not—at least we shall find her in heaven.
In death's kindly bosom our last hope remains,
The dead fear no tyrants, the grave has no chains.

LESSON XXXVI.

JACK HALYARD'S SPEECH.—Cardell.

Young men, Americans, far from you be that mean spirit,
which is satisfied with half-way excellence. Strive to gain

8*

the highest badge of honor for yourselves, and for your country. Be greatly good. Now is the time to store your minds with knowledge, and form your hearts to virtue. It is the condition of our being, that all which is most valuable is to be diligently sought. They who would win the prize, must exert themselves earnestly in the race, and not fall back, nor turn aside for small obstacles.

Young men of America, can you be ignorant of the high duties to which you are called? Will you pass away the prime of your days in careless indolence, and cheat the fair hopes of your friends? Can you be contented to crawl through the world with infamy, and die without doing anything worthy of your character as men?

My young countrymen,—your lot is cast in a land where empire is built on truth and justice; where the rights of man are cherished: you are to follow where a Washington has led, and where victory can gain no laurels in a bad cause.

LESSON XXXVII.

THE GREEK ISLANDER IN EXILE.—Mrs. Hemans.

A Greek Islander being taken to the Vale of Tempe, and called upon to admire its beautiful scenery, replied, " Yes, all is fair ; but the sea—where is the sea ?"

WHERE is the sea ?—I languish here—
    Where is my own blue sea ?
With all its barks of fleet career,
    And flags and breezes free!

I miss that voice of waves—the first
    That woke my childish glee :
The measured chime—the thundering burst—
    Where is my own blue sea ?

Oh! rich your myrtles' breath may rise,
    Soft, soft, your winds may be ;
Yet my sick heart within me dies—
    Where is my own blue sea ?

I hear the shepherd's mountain flute,
    I hear the whispering tree—
The echoes of my soul are mute—
    Where is my own blue sea ?

———

To change from the *first right*
position to the first *left*, the head is
first turned, the eye resting on the
point to which the position is to be
directed, the *left* foot then slides
forward and receives the weight of
the body, while the *right* foot follows, and at the proper distance,
rests lightly behind it. The change
from the *first left* to the *first right*
is made in precisely the same manner.

———

LESSON XXXVIII.

ADVERSITY.—Anonymous.

Adversity, thy malice cease—
In vain thy hope to wound my peace ;
    Thy shafts are idly spent :—
The full extent of grief and woe,
With all thy spite, I cannot know ;
    For I am innocent.

For innocence can make the soul,
Possessed of tranquil self-control,
    Always enjoy content :
Remorse alone can make thy dart
Corrode the sinner's guilty heart,
    And I am innocent.

Disgrace and scorn I can endure,
In conscious rectitude secure,
    And though they ne'er relent,
To every ill I am resigned,
Since *He* who sees the inmost mind
    Knows I am innocent.

LESSON XXXIX.

TO THE SEA.—KEATE.

HAIL ! thou inexhaustible source of wonder and contemplation ! Hail !—Hail thou multitudinous ocean ! How glorious ! how awful, how beautiful are the scenes thou display-
est ! when every wind is hushed, when the morning sun sil-
vers the level line of the horizon,—when its evening track is
marked with flaming gold, and thy unrippled bosom reflects
the radiance of the overarching heavens !—in thy terrors !
when the black tempest sweeps thy swelling billows, and the
boiling surge mixes with the clouds,—when death rides the
storm, and humanity drops a fruitless tear for the poor mariner.

And yet, mighty deep ! 'tis thy *surface* alone we view.—
Who can penetrate the secrets of thy wide domain ? Great
and mighty art thou, O ocean ! Terrible as a giant in his
strength. Placid and gentle art thou, O sea ! Beautiful as
a babe in its first dream. *He* permitteth thy stormy anger—
thy desolating rage ! *He* lulleth thee with the breath of
heaven !—graceth thee with the blue and the beauty of day !
He hath laid sure thy foundations—*His* voice hath said thus
far shalt thou go—here shall thy proud waves be stayed.

LESSON XL.

A SUDDEN CALM IN THE PACIFIC.—COLERIDGE.

THE fair breeze blew, the white foam flew,
    The furrow streamed off free :
We were the first that ever burst
    Into that silent sea.

Down dropt the breeze, the sails dropt down,
  'Twas sad as sad could be;
And we did speak only to break
  The silence of the sea.

All in a hot and copper sky,
  The bloody sun, at noon;
Right up above the mast did stand,
  No bigger than the moon.

Day after day, day after day,
  We struck, nor breath nor motion;
As idle as a painted ship
  Upon a painted ocean.

Water, water, everywhere,
  And all the boards did shrink;
Water, water, everywhere,
  But not a drop *to drink*.

LESSON XLI.

AMBITION FALSE AND TRUE.—Anonymous.

I WOULD not wear the warrior's wreath,
  I would not court his crown;
For love and virtue sink beneath
  His dark and vengeful frown.

I would not seek *my* fame to build
  On glory's dizzy height;
Her temple is with orphans filled;
  Blood soils her sceptre bright.

I would not wear the diadem,
  By folly prized so dear;
For want and woe have bought each gem,
  And every pearl's a tear.

I would not heap the golden chest,
  That sordid spirits crave;

For every gain,—by penury curst,—
Is gathered from the grave.

No; let my wreath unsullied be;
My fame be virtuous youth;
My wealth be kindness, charity;
My diadem be truth.

It is much to the credit of the young speaker when he comes before his audience with a neat and graceful *bow*. The figure presents the *side* view of a boy making his bow. The pupil, with a gentle but assured step, approaches to near the front of the platform, a little on the right of the centre, then pausing for a moment in the *first right* position, he casts his eyes with a diffident respect, over the audience; slides out his *left* foot on the toe, in a straight line; then, supporting the body on that foot, he draws in the *right* foot until its *heel* comes into the *middle* or hollow of the *left* foot; he then presses his legs together, and dropping his eyes modestly to the floor, brings his body into a slight and graceful curve, the *arms* hanging perfectly *free*. In this posture the body is kept for an instant; he then rises slowly to an erect attitude, and resumes the *first right* position, when he is ready to commence speaking. There should be no parade or affectation, but all marked by the manliness of a noble boy who thinks more of propriety and excellence than he does of mere show.

Some teachers instruct their pupils *to look directly in the eyes* of those to whom they are bowing; this mode, if preferred, can be adopted without any injury to the other directions here given.

LESSON XLII.

REPLY TO THE DUKE OF GRAFTON.—Thurlow.

My Lords:—I am amazed, yes, my Lords, I am amazed at his Grace's speech. The noble duke cannot look before him, behind him, or on either side of him, without seeing some noble peer, who owes his seat in this house to his successful exertions, in the profession to which I belong. Does he not feel that it is as honorable to owe it to these, as to being the accident of an accident?—To all these noble lords, the lan-

guage of the noble duke is as applicable and as insulting as it
is to myself. But I don't fear to meet it single and alone. No
one venerates the peerage more than I do—but, my lords, I must
say that the peerage solicited me,—not I the peerage. Nay
more,—I can say and will say, that as a peer of parliament,—
as speaker of this right honorable house,—as keeper of the
great seal,—as guardian of his majesty's conscience,—as
lord high chancellor of England,—nay, even in that character alone, in which the noble duke would think it an affront to
be considered—but which character none can deny *me*—as a
man, I am at this moment as respectable ; I beg leave to add
—I am, at this time as much respected, as the proudest peer
I now look down upon.

LESSON XLIII.

AN INFANT KILLED BY LIGHTNING.—CLARE.

As fearless as a cherub's rest
  Now safe above the cloud,
A babe lay on its mother's breast,
  When thunders roared aloud;
It started not to hear the crash,
  But held its little hand
Up, at the lightning's fearful flash,
  To catch the burning brand !

The tender mother stayed her breath
  In more than grief, awhile,
To think the thing that brought its death,
  Should cause the babe to smile.
Aye, it did smile a heavenly smile,
  To see the lightning play ;
Well might she shriek when it turned pale,
  And yet it smiled in clay.

O woman ! the dread storm was given
  To be to each a friend :
It took thy infant pure, to heaven—
  Left thee impure to mend.
Thus Providence will oft appear
  From God's own mouth to preach :
Ah ! would we were as prone to hear,
  As mercy is to teach.

LESSON XLIV.

ASPIRATIONS OF YOUTH.—Montgomery.

Higher, higher will we climb,
  Up the mount of glory,
That our names may live through time,
  In our country's story;
Happy, when her welfare calls,
He who conquers, he who falls.

Deeper, deeper let us toil
  In the mines of knowledge;
Nature's wealth, and learning's spoil,
  Win from school and college;
Delve we there for richer gems,
Than the stars of diadems.

Onward, onward may we press,
  Through the path of duty;
Virtue is true happiness,
  Excellence true beauty;
Minds are of celestial birth,—
Make we then a heaven of earth.

Closer, closer let us knit
  Hearts and hands together,
Where our fireside comforts sit,
  In the wildest weather;
Oh! they wander wide who roam
From the joys of life and home.

LESSON XLV.

INDIGNANT REBUKE.—Chatham.

I am astonished, my lords, to hear such principles confessed! I am shocked to hear them avowed in this House, or in this country! Principles equally unconstitutional, inhuman, and unchristian! My Lords, I did not intend to encroach again on your attention, but I cannot repress my indignation.

I feel myself impelled by every duty. My lords, we are called upon as members of this House, as men, as Christian men, to protest against such notions standing near the throne, polluting the ear of Majesty. "That God and nature put into our hands." I know not what ideas that lord may entertain of God and nature; but I know that such abominable principles are equally abhorrent to religion and humanity. What! to attribute the sacred sanction of God and nature to the massacres of the Indian scalping knife! to the cannibal savage, torturing, murdering, roasting, and eating; literally, my lords, *eating* the mangled victims of his barbarous battles! Such horrible notions shock every precept of religion, divine or natural, and every generous feeling of humanity. And, my lords, they shock every sentiment of honor; they shock me as a defender of honorable war, and a detester of murderous barbarity.

LESSON XLVI.

THE LITTLE HUSBANDMAN.—Anonymous.

I'M a little husbandman,
Work and labor hard I can;
I'm as happy all the day,
At my work, as if 'twere play;
Though I've nothing fine to wear,

THIS Figure represents a boy standing, as the pupil will see, in the *first right position*, and making what may be called *the first right hand gesture, palm up*. It is the first of a class of three. The Figure is placed above the language which the boy is supposed to be speaking. The hand begins to move at the word *for*, where this mark | is placed; it goes from the little *star* at the side of the Figure, and passes in a curved direction, as shown by the *dotted line* —this is called the *course* of the gesture; it strikes upon the word *that*, printed in italic letters—this is called the *stroke* of the gesture; and it falls to the side at the word *not*, where this mark) is placed. As here applied, it is an *emphatic* gesture; but it is proper also to *the*, denoting of objects supposed to be *near to* or *upon* the earth, and not far from the speaker's feet— as *flowers*, the *grave*, a *dog*, and the like. When thus used it is a *significant* gesture.

Yet | for *that* I do not) care.

9

When to work I go along,
Singing loud my morning song;
With my wallet on my back,
Or my wagon-whip to smack;
O, I am as happy then,
As the idle gentleman.

I've a hearty appetite,
And I soundly sleep at night;
Down I lie content, and say,
I've been useful all the day;
I'd rather be a plough-boy, than
A *useless* little gentleman.

LESSON XLVII.

THE ALARM.—Whittier.

Up the hillside, down the glen,
Rouse the sleeping citizen,
  Summon out the might of men!

Like a lion crouching low,
Like a night-storm rising slow,
Like the tread of unseen foe—

It is coming—it is nigh!
Stand your homes and altars by!
On your own free hearthstones die!

Clang the bells in all your spires!
On the gray hills of your sires,
Fling to heaven your signal fires!

O, for God and Duty stand,
Heart to heart, and hand with hand,
Round the old graves of your land;

Whoso shrinks and falters now,
Whoso to the yoke would bow,
Brand the craven on his brow.

LESSON XLVIII.

WHY WE DO NOT EXCEL IN ORATORY.—Knowles.

The principal cause of our not excelling in oratory is—our neglecting to cultivate the art of speaking—of speaking our own language. We acquire the power of expressing our ideas, almost insensibly—we consider it as a thing that is natural to us; we do not regard it as an art—it is an art—a difficult art—an intricate art—and our ignorance of that circumstance, or our omitting to give it due consideration is the cause of our deficiency.

In the infant just beginning to articulate, you will observe every inflection that is recognized in the most accurate treatise on elocution—you will observe, further, an exact proportion in its several cadences, and a speaking expression in its tones. I say, you will observe these things in almost every infant. Select a dozen men—men of education—erudition—ask them to read a piece of animated composition—you will be fortunate if you find one in the dozen, that can raise or depress his voice—inflect or modulate it as the variety of the subject requires. What has become of the inflections, the cadences, the modulation of the infant? They have not been exercised—they have been neglected—they have never been put into the hands of the artist, that he might apply them to their proper use—they have been laid aside, spoiled, abused, and, ten to one, they will never be good for anything!

LESSON XLIX.

HOW OLD ART THOU.—L. H. C.

Count not thy days that have idly flown,
   The years that were vainly spent,
Nor speak of the hours thou must blush to own,
When thy spirit stands before the throne,
   To account for the talents lent.

But number the hours redeemed from sin,
   The moments employed for heaven;

Oh! few and evil thy days have been,
Thy life a toilsome and worthless scene,
    For a nobler purpose given.

Will the shade go back on thy dial-plate?
    Will thy sun stand still on his way?
Both hasten on, and thy spirit's fate
Rests on the point of life's little date;

THIS Figure exhibits the *second or middle right hand gesture, palm up*. The hand begins to *move* the instant the word *is* drops from the lips; the *course* of the gesture is *circular* till it rises to about the height of the shoulder, when it passes to the right in *nearly a straight* line; the *stroke* comes upon the word *to-day;* and the hand falls to the side or comes to *rest,* as it is called, with the *first* word of the *next* line. The position is the same as in the Figure on page 97—the *first right;* but the pupil will notice that the *feet are a little farther apart.* This is the consequence of a *stronger* emphasis.— Supposing the speaker, as he makes the gesture, to change from the *second* right position, the *earnestness* of his admonition would necessarily occasion this difference. This gesture is well applied in asking *emphatic* questions, and it may be used also, as a *significant* gesture, in denoting persons or things at some distance from the speaker.

Then *live* while while it is | called *to-day!*

Life's) waning hours like the sybil's page,
    As they lessen, in value rise;
Oh! arouse thee and live; nor deem that man's age
Stands in the length of his pilgrimage,
    But in days that are truly wise.

LESSON L.

ON LAYING THE CORNER STONE OF THE BUNKER-HILL MONUMENT.—PIERPONT.

O, is not this a holy spot?
    'Tis the high place of freedom's birth!
God of our fathers! is it not
    The holiest spot of all the earth?

Quenched is thy flame on Horeb's side;
   The robber roams o'er Sinai now;
And those old men, thy seers, abide
   No more on Zion's mournful brow.

But on this hill, thou, Lord, hast dwelt,
   Since round its head the war-cloud curled,
And wrapped our fathers, where they knelt
   In prayer and battle for a world.

Here sleeps their dust: 'tis holy ground:
   And we, the children of the brave,
From the four winds are gathered round,
   To lay our offering on their grave.

Free as the winds around us blow,
   Free as the waves below us spread,
We rear a pile, that long shall throw
   Its shadow on their sacred bed.

But on their deeds no shade shall fall,
   While o'er their couch thy sun shall flame:
Thine ear was bowed to hear their call,
   And thy right hand shall guard their fame.

LESSON LI.

NOBLE INSPIRATION.—Hervey.

WHEN the keen eyed eagle soars above all the feathered race, and leaves their very sight below; when she wings her way with direct ascent, up the steep of heaven; and steadily gazing on the meridian sun, accounts its beaming splendors all her own: does she then regard, with any solicitude, the *mote* that is flying in the air, or the *dust* which she shook from her feet? No. Shall then this *eternal mind*, which is capable of contemplating its Creator's glory; which is intended to enjoy the visions of his countenance; shall this eternal mind, endowed with such great capacities and made for such exalted ends, be so *ignobly ambitious*, as to sigh for the tinsels of state; or so poorly covetous, as to grasp after

9*

ample territories on a needle's point? Under the influence
of such considerations, I feel my sentiments expand, and my
wishes acquire a turn of sublimity.—Too long have my affections been pinioned by vanity, and immured in this earthly
clod. But these thoughts break the *shackles*. These objects
open the door of *liberty*. My soul, fired by such noble pros-
pects, weighs anchor from this little nook, and coasts no longer
about its contracted shores, doats no longer on its painted
shells. The *immensity* of things is her range, and an *infinity*
of bliss is her aim.

LESSON LII.

ON SEEING TWINS LYING DEAD.—Montgomery.

'Twas summer, and a Sabbath eve,
    And balmy was the air,
I saw a sight that made me grieve,
    And yet that sight was fair;
For in a little coffin lay
Two lifeless babes, as sweet as May.

Like waxen dolls that infants dress,
    There little bodies were;
A look of placid happiness
    Did on each face appear;
And in a coffin short and wide
They lay together side by side.

A rosebud, nearly closed, I found
    Each little hand within,
And many a pink was strewed around,
    With sprigs of Jessamine;
But all the flowers that round them lay
Were not to me so sweet as they.

Their mother as a lily pale,
    Sat near them on a bed,
And, bending o'er them, told her tale,
    And many a tear she shed;
But oft she cried amidst her pain,
"My babes and I shall meet again."

LESSON LIII.

THE SAILOR BOY'S FAREWELL.—Mrs. Hale.

Hark! hark! 'tis the signal!
The breezes are steady,
The anchor is weighing,
And we must be ready.
Farewell, my dear mother,
I fear thou'lt be lonely—
But oh, do not sorrow,
I 'll think of thee only.

And dread not the danger,
Though I 'm on the billow;
I know my kind Savior
Will watch o'er my pillow;
The sea owns his sceptre,
When its path he was treading,
The winds and the water
Grew calm at his bidding.

We 'll trust him, we 'll trust him,
We 'll pray, and he 'll hear us,
On land or on water
Alike he 'll be near us—
Let this song bear to him
Our heart's pure devotion,
And under his guidance,
I 'll launch on the ocean.

LESSON LIV.

OUR DEAR AND NATIVE LAND.—Webster.

It is not to inflate national vanity, nor to swell a light and empty feeling of self-importance, but it is that we may judge justly of our situation, and of our own duties, that I urge the consideration of our position, and our character, among the nations of the earth. It cannot be denied, but by those who would dispute against the sun, that with America, and in America, a new era commences in human affairs. This era is distinguished by Free Representative Governments, by entire religious liberty, by improved systems of national intercourse, by a newly awakened, and an unconquerable spirit of free inquiry, and by a diffusion of knowledge through the community, such as has been before altogether unknown and unheard of. America, America, our country, fellow citizens, our own dear and native land, is inseparably connected, fast bound up in fortune and by fate, with these great interests. If they fall, we fall with them; if they stand, it will be because we have upholden them. Let us contemplate, then, this connexion, which binds the prosperity of others to our own; and let us manfully discharge all the duties which it imposes. If we cherish the virtues, and the principles of our fathers, Heaven will assist us to carry on the work of human liberty and human happiness. Auspicious omens cheer us. Great examples are before us. Our own firmament now shines brightly upon our path. WASHINGTON is in the clear upper sky. Those other stars, Adams and Jefferson, have joined the American constellation; they circle round their centre, and the heavens beam with new light. Beneath this illumination, let us walk the course of life, and at its close devoutly commend our beloved country, the common parent of us all, to the Divine Benignity.

LESSON LV.

LIBERTY.—PERCIVAL.

BENEATH our country's flag we stand,
And give our hearts to thee,
Bright power, who steel'st and nerv'st our hand,
Thou first born, Liberty!
Here, on our swords we swear to give
Our willing lives, that thou may'st live!

For thee, the Spartan youth of old,
To death devoted, fell!
Thy spirit made the Roman bold,
And fired the patriot Tell!
Our sires, on Bunker, fought for thee—
Undaunted fought, and we are free!

This is the *third right hand gesture, palm up*. The hand begins to move at the word *run*, and gradually mounts through the *course* of the gesture till it reaches the word *high*, upon which word comes the *stroke* of the gesture. The figures of this class exhibit, together, the *three* most important positions of the *arm*. The arm of the *second* Figure, is nearly *horizontal*, the hand being on a level with the shoulder; that of the *first* falls about the same distance *below*, as the arm of the *third* rises *above* it. The arm of each Fig-

ure is directed *moderately forward*, in a line *nearly* with the *right* foot, having a *very slight* bend at the elbow. The palm of the hand is *upward;* the fingers nearly straight, but not *stiffened;* the thumb turned upward; the first or *fore* finger being a *little* straighter than the others, which curve *inward* as the arm rises and the gesture becomes more emphatic. The pupil will notice that the *feet,* in this Figure, are still farther apart, than they are in that on page 100. The extension arises from the spirited elevation of the gesture.

Run up your starry flag on *high !*
No storm shall rend its folds ;
On, like a meteor, through the sky,
Its steady course it holds.
Thus high in heaven our flag unfurled—
Go, bear it, Freedom, round the world!

LESSON LVI.

A PICTURE.—Anonymous.

The farmer sat in his easy chair,
 Smoking his pipe of clay,
While his hale old wife, with busy care,
 Was clearing the dinner away :
A sweet little girl, with fine blue eyes,
 On her grandpa's knee was catching flies.

The old man placed his hand on her head,
 With a tear on his wrinkled face—

He thought how often her mother dead,
   Had sat in the same, same place :
As the tear stole down from his half-shut eye,
Don't smoke, said the child, how it makes you cry !

The house-dog lay *stretched* out on the floor,
   Where the sun, after noon, used to steal—
The busy old wife, by the open door,
   Was turning the spinning wheel—
And the old brass clock on the mantel-tree
Had plodded along to almost three.

Still the farmer sat in his easy chair,
   While close to his heaving breast ;
The moistened brow and the head so fair,
   Of his sweet grandchild were prest :
His head bent down, on her soft hair lay—
Fast asleep, were they both, on that summer day !

LESSON LVII.

SONG OF LOGAN.—Ashe.

THIS is the song of the mighty Logan: the conqueror of
white men : the pride of his nation, and the beloved of the
Author of life. He was good, valorous, and warlike; the
soul of his army, and the executor of vengeance. He was
the light of our camps and villages. His hatchet was always
raised up in their defense, and his bosom glowed with the love
of his brethren.

Logan, valiant and triumphant chieftain ; may the Great
Spirit, in whose defense you often warred, account with you
in the Land of Souls, and give you a garden of beauty and
harmony, and a pond of water like the moon in her full, on
which the sun reflects his light, and round which the birds and
beasts may delight to play!

Young warriors of Logan's tribe, bear in view the honors
he reaped when living, and the glorious recompense which
awaits him dead! May the Great Spirit prosper his work,
and never permit his enemies to be avenged of him! May his
gardens flourish beyond theirs, and may the fountain of his

waters have flavor and brightness when theirs are putrid and
dried up!

Friends of Logan, mitigate your sorrow; remember his
actions; improve by them; and let this song go down from
child to child, to commemorate his virtues and his worth!

LESSON LVIII.

A CHILD'S THOUGHTS.—ANONYMOUS.

See the sun how broad and red!
He seems to touch that elm-tree's head;
See, about him cling in crowds,
Crimson, blue, and golden clouds;
And the sky above him glows,
With a color like the rose.

This Figure stands in
the *first left position*, and
exhibits the *first left hand
gesture, palm up.* The
pupil has before been told
that the hand thus pre-
sented is said to be *su-
pine.* The hand, going
from the little *star, begins*
the gesture at the word
see, and makes its *course*
slowly in a gentle curve,
as shown by the *dotted
line;* its *stroke* comes very lightly upon the word
beads, and the hand falls
to *rest* at the word *hang.*
The pupil must remem-
ber that it is not considered proper to *commence*
speaking a piece in the
left position, nor to
make the *first gesture*
with the *left hand.*—
Neither is it in good taste
to use the *left* hand as
frequently as the *right,*
especially for the *principal* gesture; but there are
cases, where its use is
strictly correct, and these
will be explained.

| See, what little shining *beads*
Hang) upon the flowers and weeds;
All the lawn is covered quite,
With a veil of watery white,
And the distant meadows seem,
Almost hid in misty steam.

Happy birds are on the wing;
Hark! how loud and sweet they sing!
See that speck upon the sky;—
'Tis a lark; I saw her fly.
Happy birds! I 'm happy too;
I will skip and sing with you.

LESSON LIX.

THE WAR SONG.—Folsom.

Is it the welcome roar
Of thundering signal gun?—
Hark! for the sound bursts through once more,
Rending night's robe of dun:
It is the welcome sound,
The joyous call to war,
For the near bugle screams around
The cry to arms—hurrah!

See! yonder comes the foe—
Rush on with gun and glaive,
For freedom 'tis ye strike below
The banner of the brave;
On—on, until they fly,
Their fiercest daring mar—
'Tis well! fling down the brand and cry
The victor shout—hurrah!

LESSON LX.

BATTLE OF BUNKER HILL.—Webster.

It is not as a mere military encounter of hostile armies, that the battle of Bunker Hill founds its principal claim to attention. Yet, even as a mere battle, there were circumstances attending it, extraordinary in character, and entitling it to peculiar distinction.

But the consequences of the battle of Bunker Hill are greater than those of any conflict between the hostile armies of European powers. It was the first great battle of the Revolution; and not only the first blow, but the blow which determined the contest. It did not, indeed, put an end to the war, but in the then existing hostile feeling, the difficulties could only be referred to the arbitration of the sword. And one thing is certain; that after the New England troops had shown themselves able to face and repulse the regulars, it was decided that peace could never be established but upon the basis of the independence of the colonies. When the sun of that day went down, the event of independence was certain! When Washington heard of the battle, he inquired if the militia had stood the fire of the regulars? And when told that they had not only stood the fire, but reserved their own until the enemy was within eight rods, and then poured it in with tremendous effect—"Then," exclaimed he, "the liberties of the country are safe!"

LESSON LXI.

TO MY SISTER.—Thatcher.

My sister! Oh, my sister!
　All other hearts may fail,
As time and change that visit all,
　Pass o'er them like a gale,
Dashing the silvery dews of morn,
　From violets of the vale.

And mournfully, Oh, mournfully,
　The hopes of younger years,
May fall and leave me, one by one,
　In darkness and in tears,
Till I shall be the bloomless tree,
　A desert region rears.

And nothing in that wilderness,
　Though thronged by living men;
No, nothing but the memory
　Of joys that once have been,
Freshen my sultry soul, like airs
　From a fair Indian glen.

10

Yet sister! Oh, my sister!
  Thou wilt not so forget
To fan for me the sacred flame,
  In the fond bosom set
When life was green. Love on! Love on!
  It burns, it shrills me yet!

LESSON LXII.

PERSONAL INFLUENCE.—Hervey.

I HAVE taken a solitary walk on the *Western Cliffs*. At
the foot of the steep mountain, the sea all clear and smooth,
spread itself into an immense plain, and held a watery mirror
to the skies. Infinite heights above, the firmament stretched
its azure expanse, bespangled with unnumbered stars, and
adorned with the moon "walking in brightness." She seemed to contemplate herself with a peculiar pleasure, while
the *transparent surface* both received and returned her *silver
image*. Here, instead of being covered with sackcloth, she
shone with double lustre ; or rather with a lustre multiplied,
in proportion to the number of beholders, and their various
situations.

Such, methinks, is the effect of an exemplary behavior,
in persons of exalted situations. Their course, as it is nobly
distinguished, so it will be happily *influential*. Others will
catch the diffusive ray, and be ambitious to resemble a pattern, so attracting, so commanding. Their amiable qualities
will not terminate in themselves; but we shall see them *reflected* from their families and their acquaintance, just as we
may now behold another moon, trembling in the stream, glittering in the fountain, and displaying its lovely impress on
every collection of waters.

LESSON LXIII.

THE ORPHAN.—Anonymous.

"THE wintry wind blows bitter keen,
  Across the wide and dreary waste ;
The snow o'erlays the extended scene,
  O that this dismal heath were past !

In tatters clad my feeble frame
    Shrinks shivering from the piercing wind;
Could I but reach yon glimmering flame,
    Perhaps I might a shelter find."

Thus moaned the wanderer o'er the moor,
    Hastening to reach the distant cot;—
Arrived, she gently taps the door,—
    "O will they kindly hear or not?"

Wide ope's the door—the sire appears,
    With hoary head and bending form;

THIS is the *second or middle left hand gesture, palm up.* The gesture begins at the word *why,* and its course is first *circular* to the shoulder, and then in a line, a little *waving,* to the *left;* the *stroke* occurs on *why,* and is repeated, lightly, on *tears;* the hand comes to rest on the word *shelter.* In reciting this piece a sort of *picture* is to be represented. So the positions of the feet are necessarily *changed* several times. The part of the *orphan* should be done in the *first right* position. The speaker, in the narrative portions, should assume the *second right,* as denoting his own place in the picture; and the part of the *aged sire* should be done in the *first left,* agreeing with the Figure. This is a case where the *left* hand assumes the *principal* gesture with obvious propriety. And by this arrangement, each character is invested with a distinctness and life, which could hardly be given to it by any other mode.

He kindly asks—|" *Why* thus in *tears?*
    Seek'st thou a shelter) from the storm?"

"Alas!" the trembling wanderer cries,
    "My only home's the dreary wild—
My father in the cold grave lies,
    Far from his country and his child:

My mother, too, has bowed her head,
    And sunk into the cold, cold grave;
As her departing spirit fled,
    She prayed—'O heaven, my orphan save!'

Heaven sure will answer mother's prayer,
  Be you heaven's messenger to me;
Take then—O take into your care,
  An orphan-child of misery!"

No more she said—the door was closed—
  The storm howled louder o'er the scene;
But sweet compassion interposed,
  And drew the shivering orphan in.

LESSON LXIV.

AMERICA—HER EXAMPLE.—Phillips.

AMERICANS! you have a country vast in extent and embracing all the varieties of the most salubrious climes; held not by charters wrested from unwilling kings, but the bountiful gift of the Author of nature. The exuberance of your population is daily divesting the gloomy wilderness of its rude attire, and splendid cities rise to cheer the dreary desert. You have a government deservedly celebrated "as giving the sanctions of law to the precepts of reason;" presenting, instead of the rank luxuriance of natural licentiousness, the corrected sweets of civil liberty. You have fought the battles of freedom, and enkindled that sacred flame which now glows with vivid fervor through the greatest empire in Europe. We indulge the sanguine hope, that her equal laws and virtuous conduct will hereafter afford examples of imitation to all surrounding nations. That the blissful period will soon arrive when man shall be elevated to his primitive character; when illuminated reason and regulated liberty shall once more exhibit him in the image of his Maker; when all the inhabitants of the globe shall be freemen and fellow citizens, and patriotism itself be lost in universal philanthropy. Then shall volumes of incense incessantly roll from altars inscribed to liberty. Then shall the innumerable varieties of the human race unitedly " worship in her sacred temple, whose pillars shall rest on the remotest corners of the earth, and whose arch will be the vault of heaven."

LESSON LXV.

THE CHARGE.—Percival.

The horn and the trumpet are ringing afar,
  As the summons to battle are sounding;
And the steed, as he catches the signal of war,
  In the pride of his spirit is bounding.
Shrill it echoes afar, over hill and o'er plain,
And the wide distant mountains repeat it again;
And the shout of the warrior, and nearer the song,
Peal aloud as the glittering bands are hurrying along:
As on, on, on, on, pours the tide of fight,
Still aloft floats the tossing flag, in the glance of morning's
      light.

We leap to our saddles, we range us in line,
  As the voice of the trumpet is calling:

This Figure exhibits the *third left hand gesture, palm up.* It is a beautiful *significant* gesture. The hand begins to move at the word *yon;* the *dotted line* illustrates the *course* of the gesture, and the *italic* word *ridge*, shows where the *stroke* comes; the hand *begins* to descend at the word *bright,* and comes to *rest* on the word *drawn.* This is another example of an important gesture made by the *left* hand. Its propriety is obvious. The speaker *begins* in the *first right position.* At the words " leaping to the saddle," he naturally changes with a *spirited* motion to the *first left;* and the *left hand* as naturally assumes the first principal gesture. The pupil must remember, that wherever it is proper to assume the *left position of the feet,* it may be proper to use *the left hand gesture.*

On the crown of | yon *ridge,* bright their drawn) sabres shine;
  Down its slope, like a flood, they are falling.
" Give the spur to the charge, ere the foeman is nigh:
Rush amain, as the forest rings loud with your cry:
              10*

Speed on to the shock, in his midway career—
For our sires still were first in fight ; they never thought of
    fear !"
So on, on, on, on, o'er the sounding plain,
To the wild conflict fierce they rush, and together dash
    amain.

LESSON LXVI.

THE SNOW STORM.—Smith.

THE cold winds swept the mountain's height,
    And pathless was the dreary wild,
And 'mid the cheerless hours of night,
    A mother wandered with her child,
As through the drifted snow she pressed,
The babe was sleeping on her breast.

And colder still the winds did blow,
    And darker hours of night came on,
And deeper grew the drifts of snow,—
    Her limbs were chilled, her strength was gone ;
"O God," she cried in accents wild,
"If I must perish, save my child !"

She stripped her mantle from her breast,
    And bared her bosom to the storm,
As round the child she wrapped the vest,
    She smiled to think that it was warm.
With one cold kiss, one tear she shed,
And sunk upon a snowy bed.

At dawn, a traveler passed by ;
    She lay beneath a snowy vail,—
The frost of death was in her eye,
    Her cheek was cold, and hard, and pale ;
He moved the robe from off the child :
The babe looked up, and *sweetly smiled.*

LESSON LXVII.

STRIKE FOR LIBERTY.—ANONYMOUS.

ON, on, to the just and glorious strife !
　With your swords your freedom shielding—
Nay, resign, if it must be so, even life ;
　But die, at least, unyielding.

On to the strife ! for 't were far more meet
　To sink with the foes who bay you,

THIS Figure presents to the pupil *another position* of the *right hand*. The palm is *downward*. We will call this, therefore, the *first right hand gesture, palm down*. The hand, in this position, is said to be *prone* ; gestures of this kind are sometimes named *inverted* gestures. The fingers are a little farther apart than in the other position of the hand, the *first* or fore finger being almost *straight*, and the *thumb straight* and *off* from that finger. The hand begins to move at the word *than*, and makes its *course* according to the dotted line ; the *stroke* of the gesture comes upon the word *crouch*, and the hand falls to *rest* on the word *at*. This gesture is well suited to the expression of *scorn, contemptuous* feeling, *rebuke, casting down, humbling,* and the like.

|Than *crouch*, like dogs, at) your tyrant's feet,
　And smile on the swords that slay you.

Strike ! for the sires who left you free !
　Strike ! for their sakes who bore you !
Strike ! for your homes and liberty,
　And the heaven you worship o'er you !

LESSON LXVIII.

THE LIGHT OF HOME.—MRS. HALE.

MY son, thou wilt dream the world is fair,
　And thy spirit will sigh to roam,

And thou must go ;—but never, when there,
  Forget the light of home.

Though Pleasure may smile with a ray more bright,
  It dazzles to lead astray :
Like the meteor's flash, 't will deepen the night,
  When thou treadest the lonely way.

But the hearth of home has a constant flame,
  And pure as vestal fire ;
'T will burn, 't will burn, forever the same,
  For nature feeds the pyre.

The sea of Ambition is tempest-tost,
  And thy hopes may vanish like foam ;
But when sails are shivered and rudder lost,
  Then look to the light of home.

And there, like a star through the midnight cloud,
  Thou shalt see the beacon bright ;
For never, till shining on thy shroud,
  Can be quench'd its holy light.

The sun of Fame, 't will gild the name,
  But the heart ne'er feels its ray ;
And fashion's smiles, that rich ones claim,
  Are like beams of a wintry day :

And how cold and dim those beams would be,
  Should life's poor wanderer come !
But, my son, when the world is dark to thee,
  Turn, *turn* to the light of home.

LESSON LXIX.

GOD'S CARE OVER US.—Chalmers.

How finely diversified, and how multiplied into many
thousand distinct exercises, is the attention of God! His
eye is upon every hour of my existence. His spirit is inti-
mately present with every thought of my heart. His inspiration gives birth to every purpose within me. His hand

impresses a direction on every footstep of my goings. Every breath I inhale is drawn by an energy which God deals out to me. This body, which upon the slightest derangement, would become the prey of death, or of woeful suffering, is now at ease, because he at this moment is warding off from me a thousand dangers, and upholding the thousand movements of its complex and delicate machinery. His presiding influence keeps by me through the whole current of my restless and ever-changing history. When I walk by the wayside, he is along with me. When I enter into company, amidst all my forgetfulness of Him, he never forgets me. In the silent watches of the night, when my eyelids have closed, and my spirit has sunk into unconsciousness, the observant eye of Him who never slumbers, is upon me. I cannot fly from his presence. Go where I will, he leads me, and watches me, and cares for me; and the same Being who is now at work in the remotest domains of nature and of providence, is also at my right hand to eke out to me every moment of my being, and to uphold me in the exercise of all my feelings, and of all my faculties.

LESSON LXX.

THE ATHEIST AND ACORN.—Watts.

"Methinks the world seems oddly made,
   And every thing amiss;"
A dull, complaining atheist said,
As stretched he lay beneath the shade,
   And instanced it in this:

"Behold," quoth he, "that mighty thing,
   A pumpkin large and round,
Is held but by a little string,
Which upwards cannot make it spring,
   Nor bear it from the ground.

While on this oak an acorn small,
   So disproportioned grows,
That whosoe'er surveys this all,
This universal casual ball,
   Its ill contrivance knows.

My better judgment would have hung
   The pumpkin on the tree,
And left the acorn slightly strung,
'Mong things that on the surface sprung,
   And weak and feeble be."

No more the caviler could say,
   No further faults descry ;
For upward gazing, as he lay,
An acorn, loosened from its spray,
   Fell down upon his eye.

The wounded part with tears ran o'er,
   As punished for that sin;

THIS Figure exhibits the *second* or *middle right hand gesture, palm down.*— The hand, from this mark | sweeps swiftly round to the shoulder, in its *course,* making its *stroke* in nearly a *horizontal* line upon the word *fool ;* it falls to *rest* with some *emphasis,* immediately after the word *pumpkin.* The palm should be a little more *inward,* and the fingers rather closer together than in the *first* gesture of this class. In the example which it illustrates, it expresses *contempt;* but the language of *authority* and *command* is also well enforced by it,—as, " *Drive that monster from the land.*" It may be used, likewise, to describe *extent* of *land* or *water,* or any *moving spectacle,* thus " *Before him marched the princes and noble foreigners of the countries he had conquered.*"

| *Fool !* had that bough a pumpkin) bore,
Thy whimseys would have worked no more,
   Nor skull have kept them in.

LESSON LXXI.

READ THE SKY.—MISS ROSCOE.

Go forth when midnight winds are high,
   And ask them whence they come ;
Who sent them raging through the sky,
   And where is their far home !

Ask of the tempest if its bound
   Is fix'd in Heaven's decree,
When storm and thunders burst around
   In awful revelry.

The winds may keep their midnight way—
   The tempest know its power ;
But, trembling mortal, canst thou say
   Where ends thy destined hour ?

Whence didst thou spring, and whither tend ?
   Is thine this atom world ?
What is thy being's aim and end,
   On time's swift pinion hurl'd ?

Thou know'st not—no ; thou may'st not know—
   But read that glorious sky,—
Look up ! those million planets glow
   With marks of Deity !

Yes, trace him there—exulting trace !
   The soul that soars to God,
And follows the immortal race
   Those shining stars have trod,—

Can never falter in its faith—
   Can never bow to fears ;
The conquest over Time and Death,
   It reads in yon bright spheres !

LESSON LXXII.

ADAMS AND JEFFERSON.—Webster.

Adams and Jefferson are no more. On our fiftieth anniversary, the great day of National Jubilee, in the very hour of public rejoicing, in the midst of echoing and reechoing voices of thanksgiving ; while their own names were on all tongues, they took their flight, together, to the world of spirits.
Adams and Jefferson are no more. As human beings, indeed, they are no more. They are no more as in 1776,

bold and fearless advocates of independence; no more, as on
subsequent periods, the head of the government; no more,
as we have recently seen them, aged and venerable objects
of admiration and regard.

They are no more. They are dead. But how little is
there of the great and good, which can die! To their country
they yet live, and live forever. They live in all that perpet-
uates the remembrance of men on earth; in the recorded
proofs of their own great actions—in the offspring of their
intellect—in the deep engraved lines of public gratitude, and
in the respect and homage of mankind. A superior and
commanding human intellect, a truly great man, when
Heaven vouchsafes so rare a gift, is not a temporary flame,
burning bright for awhile, and then expiring, giving place to
returning darkness. It is rather a spark of fervent heat, as
well as radiant light, with power to enkindle the common
mass of human mind; so that when it glimmers, in its own
decay, and finally goes out in death, no night follows, but it
leaves the world all light, all on fire, from the potent con-
tact of its own spirit.

LESSON LXXIII.

APPLAUSE OF WAR.—Knowles.

What species of beings are we, that we laud to the skies
those men whose names live in the recollection of a field of
carnage, a sacked town, or a stormed citadel?—That we celebrate, at our convivial meetings, the exploits of him, who,
in a single day, has more than trebled the ordinary havoc of
death? that our wives and daughters weave garlands for the
brow, whose sweat has cost the groans of widows and of orphans?—and that our very babes are taught to twine the
arms of innocence and purity about the knees that have been
used to wade in blood?—I say, what species of beings are
we, that we give our praise, our admiration, and our love, to
that which reason, religion, interest, every consideration,
should persuade us to condemn—to avoid—to abhor!

I do not mean to say, that war ought never to be waged—
there are at times, occasions, when it is expedient—necessary—justifiable. But who celebrates with songs of triumph

those commotions of the elements that call the awful lightning into action—that hurl the inundating clouds to earth—and send the winds into the deep to rouse its horrors? These things are necessary; but we hail them not with shouts of exultation; we do not clap our hands as they pass by us; we shudder as we behold them! What species of beings are we? We turn with disgust from the sight of the common executioner, who, in his time, has despatched a score or two of victims; and press to the heels of him, that in a single day, has been the executioner of thousands!

LESSON LXXIV.

VENGEANCE.—PERCIVAL.

VENGEANCE calls you! quick, be ready:—
Rouse ye, in the name of God:
Onward, onward! strong and steady—

THIS Figure presents the *third right hand gesture, palm down*. The pupil will notice *two* dotted lines; that going from the *star* denotes an *upward* movement—which, with the pause of the hand for an instant, forms a *suspending* gesture;—these gestures are so named because they hold the audience in suspense, by the preparation which they make for the *stroke*;—the other line denotes a *downward* movement;—

these movements are the *course* of the gesture; previous to the *downward* movement, the hand is thrown back *quickly*, a *few inches*, from the point which it occupies in the picture, that it may make the *stroke* upon the word *dash* with the greater *force*; the hand comes to *rest* immediately after the word *earth*. This gesture is proper to the language of *reprehension, denunciation, extermination, anger*, and the like.

(*Dash* to earth) the oppressor's rod.
Vengeance calls! ye brave, ye brave!
Rise, and spurn the name of slave.

11

Grasp the sword !—its edge is keen ;
    Seize the gun ! its ball is true ;
Sweep your land from tyrants clean—
    Haste, and scour it through and through.
Onward, onward !—vengeance cries,
Rush to arms—the tyrant flies.

Vengeance calls you ! quick, be ready—
    Think of what your sires have been :
Onward, onward ! strong and steady—
    Drive the tyrant to his den.
On, and let the watch-word be :
Country, home, and liberty !

LESSON LXXV.

STORY OF JOSEPH.—Sprague.

THE story of Joseph, of which these words are a part,—
"Now, therefore, be not grieved nor angry with yourselves
that ye sold me hither ; for God did send me before you to
preserve life,"—may perhaps be considered, in some respects,
as the master-piece even of inspiration. It is so simple, as to
be entirely appropriate to the nursery ; and yet so beautiful,
that the man of taste can never ponder it enough ; so tender,
that the stoic can scarcely read it with an unmoistened eye ;
and withal, so illustrative of the great principles of human
nature, as to be an edifying subject of contemplation to the
philosopher and the sage. We meet Joseph, at the point,
perhaps, of the greatest interest—in the act of discovering
himself to his brethren. With one breath, he let out the as-
tounding secret that he was Joseph, whom they had sold into
Egypt, and with the next, endeavored to soothe their troubled
spirits, by referring to the benevolent end which God had
accomplished by their unnatural conduct. He saw the per-
plexity, the terror, the agitation, which had come over them,
and his eye affected his heart ; and though he knew that they
had deserved all, and more than all that they suffered, yet
the heart of the injured brother rose as their apologist ; and
he said—" Now, therefore, be not grieved, nor angry with
yourselves, that ye sold me hither ; for God did send me be-

fore you to preserve life." Admirable triumph of the best feelings of the heart! Noble example of a forgiving and generous spirit in a young man!

LESSON LXXVI.

ULYSSES'S DOG.—Anonymous.

FORGOT by all his own domestic crew,
The faithful dog alone his master knew :

This is the *first* of another class of three gestures of the left hand. It is the *first left hand gesture, palm up, off.* The peculiarity is, that the *left* hand makes the gesture, though the Figure stands in the first *right* position. Thus we say the gesture is *off*. The position should be *strongly* made. In the sentence supposed to be spoken, the hand begins its *course* directly after the utterance of the word *unhoused*, and makes its *stroke* in a smooth *curve* upon the word *neglected*, retaining its position till the word *lay* has been pronounced, when it comes to *rest*. This is chiefly used as a *significant* gesture. It is associated in the mind with things *aside, passed by, depressed, neglected,* and the like. When well done it is graceful.

Unfed, unhoused, |*neglected*, on the clay,
Like an old servant, now cashiered he lay ;)
Touched with resentment to *ungrateful* man,
And longing to behold his ancient lord again ;
Him when he saw he rose and crawled to meet,
—'T was all he could—and fawned, and licked his feet ;
Seized with dumb joy—then, falling by his side,
Owned his returning lord, looked up, and died !
Hence learn *fidelity ;*—with grateful mind
Repay the courteous ; to your *friends* be *kind ;*
Whatever fortune on your life attend,
The best of treasures is a *faithful friend.*

LESSON LXXVII.

THE WARRIOR'S WREATH.—Anonymous.

BEHOLD the wreath which decks the warrior's brow,
Breathes it a balmy fragrance sweet? Ah, no!
    It rankly savors of the grave!
'T is *red*—but not with roseate hues;
      'T is crimsoned o'er
      With human gore!
'T is *wet*—but not with heavenly dews;

'T is drenched in tears by widows, orphans shed,
Methinks in sable weeds I see them clad,
    And mourn in vain, for husbands slain,
Children beloved, or brothers dear,
      The fatherless
      In deep distress
Despairing, shed the scalding tear.

I hear, 'mid dying groans, the cannon's crash,—
I see, 'mid smoke, the musket's horrid flash—
    Here famine walks—there carnage stalks—
Hell in her fiery eye, she stains
      With purple blood
      The crystal flood,
Heaven's altars and the verdant plains!

Scenes of domestic peace and social bliss
Are changed to scenes of woe and wretchedness;
    The votaries of vice increase—
Towns sacked, whole cities wrapped in flame!
      Just Heaven! say,
      Is this the *bay*,
Which warriors gain—is this called Fame!

LESSON LXXVIII.

ADVOCATING THE REVOLUTION.—Quincy.

BE not deceived, my countrymen. Believe not these ve-
nal hirelings, when they would cajole you by their subtleties

into submission, or frighten you by their vaporings into compliance. When they strive to flatter you by the terms "moderation and prudence," tell them that calmness and deliberation are to guide the judgment; courage and intrepidity command the action. When they endeavor to make us "perceive our inability to oppose our mother country," let us boldly answer:—"In defence of our civil and religious rights, we dare oppose the world; with the God of armies on our side! even the God who fought our fathers' battles! we fear not the hour of trial, though the hosts of our enemies should cover the field like locusts. If this be enthusiasm, we will live and die enthusiasts."

Oh, my countrymen! what will our children say, when they read the history of these times, should they find that we tamely gave away, without one noble struggle, the most invaluable of earthly blessings! As they drag the galling chain, will they not execrate us? If we have any respect for things sacred,—any regard to the dearest treasure on earth; if we have one tender sentiment for posterity; if we would not be despised by the whole world,—let us, in the most open, solemn manner, and with determined fortitude, swear—*We will die, if we cannot live freemen!*

While we have equity, justice, and God on our side, tyranny, spiritual or temporal, shall never ride triumphant in a land inhabited by Englishmen.

LESSON LXXIX.

DEATH AND THE YOUTH.—Miss Landon.

"Not yet,—the flowers are in my path;
    The sun is in my sky;—
Not yet,—my heart is full of hope,
    I cannot bear to die.

Not yet,—I never knew till now,
    How precious life could be;—
My heart is full of love,—Oh! Death,
    I cannot go with thee."

11*

But *love* and *hope*, enchanted twain,

THIS Figure exhibits the *second or middle left hand gesture, palm up, off.* As mentioned in the description of the *first* gesture of this class, the pupil must be sure to stand well *inclined* in the first right position. The *course* of this gesture begins immediately after the word *twain,* and makes its *stroke* upon the word *passed;* the movement is *circular* to about the shoulder, and then glides in a graceful *wave* to the left; the hand comes to *rest* on the word *by.* The pupil will be careful—of which he has been instructed before—to keep the fingers of the gesturing hand a little *apart,* the *fore* finger a little *straighter* than the rest, the *little* finger rather more *curved* than the middle and third, and the *thumb up* but not stiff. This gesture is expressive in denoting *past time or events, objects at a distance, persons and things behind,* sometimes mingled with *scorn;* as, " *We left the coward slave behind.*"

|*Passed* in their falsehood by:—)
Death came again,—and then he said,—
" I'm ready now to die."

LESSON LXXX.

SPEECH OF JUDAS.—JOSEPHUS.

MY fellow soldiers and companions, we shall never again have such an opportunity of showing our bravery in the defense of our country, and the contempt of all dangers as we have now before us ; for, upon the issue of to-morrow's combat, depends not only our liberty, but all the comforts and advantages that attend it; and over and above the blessings of such a freedom, our very *religion* lies at stake with it too ; nor can we secure the one but by preserving the other. Bethink yourselves well, therefore, what it is you are to contend for, and you will find it to be no less than the sum and substance of the greatest happiness you ever enjoyed ; that is to say, the peaceable possession of your ancient laws, rights, and discipline. Now, whether you will rather choose to perish with infamy, and involve the miserable remainder of your countrymen in the same ruin, or venture one generous effort for the redemption of yourselves and your friends, is the point in question. *Death* is the same thing to the *coward* that it is to the *man* of *valor*, and as certain to *one* as the *other;* but there is a wide difference between them, in point of *honor* and *everlasting fame.* The gallant man, who falls in vindication of his religion, laws, and country, dies to be perpetuated with *honor;* the pusillanimous coward, at his exit is consigned to *infamy.* Take these considerations into your thoughts, and make this use of the meditation. You have nothing to trust to but the providence of God, and your own concurring resolutions, and, at the worst, while we contend for *victory*, we can never fail of *glory!*

LESSON LXXXI.

THE BUTTERFLY BEAU.—Anonymous.

I'm a volatile thing, with exquisite wing,
   Sprinkled o'er with the tints of the rainbow;
All the butterflies swarm to behold my sweet form,
   Though the grubs may all vote me a vain beau.
I my toilet go through with rose-water dew,
   And each blossom contributes its essence;
Then—all fragrance and grace, not a plume out of place,
   I adorn the gay world with my presence—
      In short, you must know,
      I'm the butterfly beau.

At first I enchant a fair Sensitive plant,
   Then I flirt with the Pink of perfection:
Then I seek a sweet Pea, and I whisper " for thee
   I have long felt a fond predilection:"
A Lily I kiss, and exult in my bliss,
   But I very soon search for a new lip;
And I pause in my flight, to exclaim with delight,
   "O, how dearly I *love* you, my Tulip!"
      In short, you must know,
      I'm the butterfly beau.

Thus forever I rove, and the honey of love
   From each delicate blossom I pilfer,—

But though many I see pale and pining for me,
  I know none that are worth growing ill for:
And though I must own, there are some that I've known,
  Whose external attractions are splendid ;
On myself *I* must dote, for in my pretty coat,
  All the tints of the garden are blended ;—
      In short, you must know,
      I'm the *butterfly beau.*

LESSON LXXXII.

VIRTUE.—Price.

Virtue is the foundation of honor and esteem, and the
source of all beauty, order, and happiness in nature. It is
what confers value on all the other endowments and qualities
of a reasonable being; it reaches through all the periods and
circumstances of our being. Many of the endowments and
talents we now possess, and of which we are too apt to be
proud, will cease entirely with the present state; but this
will be our ornament and dignity in every future state to
which we may be removed. Beauty and wit will die; learning will vanish away, and all the arts of life be soon forgot;
but *virtue* will remain forever. This unites us to the whole
rational creation, and fits us for conversing with any order of
superior natures, and for a place in any part of God's works.
Superior beings of all ranks, are bound by it no less than ourselves. It has the same authority in all worlds, that it has
in this. 'Tis the law of the whole universe: it stands first
in the estimation of the Deity; its original is his nature; and
it is the very object that makes him lovely. Such is the importance of virtue. Of what consequence, therefore, is it
that we practise it! There is no argument, or motive, which
is at all fitted to influence a reasonable mind, which does not
call us to this. One virtuous disposition of soul is of more
value than all the treasures of the world. If you are wise,
then, study virtue, and contemn every thing that can come
into competition with it. Remember, that nothing else deserves our anxious thought, or wish. Remember, that this
alone is honor, glory, wealth, and happiness. *Secure* this,
and you secure everything ; *lose* this, and all is lost.

LESSON LXXXIII.

FRIENDS SEPARATED BY DEATH.—MONTGOMERY.

FRIEND after friend departs;
  Who has not lost a friend?
There is no union here of hearts,
  That finds not here an end;
Were this frail world our final rest,
Living or dying none were blest.

Beyond the flight of time—
  Beyond the reign of death—
There surely is some blessed clime
  Where life is not a breath;
Nor life's affections transient fire,
Whose sparks fly upward and expire.

There is a world above,
  Where parting is unknown;
A long eternity of love,
  Formed for the good alone;
And Faith beholds the dying here,
Translated to that glorious sphere.

THIS Figure exhibits the *third left hand gesture, palm up, off.* The hand makes its *course* in a graceful *curve* from the word *thus;* the *stroke* comes upon the word *star,* and is suspended, till it falls to *rest* at the word *all.* The pupil will notice that the position of the feet is *extended,* nearly all the weight of the body being supported on the *right* foot, while the ball of the *left great toe* but lightly touches the floor. It is a beautiful gesture, and employed here to carry the mind up, better than the words alone could, to those sublime objects—the *stars* of Heaven.— *Ideas of God, eternity, immortality,* and the like, may be appropriately aided by this gesture.

|Thus *star* by star declines,
  Till all) are past away;

As morning high and higher shines,
  To pure and perfect day :
Nor sink those stars in empty night,
But hide themselves in heaven's own light.

LESSON LXXXIV.

THE EXISTENCE OF GOD.—MAXCY.

A FIRM belief in the existence of God, will heighten all the enjoyments of life, and, by conforming our hearts to his will, will secure the approbation of a good conscience, and inspire us with the hopes of a blessed immortality. Never be tempted to disbelieve the existence of God, when every thing around you proclaims it in a language too plain not to be understood. Never cast your eyes on creation, without having your souls expanded with this sentiment,—"There is a God." When you survey this globe of earth, with all its appendages; when you behold it inhabited by numberless ranks of creatures, all moving in their proper spheres; all verging to their proper ends, all animated by the same great source of life, all supported at the same great bounteous table; when you behold, not only the earth, but the ocean, and the air, swarming with living creatures, all happy in their situation; when you behold yonder sun darting an effulgent blaze of glory over the heavens, garnishing mighty worlds, and waking ten thousand songs of praise; when you behold unnumbered systems diffused through vast immensity, clothed in splendor, and rolling in majesty; when you behold these things, your affections will rise above all the vanities of time; your full souls will struggle with exstacy, and your reason, passions, and feelings, all united, will rush up to the skies, with a devout acknowledgment of the existence, power, wisdom, and goodness of God. Let us behold Him, let us wonder, let us praise and adore. These things will make us happy.

LESSON LXXXV.

THE LOST BOY.—Anonymous.

The little boy wandered away,
   Nor thought what might betide him ;
For he loved to ramble and play,
   With his faithful dog beside him :
The flowers were gay, the trees were green,
A pleasanter day was never seen,—
The birds were singing on every spray,
As if they would flatter the boy away,
   When he 'd none but his dog to guide him.

They rambled, *rambled* on,—

This Figure exhibits the first of another class of single gestures. A gesture is said to be *single* when it is made with *one* hand only. This gesture may be called the *first left hand gesture, index finger.* The pupil will observe that the *fore*-finger is *extended*, while the others are moderately *curved* inward, the *thumb* standing easily *off* from them. In the passage illustrated, the gesture begins at the word *and*, making its *course* in a *curve*, as seen in the *dotted line ;* the stroke comes upon the word *dog*, and the hand falls to *rest* at the word *many*. The reciter is in the *first right* position during the first nine lines ; at the second word *rambled*, he changes,—obeying the idea of *motion*,—to the *first left ;* at the word *and* he slides into the *second* left. The use of this class of gestures is, in *noting*, in expressing *scorn*, but particularly, in pointing out *single* objects, as in our example.

The boy | and *dog*, together,
In many) a pleasant path they run,
   Nor knew, nor heeded whither ;—
But the sun is set, and a storm seems near,
And the poor little boy is pale with fear :
He thought the old trees grew dark and tall,
And as he ran, you might hear him call,—
   " Oh, mother, do come hither !"

His mother is all alone,
   And sadly, sadly weeping ;

The father to seek his son has gone,
  And how can she think of sleeping ?
She watches the clock, she watches the skies,—
"Oh! where is my poor little boy ?"—she cries;
"Oh! where will he pillow his little head ?—
And where can he find a sheltered bed,
  When the storm in its wrath is sweeping ?"

The morning is fresh and fair,
  There's silver dew on the blossom,—
The mother she sits in her easy chair,
  With her little boy on her bosom :—
"Oh, mother! dear mother! don't weep, I pray,
For never again will I ramble away—
I'll remember to ask if I wish to go,"—
And each little boy must remember it too,
  Lest his mother should grieve to lose him.

LESSON LXXXVI.

DEATH AND IMMORTALITY.—Anonymous.

WHILE enjoying the blessings of health, and the festivities
of youth, we stand on this bridge of life, careless of the rapid
currents of yesterdays and to-morrows; yet reflection teaches
that the hour is rapidly hastening, when " the cloud-capped
towers; the gorgeous palaces; the solemn temples; yea, the
great globe itself, with all which it inherits, shall dissolve,
and like the baseless fabric of a vision, leave not a wreck behind." We shall survive—

  " An angel's arm can't snatch us from the grave ;
  Legions of angels can't confine us there."

  The trump of God shall sound ; then shall He, who once
said, " Lazarus, come forth !" descend from heaven, with a
mighty shout. Then shall the dead hear ; then shall they
burst the bands of death, and rise, never to sleep again.
Then shall this mortal put on immortality, and death be swallowed up of life. We shall be present at this august resur-
rection !
  Soon shall we cease to see the blue canopy of day, and
the starred curtain of the night ; to hear the rolling of the

thunder, or see the lightning of the heavens,—scenes, which now impress us with awe and delight. We look round creation, and see all living nature, below our rank, dissolving to dust; never to revive. We see the flowers of spring die, and the leaves of autumn fade, never to resume their beauty and verdure. But, contemplating the soul of man, we are led to the language of the poet,—

See truth, love, and mercy, in triumph descending,
And nature all glowing in Eden's first bloom;
On the cold cheek of death, smiles and roses are blending,
And beauty immortal awakes from the tomb.

LESSON LXXXVII.

ROLLA'S SPEECH.—Sheridan.

My brave associates!—partners of my toil, my feelings, and my fame!—Can Rolla's words add vigor to the virtuous energies which inspire your hearts?—No—you have judged as I have, the foulness of the crafty plea by which these bold invaders would delude you.—Your generous spirit has compared, as mine has, the motives, which in a war like this, can animate *their* minds and *ours*.—*They*, by a strange frenzy driven, fight for power, for plunder,—and extended rule: —*We* for our country, our altars, and our homes.—*They* follow an adventurer whom they fear—and obey a power which they hate:—*We* serve a monarch whom we love—a God whom we adore. Whene'er they move in anger, desolation tracks their progress!—Where'er they pause in amity, affliction mourns their friendship!—They boast they come but to improve our state, enlarge our thoughts, and free us from the yoke of error!—Yes,—*they* will give enlightened freedom to *our* minds, who are *themselves* the slaves of passion, avarice and pride.—They offer us their protection—yes, such protection as vultures give to lambs, covering and devouring them!—They call on us to barter all of good we have inherited and proved, for the desperate chance of something better, which they promise.—Be our plain answer this: The throne *we* honor is the people's choice—the laws *we* reverence are our brave fathers' legacy—the faith *we* follow teaches us to

12

live in bonds of charity with all mankind, and die with hope of bliss beyond the grave.—Tell your invaders this, and tell them too, we seek no change ; and, least of all, such change as *they* would bring us.

LESSON LXXXVIII.

DREAMING IN CAPTIVITY.—Mrs. Hemans.

I DREAM of all things free !
   Of a gallant, gallant bark,
That sweeps through storm and sea

THIS Figure exhibits the *second right hand gesture, index finger.* It stands in the *first right* position, and gesticulates with the *right* hand. It differs in these respects from the Figure of this class, page 131, but the *nature* of the gesture is the same. It would not be well to stand in the *left* position, because it is too near the *beginning* of the piece ; it would not be well to use the *left* hand, because the idea to be illustrated implies too much *strength* and *swiftness.* Much of the *propriety* of gesture depends on considerations like these.—The instant the hand *begins* its *course*, at the word *like*, the speaker slides into the *second* right position ; as it shoots on to its *stroke* upon the word *arrow*, he comes again into the *first* right. Both motions are *swift*, but that on *arrow* like lightning. As the hand goes to the shoulder, the palm is *inward ;* as it darts from that point it is *upward ;* the *fore* finger and *thumb* are *straight* and rigid. The hand comes to *rest* on the word *mark.*

(Like an *arrow* to its mark !)
   Of a stag that o'er the hills,
     Goes bounding in its glee ;
   Of a thousand flashing rills—
     Of all things glad and free.

I dream of some proud bird,
   A bright eyed mountain thing !
In my visions I have heard
   The rustling of his wing.

I follow some wild river,
  On whose breast no sail may be ;
Dark woods around it shiver—
  I dream of all things free !—

Of a happy forest child,
  With the fawns and flowers at play ;
Of an Indian midst the wild
  With the stars to guide his way ;
Of a chief his warriors leading,
  Of an archer's greenwood tree :—
My heart in chains is bleeding,
  And I dream of all things free.

LESSON LXXXIX.

RESPONSIBILITY OF THE AMERICAN CITIZEN.—WEBSTER.

LET us cherish, fellow citizens, a deep and solemn conviction of the duties which have devolved upon us. This lovely land, this glorious liberty, these benign institutions, the dear purchase of our fathers, are ours ; ours to enjoy, ours to preserve, ours to transmit. Generations past, and generations to come, hold us responsible for this sacred trust. Our fathers, from behind, admonish us, with their anxious paternal voices ; posterity calls out to us, from the bosom of the future ; the world turns hither its solicitous eyes—all, all conjure us to act wisely, and faithfully, in the relation which we sustain. We can never, indeed, pay the debt which is upon us ; but by virtue, by morality, by religion, by the cultivation of every good principle and every good habit, we may hope to enjoy the blessing, through our day, and to leave it unimpaired to our children. Let us feel deeply how much of what we are and of what we possess, we owe to this liberty, and these institutions of government. Nature has, indeed, given us a soil, which yields bounteously to the hands of industry ; the mighty and fruitful ocean is before us, and the skies over our heads shed health and vigor. But what are lands, and seas, and skies, to civilized men, without society, without knowledge, without morals, without religious culture ; and how can these be enjoyed, in all their extent, and all their excellence, but under the protection of wise institutions

and a free government? Fellow citizens, there is not one of
us, there is not one of us here present, who does not, at this
moment, and at every moment, experience in his own condition, and in the condition of those most near and dear to him,
the influence and the benefit of this liberty, and these institutions. Let us then acknowledge the blessing, let us feel it
deeply and powerfully, let us cherish a strong affection for it,
and resolve to maintain and perpetuate it. The blood of our
fathers, let it not have been shed in vain; the great hope of
posterity, let it not be blasted.

LESSON XC.

GLORY OF WASHINGTON.—Brougham.

This is the consummate glory of Washington;—a triumphant warrior where the most sanguine had a right to despair; a successful ruler in all the difficulties of a course
wholly untried; but a warrior, whose sword only left its
sheath when the first law of our nature commanded it to be
drawn, and a ruler who, having tasted of supreme power,
gently and unostentatiously desired that the cup might pass
from him, nor would suffer more to wet his lips than the
most solemn and sacred duty to his country and his God re-
quired!

To his latest breath did this great patriot maintain the noble character, of a captain the patron of peace, and a states-
man the friend of justice. Dying, he bequeathed to his heirs
the sword which he had worn in the war for liberty, and
charged them "Never to take it from the scabbard but in
self-defense, or in the defense of their country and her freedom;" and commanded them, that "when it should be thus
drawn, they should never sheath it nor ever give it up, but
prefer falling with it in their hands to the relinquishment
thereof,"—words, the majesty and simple eloquence of which
are not surpassed in the oratory of Athens and Rome.

It will be the duty of the historian and the sage in all ages
to let no occasion pass, of commemorating this illustrious
man; and until time shall be no more, will a test of the progress which our race has made in wisdom and in virtue be
derived from the veneration paid to the immortal name of
Washington!

LESSON XCI.

HOME.—Anonymous.

Home! How that blessed word thrills the ear!
  In it what recollections blend!
It tells of childhood's scenes so dear,
  And speaks of many a cherished friend.

O, through the world, where'er we roam,
  Though souls be pure and lips be kind,
The heart with fondness *turns* to home—
  Still turns to those it left behind.

This Figure exhibits the *third left hand gesture, index finger.* The gesture *begins* at the word *the,* making its *course* according to the *dotted line,* till its *stroke* comes upon the word *bird;* it is *suspended* till the utterance of the word *downward,* with which word it *descends* and comes to *rest* at the word *to.* To effect this gesture properly, the speaker takes the *first left* position at the word *turns,* in the second stanza, and slides into the *second* left at the word *the,* the instant the hand *begins* to move. Some cases have been pointed out to the pupil where it is proper to assume the *left* position. It is proper in these cases,—to mark a *new train of thought;* where persons addressed or objects referred to are on *the left hand;* sometimes for the sake of *variety;* and, certainly, as a mark of *respect* to that portion of the audience who sit *on the left side of the room.* In all these cases it *may* be proper to use the left gesture.

|The *bird* that soars to yonder skies,
  Though nigh to heaven, still seems unblessed;
It leaves them, and with rapture flies
  Downward to) its own much loved nest.

Though beauteous scenes may meet its view,
  And breezes blow from balmy groves,
With wing untired and bosom true,
  It turns to that dear spot it loves.

When heaven shall bid this soul depart,
  This form return to kindred earth,

12*

May the last throb, which swells my heart,
  Heave, where it started into birth.

And should affection shed one tear;
  Should friendship linger round my tomb;
The tribute will be doubly dear,
  When given by those of "home, sweet home."

LESSON XCII.

THE NURSERY TALE.—BAYLEY.

OH! did you not hear in your nursery,
  The tale that the gossips tell,
Of two young girls that came to drink
  At a certain fairy well?
The words of the youngest were as sweet
  As the smile of her ruby lip,
But the tongue of the eldest seemed to move
  As if venom were on its tip!

At the well a beggar accosted them,
  A sprite in a mean disguise ;—
The eldest spoke with a scornful brow,
  The youngest with tearful eyes ;
Cried the Fairy, "Whenever *you* speak, sweet girl,
  Pure gems from your lips shall fall ;
But whenever *you* utter a word, proud maid,
  From your tongue shall a serpent fall."

And have you not met with these sisters oft,
  In the haunts of the old and young ?
The first with her pure and unsullied lip?
  The last with her serpent tongue ?
Yes—the first is *Good Nature*—diamonds bright
  On the darkest theme she throws ;
And the last is *Slander*—leaving the slime
  Of the snake wherever she goes!

LESSON XCIII.

UNION—WASHINGTON.—Russell.

IF we are united, we shall have nothing to fear. Union is the heart, through which must circulate those streams of life, of health, of joy, which shall animate every member, which shall heal every disease, and which shall give a zest to every blessing. United you may sit securely, like a mighty giant, on your mountains, and bending a stern regard upon the ocean, dare the coming of the proudest foe. Policy, genius, nature herself invites to union. Be united!—was the last injunction which trembled from the lips of our departed Washington. At the name of Washington does not a melancholy pleasure sadden and delight your souls? He has filled the world with his and our glory. The *Tartar* and the *Arab* converse about him in their tents. His form already stands in bronze and marble among the worthies of ancient and modern times. The fidelity of history has already taken care of the immortality of his fame. His example shall animate posterity, and should faction tear, or invasion approach our country, his spirit shall descend from the Divinity, and inspire tranquility and courage. Death has not terminated his usefulness—he has not, he can never cease to do good; even now he holds from his tomb a torch which cheers and enlightens the world. Be united, was his last injunction. Washington *loved* truth!—Let us love it—let us seek it with a sincere and single heart. It will reward the search. It is great, immutable and eternal. The fugitive falsehoods of the moment shall perish; party and passion may write their names upon the plaister; but this shall one day moulder, and Truth remain forever inscribed upon the marble.

LESSON XCIV.

THE DOG.—Mrs. Sigourney.

" *He will not come,*" said the gentle child,
    And she patted the poor dog's head,
And she pleasantly called him and fondly smiled,
But he heeded her not, in his anguish wild,
    Nor arose from his lowly bed.

We come now to the *double* gestures. Double gestures are those which require the action of *both* hands at the same time. The Figure exhibits the *first double gesture, palms up.* The gesture *begins* at the word *masters,* and making its *course* in a gentle *curve,* its *stroke* comes upon the word *grave;* the hands retain their position till the word *guarded* has been pronounced, when they fall to *rest.* The *use*

of this gesture is similar to that of the *first single* gesture on page 79; this, however, generally implies the idea of *space* or *local extent,* while that, as a *significant* gesture, has no connection at all with such a thought. This comes also to the relief of the first single gesture, of *either* hand to prevent *sameness;* or it may be used, as a *terminating* gesture, to *grace* a concluding sentence.

'Twas his | master's *grave* where he chose to rest ;
 He guarded) it night and day ;
The love that glowed in his grateful breast,
For the friend who had fed, controlled, and carest,
 Might never fade away.

So there through the Summer's heat he lay,
 Till Autumn nights grew bleak,
Till his eye grew dim with his hope's decay,
And he pined, and pined, and wasted away,
 A skeleton gaunt and weak.

Cold Winter came with an angry sway,
 And the snow lay deep and sore,
Then his moaning grew fainter day by day,
Till close where the broken tombstone lay,
 He fell, to rise no more.

And when he struggled with mortal pain,
 And Death was by his side,
With one loud cry that shook the plain,
He called for his master,—but all in vain ;—
 Then stretched himself, and died.

LESSON XCV.

THE BEGGAR AND HIS DOG.—Wolcot.

WELCOME, thou man of sorrows, to my door!
  A willing balm thy wounded heart shall find,
Thou and thy guiding dog my cares implore!
  O haste and shelter from the unfeeling wind.

Alas! shall misery seek my cot with sighs,
  And humbly sue for piteous alms my ear:
Yet disappointed go with lifted eyes,
  And on my threshold leave the upbraiding tear?

Thou *bowest* for the pity I bestow:
  Bend not to me, because I mourn distress;
I am thy debtor—much to thee I owe:
  For learn—the *greatest blessing* is to *bless.*

Thy sightless orbs and venerable beard—
  And pressed by weight of years that palsied head,
Though silent, speak with tongues that must be heard,
  Nay, must be *felt,* if virtue be not dead.

O let me own that heart which pants to bless,
  That nobly scorns to hide the useless store;
But looks around for objects of distress,
  And triumph's in a pity for the poor!

When heaven on man is pleased its wealth to shower,
  Ah! what an envied bliss doth heaven bestow,
To raise pale Merit in her hopeless hour,
  And lead Despondence from the tomb of woe.

LESSON XCVI.

THE DEATH OF THE FLOWERS.—Miss Bowles.

How happily, how happily the flowers die away!
Oh! could we but return to earth as easily as they!
Just live a life of sunshine, of innocence and bloom,
Then drop without decrepitude, or pain, into the tomb!

The gay and glorious creatures! they neither "toil nor spin;"

THIS Figure exhibits the *second or middle double gesture, palms up*. In preparing for the gesture, the speaker, at the word *lo !* slides into the *second right* position, with an expression of *pleased surprise ;* the hands *begin* the *course* of the gesture at the word *what*, and having performed it according to the *dotted lines*, its *stroke* comes upon the word *apparelled ;* the hands fall to *rest* after the word *in*. The speaker resumes the *first right* position on the word *tears*. This gesture, like the former of its class, is excellent to describe objects *occupying space ;* as a *landscape*, the *earth*, the *ocean ;* or large *assemblages* of persons, and the like ; as, "*Look at the men who have swelled out this vast procession.*" In this, as well as in the other gestures described, the pupil should be careful to keep the arms well from the body.

Yet, lo! |what goodly raiment they are all *apparelled* in ;)
No tears are on their beauty, but dewy gems more bright
Than ever brow of eastern queen endiademed with light.

The young rejoicing creatures! their pleasures never pall ;
Nor lose in sweet contentment, because so free to all !—
The dew, the showers, the sunshine, the balmy, blessed air,
Spend nothing of their freshness, though all may freely share.

The happy careless creatures ! of time they take no heed ;
Nor weary of his creeping, nor tremble at his speed ;
Nor sigh with sick impatience, and wish the light away ;
Nor when 'tis gone, cry dolefully, " would God that it were
      day !"

And when their lives are over, they drop away to rest,
Unconscious of the penal doom, on holy Nature's breast ;
No pain have they in dying—no shrinking from decay—
Oh! could we but return to earth as easily as they !

LESSON XCVII.

WE MUST FIGHT.—Henry.

I have but one lamp by which my feet are guided, and that is the lamp of experience. I know of no way of judging of the future but by the past. And judging by the past, I wish to know what there has been in the conduct of the British ministry for the last ten years, to justify those hopes with which gentlemen have been pleased to solace themselves and the House? Is it that insidious smile with which our petition has been lately received? Trust it not, Sir; it will prove a snare to your feet. Suffer not yourselves to be betrayed with a kiss. Let us not, I beseech you, deceive ourselves longer. We have done every thing that could be done, to avert the storm which is now coming on. We have petitioned—we have remonstrated—we have supplicated, we have prostrated ourselves before the throne, and have implored its interposition to arrest the tyrannical hands of the ministry and parliament. Our petitions have been slighted; our remonstrances have produced additional violence and insult; our supplications have been disregarded; and we have been spurned, with contempt, from the foot of the throne. In vain after these things, may we indulge the fond hope of peace and reconciliation. *There is no longer any room for hope.* If we wish to be free—if we mean to preserve inviolate those inestimable privileges for which we have been so long contending—if we mean not basely to abandon the noble struggle in which we have been so long engaged, and which we have pledged ourselves never to abandon, until the glorious object of our contest shall be obtained—we must *fight!*—I repeat it, Sir, we *must fight!!* An appeal to arms and to the God of Hosts is all that is left us!

LESSON XCVIII.

THE BLIND MOTHER.—Anonymous.

I saw a mother! In her arms
  Her infant child was sleeping;

The mother, while the infant slept,
  Her guardian watch was keeping.

Around its little tender form,
  Her snow white arm was flung;
And o'er its little infant head
  Her bending tresses hung.

"Sleep sweetly on, my darling babe,
  My own, my only child;"
And as she spoke the infant woke,
  And on its mother smiled.

But, ah! no fondly answering smile
  The mother's visage graced,
For she was blind, and could not see
  The infant she embraced.

But now he lisped his mother's name,
  And now the mother pressed
Her darling, much beloved boy,
  Unto her widowed breast.

But sudden anguish seized her mind,
  Her voice was sweetly wild;
"My God!" she cried, "but grant me sight,
  One hour to see my child!

To look upon its cherub face,
  And see its father's there;
But pardon if the wish be wrong,
  A widowed mother's prayer."

And as she spoke her anguish grew
  Still louder and more wild:
And closer to her aching breast
  She clasped her orphan child.

LESSON XCIX.

THE HILLS.—Anonymous.

The hills ! the everlasting hills !
How peerlessly they rise,
Like earth's gigantic sentinels
Discoursing in the skies.

This Figure exhibits the *third double gesture, palms up*. At this mark | the speaker throws himself into the *second* right position; the *course* of the gesture also *commences*, and the hands *ascend* upon the word *hail* with an emphatic and rather rapid motion, till they are about on a level with the shoulders ; they then *finish* the course *slowly* in a *curve*, making the *stroke* upon the word *fortresses ;* on the second word *hail*, the hands separate a little *wider*, and,—making a descending *stroke* upon the word *masonry*, come to *rest* upon the word *God*. The objects addressed—" the everlasting hills"— are magnificent, and the corresponding *emotion*, occasions an *extended* position of the feet, and a *spirited* elevation of the hands and arms. This gesture is appropriate to the description of *grand* and *lofty* objects, or to the enforcement of *sublime* and *inspiring* thoughts.

| Hail ! Nature's storm-proof *fortresses*,
By Freedom's children trod ;
Hail ! the invulnerable walls
The *Masonry* of God !)

Glorious ye are, when Noon's fierce beams
Your naked summits smite,
As o'er ye Day's great lamp hangs poised
In cloudless chrysolite ;
Glorious, when o'er ye sunset clouds,
Like broidered curtains lie—

Sublime, when through dim moonlight looms
 Your special majesty.

When the dismantled pyramids
 Shall blend with desert dust,
When every temple ' made with hands'
 Is faithless to its trust,
Ye shall not stoop your Titan crests—
 Magnificent as now !
Till your Almighty architect
 In thunder bids you bow !

LESSON C.

EULOGIUM ON DR. FRANKLIN.—MIRABEAU.

FRANKLIN is dead.—The genius who freed America, and poured a copious stream of knowledge throughout Europe, is returned into the bosom of the Divinity.

The sage to whom two worlds lay claim, the man for whom science and politics are disputing, indisputably enjoyed an elevated rank in human nature.

The cabinets of princes have been long in the habit of notifying the death of those who were great, only in their funeral orations. Long hath the etiquette of courts proclaimed the mourning of hypocrisy. Nations should wear mourning for none but their benefactors. The representatives of nations should recommend to public homage, only those who have been the heroes of humanity.

The Congress of America hath ordered, in the fourteen confederate states, a mourning of two months for the death of Benjamin Franklin ; and America is at this moment paying that tribute of veneration to one of the fathers of her constitution.

Were it not worthy of us, gentlemen, to join in the same religious act, to pay our share of that homage now rendered in the sight of the universe, at once to the rights of man, and to the philosopher who most contributed to extend the conquest of liberty over the face of the whole earth?

Antiquity would have raised altars to that vast and mighty genius, who, for the advantage of human kind, embracing earth and heaven in his ideas, *he could tame the rage of thunder and of despotism.* France, enlightened and free, owes at least some testimony of remembrance and regret to one of the greatest men who ever served the cause of philosophy and liberty.

LESSON CI.

THE CHILD'S WISH IN JUNE.—Mrs. Gilman.

Mother, mother, the winds are at play,
Prithee, let me be idle to day.

This Figure exhibits the first of another class of *double* gestures. It is the *first double gesture, palms down*. The *effect* of any gesture depends in a great measure upon its *quality*, or manner of motion. In this, the hands *begin* to move at the word *flowers*, and make the *course* of the gesture, as the *dotted lines* show, in a *curve*, passing at an equal rate *slowly* till they reach the upper line of the arm, upon the word *lie*, when—illustrative of the word *languidly* —they make the *stroke*, by *dropping*,

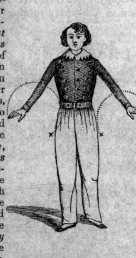

as it were, through the remaining part of the curve, upon the syllable *lan*, and, with a very slight suspension, fall lifelessly to *rest* upon the other syllables of that word. The *stroke* of gesture is to the *eye*, what *emphasis* of voice is to the *ear*,— both should come exactly upon the accented syllable of the emphatic word. This gesture may be *applied* to nearly the same ideas as those on page 115 ; it is used instead of that to prevent *repetition*, and, independently, to mark a stronger sentiment, or a more fervid emotion.

Look, dear mother, the | flowers all lie
Languidly) under the bright blue sky.
See, how slowly the streamlet glides ;
Look, how the violet roguishly hides ;
Even the butterfly rests on the rose,
And scarcely sips the sweets as he goes.

Poor Tray is asleep in the noonday sun,
And the flies go about him, one by one ;
And Pussy sits near, with a sleepy grace,
Without ever thinking of washing her face.

There flies a bird to a neighboring tree,
But very lazily flieth he,

And he sits and twitters a gentle note,
And scarcely ruffles his little throat.

You bid me be busy ; but mother, hear
How the humdrum grasshopper soundeth near ;
And the soft west wind is so light in its play,
It scarcely moves a leaf on the spray.

I wish, oh, I wish I was yonder cloud
That sails about with its misty shroud ;
Books and work I no more should see,
And I'd come and float dear mother o'er thee.

LESSON CII.

THE PAUPER'S DEATH-BED.—Mrs. Southey.

TREAD softly—bow the head—
In reverent silence bow—
No passing bell doth toll—
Yet an immortal soul
    Is passing now.

Stranger! however great,
With lowly reverence bow ;
There 's one in that poor shed—
One by that paltry bed—
    Greater than thou.

Beneath that beggar's roof,
Lo! Death doth keep his state :
Enter—no crowds attend—
Enter—no guards defend
    This palace gate.

That pavement, damp and cold,
No smiling courtiers tread ;
One silent woman stands,
Lifting with meager hands
    A dying head.

No mingling voices sound—
An infant wail alone ;

A sob suppressed—again
That short deep gasp, and then
    The parting groan.

Oh! change—oh! wondrous change—
Burst are the prison bars—
This moment there, so low,
So agonized, and now
    Beyond the stars.

Oh! change—stupendous change!
There lies the soulless clod:
The Sun eternal breaks—
The new Immortal wakes—
    Wakes with his God.

LESSON CIII.

MAN IMMORTAL.—Montgomery.

MAN, to this narrow sphere confined,
Dies when he but begins to live.
Oh! if there be no world on high

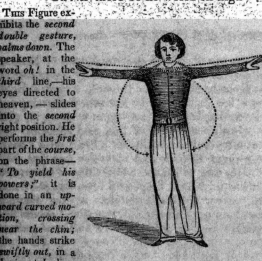

THIS Figure exhibits the *second double gesture, palms down*. The speaker, at the word *oh!* in the *third* line,—his eyes directed to heaven, — slides into the *second* right position. He performs the *first* part of the *course*, on the phrase— "*To yield his powers;*" it is done in an *upward curved motion,* *crossing near the chin;* the hands strike *swiftly out,* in a *horizontal* line, *completing* the *course;* the *stroke* comes upon the syllable *fet,* the speaker at the same *instant* resuming the *first* right position; the hands come to *rest* after the word *man.* This gesture is suitable to expressions in which the idea of *speed* and *extent* are combined, as in the example. It *discards, repels* with violence, and the like; as, "We swept them from the shore!"

|To yield his powers *unfettered* scope;
If man) be only born to die,

13*

Whence this inheritance of hope ?
Wherefore to him alone were lent
Riches that never can be spent ?
Enough, not more, to all the rest,
For life and happiness, was given ;
To man, mysteriously unblest,
Too much for any state but heaven.

It is not thus ;—it cannot be
That one so gloriously endowed
With views that reach eternity,
Should shine and vanish like a cloud :
Is there a God ?   All nature shows
There is,—and yet no mortal knows :
The mind that could this truth conceive,
Which brute sensation never taught,
No longer to the dust would cleave,
But grow immortal with the thought.

LESSON CIV.

THE QUEEN OF FRANCE.—Burke.

It is now sixteen years since I saw the Queen of France,
then the dauphiness, at Versailles ; and surely never lighted
on this orb, which she hardly seemed to touch, a more delightful vision. I saw her just above the horizon, decorating and
cheering the elevated sphere she just began to move in, glittering like the morning star, full of life, and splendor, and
joy.   Oh ! what a revolution ! and what a heart must I have,
to contemplate without emotion that elevation and that fall!
   Little did I dream that, when she added titles of veneration
to those of enthusiastic, distant, respectful love, that she could
ever be obliged to carry the sharp antidote against disgrace
concealed in that bosom ; little did I dream that I should live
to see such disasters heaped upon her in a nation of gallant
men, in a nation of men of honor and of cavaliers. I thought
ten thousand swords must have leaped from their scabbards
to avenge even a look that threatened her with insult. But
the age of chivalry has gone. That of sophisters, econ-
omists, and calculators, has succeeded ; and the glory of

Europe is extinguished for ever. Never, never more shall we behold that generous loyalty to rank and sex, that proud submission, that dignified obedience, that subordination of the heart, which kept alive, even in servitude itself, the spirit of an exalted freedom.

The unbought grace of life, the cheap defense of nations, the nurse of manly sentiment and heroic enterprise, is gone! It is gone, that sensibility of principle, that chastity of honor, which felt a stain like a wound, which inspired courage, while it mitigated ferocity, which ennobled whatever it touched, and under which vice itself lost half its evil, by losing all its grossness.

LESSON CV.

OUR FLAG.—Percival.

Lift, lift the eagle banner high,
    Our guide to fame;
On ocean's breezes bid it fly
Like meteors wafting through the sky
    Their pomp and flame;
Till wide on every sea unfurled,
It tell to an admiring world
    Our name.

O! proudly burns its beacon light
    On victory's path;
Through freedom's dawn, through danger's night,
Onward, still onward, rolling bright,
    It swept in wrath;
Still lightning-like to him who dares
Confront the terrors of our stars,
    Its scath.

Still heavenward mounts the generous flame,
    And never tires;
Does Envy dare insult our name,
Or lurking Falsehood brand with shame,
    Our buried sires?
The armed Colossus thunders by,

This Figure exhibits the *third double gesture, palms down.* In the performance of this gesture, there is an *upward* and a *downward course,* and a *second stroke.* The hands ascend upon the word *dastard,* making a smart emphasis upon the word *lie;* at this point, as represented in the picture, it is a *suspending gesture;* a preparation is made for the concluding movement, by throwing the hands a little *back* upon the syllable *ex*—they descend with a *swift motion* and *considerable force,* upon the syllable *pires,* and thus make a *terminating emphatic* gesture. In the management of a good speaker, this is an admirable gesture: it might be applied with great effect upon that memorable phrase of Patrick Henry, as related by Mr. Wirt—"*Give me liberty, or give me death.*" Admiration, *surprise, amazement,* and the like, are well expressed by the *suspending* part of this gesture.

Wide wave our stripes—the |dastard *lie*
    Expires.)

LESSON CVI.

THE BLIND BOY.—Hawkes.

"Dear Mary," said the poor blind boy,
    That little bird sings very long ;
Say, can you see him in his joy,
    And is *he* pretty as his song ?"

"Yes, Edward, yes," replied the maid ;
    "I see the bird on yonder tree."
The poor boy sighed, and gently said,
    "Sister, I wish that I could see.

The flowers, you say, are very fair,
    And bright green leaves are on the trees,
And pretty birds are singing there—
    How beautiful for one who sees !

Yet I the fragrant flower can smell,
    And I can feel the green leaf's shade,

And I can hear the notes that swell
  From these dear birds that God has made.

So, sister, God to me is kind,
  Though sight, alas! he has not given;
But tell me, are there any blind
  Among the children up in Heaven?"

"No, dearest Edward; there all see;
  But why ask me a thing so odd?"
"Oh, Mary! He's so kind to me,
  I thought I'd like to *look* at God."

Ere long, disease his hand had laid
  On that dear boy, so meek and mild;
His widowed mother wept and prayed
  That God would spare her sightless child.

He felt her warm tears on his face,
  And said, "Oh, never weep for me;
I'm going to a bright, bright place,
  Where, Mary says, I God shall see:

And you'll come there—dear Mary too;
  But, mother, when you get up there,
Tell Edward, mother, that 'tis you—
  You know I never saw you here."

He spake no more, but sweetly smiled,
  Until the final blow was given,
When God took up that poor blind child,
  And opened first his eyes in Heaven.

LESSON CVII.

THINK ON THE POOR.—Anonymous.

As you sit in warm circles, secure from the tempest,
  Nor feel the keen storm, as it drifts on the moor;
Yet shut not your door 'gainst the wandering stranger,
  But learn from your blessings to pity the poor.

When the cold northern blast blows both chilly and rudely,
And the rain patters hard at your windows and door ;
As you hear the blast howl, look around on your comforts

THIS Figure represents a boy with his *hand upon his heart*. In the expression to which the gesture is applied, the *course* begins at the word *heave*, the *stroke* comes upon the word *sigh*, and the hand falls to *rest* upon the word *poor*. *The pressure of the hand upon the breast*, is the stroke. Boys, when they first attempt to make this gesture, are apt to press the *elbow down to the side ;* this is inelegant ; the hand should be brought up in a graceful *curve* and the arm *rounded easily out*. The hand will be properly placed if the middle of the fingers is directly on the spot where the beating of the heart is felt. This gesture is appropriate to expressions of *pity, compassion, appeals to heaven*, and the *personal feelings* of the speaker.

And | heave a kind *sigh* for the indigent poor.)

Oft lift up the latch of chill poverty's dwelling,
Explore the sad mansion where care sits obscure ;
Behold ! tears of want wash the withering bosom,
Then think of your plenty, and give to the poor.

The winter presents a sad gloomy aspect—
In clusters the icicles hang at the door ;
Red berries adorn the brown thorn for the songster,
But you must relieve the hard fate of the poor.

Remember that soon we must sink in that dwelling,
Where riches no sort of distinction procure ;
That leveler, Death, and the grave, our last mansion,
Must mingle the dust of the rich and the poor.

LESSON CVIII.

INFLUENCE OF SUPERIOR MINDS.—SPRAGUE.

IT belongs to cultivated men to construct, and put in motion, and direct the complex machinery of civil society. Who

originated these free institutions,—the arteries through which
the life-blood of our country's prosperity circulates? Who
built and rocked the cradle of American liberty, and guarded
the infant angel, until she walked forth in the vigor of a glorious maturity? Whom do we welcome to the helm of state,
when the storm of faction beats, or dark clouds hang about
the heavens? Who speak, trumpet-tongued, to a nation's
ear, in behalf of a nation's rights? Who hold the scales of
equity, measuring out a portion both to the just and the unjust? Are they men who have been nursed in the lap of
ignorance, or are they not rather your great and cultivated
minds—your Franklins and Madisons, and Adamses and
your Kents, and Spencers, and Storys? And then again,
who framed that social system,—if system it could be called,
—which exploded in the horrors of the French revolution;
sporting with time-hallowed associations, and unsealing all
the fountains of blood? Think you that ignorance was the
presiding genius in that war of elements? Oh, no; the
master-spirits had many of them been known as standard
bearers in the empire of letters; they partook at once of the
strength of the angel, and the depravity of the fiend. And
as it is in these opposite cases that I have mentioned, so it is
always and every where,—men with cultivated minds will
ultimately have the power, whether they use it in the spirit
of a lofty patriotism, or pervert it to do homage to faction,
and tear society in pieces.

———

LESSON CIX.

THE ORPHAN.—Anonymous.

My father and mother are dead,
  No friend or relation I have;
And now the cold earth is their bed,
  And daisies grow over their grave.

I cast my eyes into the tomb,
  The sight made me bitterly cry;
I said, and is this the dark room
  Where my father and mother must lie!

I cast my eyes round me again,
  In hopes some protector to see;

Alas! but the search was in vain,
For none had compassion on me.

I cast my eyes up to the sky,
I groaned though I said not a word;
Yet God was not deaf to my cry—
The friend of the fatherless heard.

O, yes—and he graciously smiled,
And he bid me on him to depend;
He whispered—fear not, little child,
For I am thy father and friend.

LESSON CX.

SAUL, BEFORE HIS LAST BATTLE.—Byron.

Warriors and Chiefs! should the shaft or the sword

This Figure exhibits a gesture very similar to the preceding one. The *thumb*, instead of the open hand, is placed at the heart. The *course* of the gesture *begins* at, and the *stroke* comes upon, the word *pierce;* the hand is *thrown off*, with some emphasis, from the breast, on the word, *heed*, and comes to *rest* after the word *corse*. As the hand comes up, the fingers close upon the palm, and the *thumb* being quite *straight*, strikes with its *end*, upon the breast. This gesture is, generally, applied to denote *dark feeling, guilt, remorse, troubled conscience*, and the like; as, "*Conscience!* 'twas that made Cæsar pause upon the brink of the Rubicon."

⎰Pierce me in leading the hosts of the Lord,
 Heed not the corse,) though a king's, in your path;
 Bury your steel in the bosom of Gath!

Thou who art bearing my buckler and bow,
Should the soldiers of Saul look away from the foe,
Stretch me that moment in blood at thy feet!
Mine be the doom which they dared not to meet!

Farewell to others, but never we part,
Heir to my royalty, son of my heart!
Bright is the diadem, boundless the sway,
Or kindly the death which awaits us to-day.

———

LESSON CXI.

SUMMER.—Hunt.

THE months we used to read of
  Have come to us again,
With sunniness and sunniness
  And rare delights of rain;
The lark is up, and says aloud,
  East and west I see no cloud.

The lanes are full of roses,
  The fields are grassy deep;
The leafiness and floweriness
  Make one abundant heap;
The balmy, blossom-breathing airs,
  Smell of future plums and pears.

The sunshine at our waking,
  Is still found smiling by;
With beamingness and earnestness,
  Like some beloved eye;
And all the day it seems to take
  Delight in being wide awake.

The lasses in the gardens
  Show forth their heads of hair,
With rosiness and lightsomeness
  A chasing here and there;
And then they'll hear the birds, and stand,
  And shade their eyes with lifted hand.

And then again they're off there,
  As if their lovers came,
With giddiness and gladsomeness
  Like doves but newly tame.
Ah! light your cheeks at nature, do,
  And draw the whole world after you.

14

LESSON CXII.

THE LIFE-BOAT.—Mrs. Osgood.

The thunder-spirits sound on high
  The storm's wild tocsin, loud and deep,
And winds and waves, with maddening cry,
  Fierce at the summons leap.

Wide flashed through heaven the lightning's wing;
  The blinding rain did swiftly pour;
And the noble ship, a helpless thing,
  Lay tossing towards the shore!

Then shrieked the crew, "In mercy save!"
  And rushing headlong to her side,
They launch the life-boat on the wave,
  And tempt the fearful tide.

And there was He, *above* the storm,
  Who smiled upon the shallop light,
And sent an angel's viewless form
  To guide the bark aright!

This Figure exhibits a gesture made by bringing *both* hands to the heart. When properly applied and well executed, it is expressive and beautiful. In the passage selected to show its *use*, the *course* of the gesture *begins* at the word *that*; the *stroke*—made by the *pressure* of the hands—comes upon the word *soul*; the hands spring from the breast with an *emphatic, circular* motion upon the words *quail not*, and then falls to *rest* upon the word *life-boat*. In performing this gesture, both hands ascend at the same time, the *left* hand coming *under* upon the breast, with the *fingers* of the right *pressing* upon it. The use of it is to express *intense emotion, solemn asseveration, appeals to the Deity*, and the like. It should never occur more than *once* in any piece which a boy might be called upon to recite.

Boy! in the storms | that shake the *soul*,
  Quail not! there's still a life)-boat nigh;
And there may Angel-Faith's control,
  Grief's wildest waves defy!

LESSON CXIII.

THE PERFECT SPEAKER.—Anonymous.

IMAGINE to yourselves a Demosthenes addressing the most illustrious assembly in the world, upon a point whereon the fate of the most illustrious of nations depended.—How awful such a meeting! How vast the subject! Is man possessed of talents adequate to the great occasion? Adequate—yes, superior. By the power of his eloquence, the augustness of the assembly is lost in the dignity of the orator; and the importance of the subject for a while superseded, by the admiration of his talents.—With what strength of argument, with what powers of the fancy, with what emotions of the heart, does he assault and subjugate the whole man, and, at once, captivate his reason, his imagination, and his passions!—To effect this, must be the utmost effort of the most improved state of human nature.—Not a faculty that he possesses is here unemployed; not a faculty that he possesses but is here exerted to its highest pitch. All his internal powers are at work; all his external testify their energies. Within, the memory, the fancy, the judgment, the passions, are all busy; without, every muscle, every nerve, is exerted; not a feature, not a limb, but speaks. The organs of the body, attuned to the exertions of the mind, through the kindred organs of the hearers, instantaneously as it were with an electrical spirit, vibrate those energies from soul to soul.—Notwithstanding the diversity of minds in such a multitude, by the lightning of eloquence, they are melted into one mass—the whole assembly actuated in one and the same way, become as it were, but one man, and have but one voice. The universal cry is—" Let us march against Philip—let us fight for our liberties—let us conquer—or die."

LESSON CXIV.

THE PIRATE'S SONG.—Anonymous.

BLOW on! blow on! we love the howling
Of winds that waft us o'er the sea;

As fearless as the wolf that's prowling
Upon our native hills are we.

This Figure exhibits the *suspending* part of an emphatic *significant* gesture. The hand *begins* to move at the word *the*, and reaches the position shown in the picture—with some emphasis—upon the word *terror;* the stroke is made by projecting the arm at full length, upon the word *fly;* the hand retaining its *inverted* position, with the thumb and fingers *straight* and considerably *apart;* the gesture *terminates* immediately after the word *before*. The purpose for which the speaker designs any gesture being *completed,* the arm should drop instantly to the side—any *suspending* after this, only weakens the effect. To *repulse,* to *discard* with *indignation,* and the like ; or to express the idea of *speed* and *force,* is the office of this gesture.

The doomed in terror *fly* before) us,
    We've nailed the black flag to the mast !
It there shall float triumphant o'er us,
    We will defend it to the last !

Roll on ! roll on ! we love the motion
    Of waves that bear us on our way ;
No swifter bark e'er sailed the ocean,
    No skiff more lightly skims the bay.
The lightning from the sky is flashing !
    The thunder's distant roar we hear,
But while o'er seas we thus are dashing,
    We, waves, nor winds, nor lightning's fear !

LESSON CXV.

THE IMPRISONED EAGLE.—Anonymous.

Oh ! 'twas a mean and dastard thing,
To bind the mountain-eagle's wing :
A tyrant's forge the fetters framed,
And tyranny the deed proclaimed.

My spirit sickens when I see
That noble bird in his misery.
    Break, break, the kingly eagle's chain,
    And give him to the skies again.

His powerful wing that nature gave,
Sublime o'er mountain tops to wave,
Far sailing round the loftiest peak,
The home of princely sires to seek;
That powerful wing now drooping low,
Folds round him like a robe of woe.
    O break the kingly eagle's chain,
    And give him to the skies again.

Once he loved on the sun to gaze,
But now he shuns the dazzling blaze;
His eye is dimmed, a feebler light
Suits best the captive eagle's sight.
Oh! were he free, his glance would dare
The vivid lightning's fervid glare.
    Break, break, the kingly eagle's chain,
    And give him to the skies again.

'Twas the thought of a dastard mind,
The eagle's free-born wing to bind;
Freeman, if freedom's honored name,
The homage of thy heart can claim,
Unclose the prisoner's grated door,
And let him far and freely soar.
    Break, break, the kingly eagle's chain,
    And give him to the skies again.

LESSON CXVI.

THE SAILOR BOY'S DREAM.—Anonymous.

On the midnight ocean sleeping the youthful sailor lies,
While scenes of happy childhood in his dreaming soul arise;
Still chiming seems the Sabbath bell, as sweetly as of yore,
And once again he roams the fields, and sees the cottage door.
In her arms his mother folds him, with affection's fond caress,
His gentle bright-eyed sisters, too, in rapture round him press;

14*

His aged father meets him, and his young companions come,
To welcome him once more to share the dear delights of home.

This Figure repre-
sents a boy in the atti-
tude of *listening*. The
hand comes rapidly up
upon the word *hark*,
performing at the same
time the principal
stroke of the gesture;
then there is a return-
ing downward *course*,
making an *emphasis*
upon the word *shriek*;
the hand comes to *rest*
upon the word *dispels*.
In this action, the *ear*
is turned towards the
point whence the
sound comes; the eyes
are bent on *vacancy*,
as it is called—seem-
ing to look on nothing
—and the body *leans
forward*, more or less,
according to the ear-
nestness of the atten-
tion.

| *Hark!* what wild *shriek* dispels) his dream? whence sound
        those cries of wo?
With the storm loud thunders mingle—o'er the ship the bil-
        lows flow;
From his hammock starts the sleeper! he rushes to the deck!
The vessel's sails with lightning blaze! she sinks a burning
        wreck!
To a mast the winds have riven the sailor madly clings;
His fearful parting knell of death the tempest loudly rings;
All is dark and drear around—not a star beams o'er the wave,
As ocean spirits bear him to the sailor's shroudless grave!
Oh! never at the cottage hearth shall he again be seen,
Nor meet his playmates merrily to sport upon the green:
In vain for him the birds shall sing—the hawthorn deck the
        tree;
For slumb'ring on the sand he lies beneath the swelling sea.
Where now are happy childhood's scenes? oh, where the
        chiming bell?
The fields o'er which he used to stray, the cot he loved so well?
For ever lost! yet still he finds a home of peace and joy,
Where neither stormy wind nor wave can wreck the sailor
        boy.

LESSON CXVII.

THE WARRIOR FATHER.—Mrs. Hale.

Now fly, as flies the rushing wind—
  Urge, urge thy lagging steed!
The savage yell is fierce behind,
  And life is on thy speed.

And from those dear ones make thy choice;
  The group he wildly eyed,
When "father!" burst from every voice,
  And "child!" his heart replied.

Ambition goads the conqueror on,
  Hate points the murderer's brand;
But love and duty, these alone
  Can nerve the good man's hand.

The hero may resign the field,
  The coward murderer flee;
He cannot fear—he will not yield,
  That strikes, sweet love, for thee.

They come, they come—he heeds no cry,
  Save the soft child-like wail;
"Oh father, save!" "My children, fly!"
  Were mingled on the gale.

And firmer still he drew his breath,
  And sterner flashed his eye,
As fast he hurls the leaden death,
  Still shouting, "Children, fly!"

No shadow on his brow appeared,
  Nor tremor shook his frame,
Save when at intervals he heard
  Some trembler lisp his name.

In vain the foe, those fiends unchained,
  Like famished tigers chafe;
The sheltering roof is neared, is gained,
  All, all the dear ones safe!

LESSON CXVIII.

MARY'S GRAVE.—Roscoe.

The summer winds sing lullaby
  O'er Mary's little grave ;
And the summer flowers spring tenderly,
  O'er her their buds to wave.
For oh ! her life was short and sweet
As the flowers which blossom at her feet.

A little while the beauteous gem
  Bloomed on the parent's breast ;
Ah ! then it withered on the stem,
  And sought a deeper rest ;
And we laid on her gentle frame the sod,

THIS Figure exhibits another example of the *index finger*. The *course* of the gesture *begins* at the word *the* ; the *stroke* comes upon the word *spirit*, the hand gradually ascending till it pauses upon the word *God;* it then descends in a gentle *curve*, and comes to *rest* upon the word *loved*. It may be used to describe any thing rising in a *perpendicular* direction ; as, an *arrow*, the *sky-lark*, a *rocket*, and the like ; it is appropriate also, in allusion to the "*heavens above*," or to the *great Being* who made them.

But we know that |the *spirit* was fled to God.

The birds she loved) so well to hear,
  Her parting requiem sing,
And her memory lives in the silent tear
  Which the heart to the eye will bring ;
For her kind little feelings will ne'er be forgot
By those who have mourned her early lot.

LESSON CXIX.

GOD GOVERNS IN THE AFFAIRS OF MEN.—Franklin.

Mr. President.—The small progress we have made after four or five weeks close attendance and continual reasonings with each other—our different sentiments on almost every question, several of the last producing as many noes, as ayes—is, methinks, a melancholy proof of the imperfection of the human understanding. We indeed, seem to feel our own want of political wisdom, since we have been running about in search of it. We have gone back to ancient history for models of government, and examined the different forms of those republics, which, having been formed with the seeds of their own dissolution, now no longer exist. And we have viewed modern states all round Europe, but find none of their constitutions suitable to our circumstances.

In this situation of this Assembly, groping as it were in the dark to find political truth, and scarce able to distinguish it when presented to us, how has it happened, Sir, that we have not hitherto once thought of humbly applying to the Father of lights, to illuminate our understandings? In the beginning of the contest with great Britain, when we were sensible of danger, we had daily prayer in this room for the divine protection. Our prayers, Sir, were heard, and they were graciously answered. All of us who were engaged in the struggle must have observed frequent instances of a superintending Providence in our favor. To that kind providence we owe this happy opportunity of consulting in peace on the means of establishing our future national felicity. And have we now forgotten that powerful friend? or do we imagine that we no longer need his assistance? I have lived, Sir, along time, and the longer I live, the more convincing proofs I see of this truth—*that God governs in the affairs of men.* And if a sparrow cannot fall to the ground without his notice, is it probable that an empire can rise without his aid? We have been assured, Sir, in the sacred writings, that "except the Lord build the house they labor in vain that build it." I firmly believe this; and I also believe that without his concurring aid we shall succeed in this political building no better than the builders of Babel. We shall be divided by our little partial local interests; our projects will be confounded; and we ourselves shall become a reproach and by-word down to future ages. And what is worse, mankind may hereafter, from this unfortunate instance, despair of establishing governments by human wisdom, and leave it to chance, war, and conquest.

I therefore beg leave to move—that henceforth prayers imploring the assistance of Heaven, and its blessings on our deliberations, be held in this Assembly every morning before we proceed to business, and that one or more of the clergy of this city be requested to officiate in that service.

LESSON CXX.

THE NOBLE SAILOR.—Rindge.

It was a fearful night,
The strong flame sped
From street to street, from spire to spire,
And on their treasures tread ;

Hark ! 'tis the mother's cry,
High o'er the tumult wild,
As rushing toward her flame wrapt home,

This Figure exhibits an attitude expressive of *anguish of mind.* The pupil will notice that the position of the *feet* is *extended*, the *eyes raised to heaven*, and the *hands clasped with energy.* The fingers of one hand at the second joint are laid between the thumb and forefinger of the other, and then the fingers of both hands are *pressed tightly down*. This arrangement of the hands is sometimes called *fold-ed*, to distinguish it from that in which the fingers are all *inserted between each other.* In the passage to which the gesture is here applied, the *course* begins at the word *shrieked,* the hands come together, making the *stroke* upon the word *child,* and fall to *rest* upon the word *wanderer. Sudden impulses* of distress, agony, despair, and the like, find a natural expression in this action.

She |shrieks—"my *child !* my child !

A wanderer) from the sea,
A stranger marked her woe ;

And in his bosom woke,
The sympathetic glow.

Swift up the burning stairs
With daring feet he flew,
While sable clouds of stifling smoke,
Concealed him from the view.

Fast fell the burning beam
Across the dangerous road,
Till the far chamber where he groped
Like fiery oven glowed.

But what a pealing shout
When from the wreck he came,
And in his arms a smiling babe
Still toying with the flame.

The mother's raptured tears
Forth like a torrent sped,
But ere the throng could learn his name,
That noble tar *had fled*.

Not for the praise of man,
Did he this deed of love,
But on the bright unfading page
'Tis registered above.

LESSON CXXI.

THE BOY'S RETURN TO HIS HOME.—Waterman.

When shall I leave these mountains rude,
Rearing their giant dome,
When shall I leave this deep'ning wood,
When shall I be at home;
Bear me ye winds on tireless wing,
Bear me to love and joy,
Unto the scenes of youthful spring,
Bear back this wandering boy.

But I am near them, nearer still,
  Here are my haunts of play,
Here is the rock, the towering hill,
  Washed by the foaming spray.
There is the cliff, the shadowing cliff,
  The streamlet round its base ;
Oft I have manned my little skiff
  Over that watery space.

These are my rambling scenes of play,
  Where I have loved to roam,
But bear me, bear me on, I pray,
  Back to my mother's home ;
Bear me upon your wings, O wind !
  Back to my home of joy,
Scenes with my mother's memory shrin'd
  That she may bless her boy.

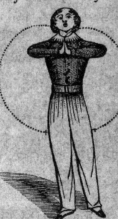

This Figure exhibits a *reverential* or *devotional* posture. As here adapted it is to express *affectionate* and *delighted gratitude.* The hands in this position are said to be *applied.* The fingers and thumbs are *laid to each other* and the hands *pressed together.* The arms are not kept down, but somewhat *raised* and *rounded outward.* So in the Fig. on page 165. In the passage which this gesture illustrates, the *course* begins immediately after the word *air;* the hands come together upon the word *thrice,* making the *stroke,* and are kept in this position till the speaker pronounces the word *soon,* when they part in an *outward curve,* and fall to *rest* on the word *feet.* Addresses to the Deity, particularly if imbued with *love* and *thankfulness* for his *mercy* and *goodness,* are appropriate to this form of gesture.

Bless thee ! oh bless thee, wandering air !
  | *Thrice* blessed my heavenly guide !
Soon will my weary feet) be where
  My heart long since has hied.

LESSON CXXII.

IMPORTANCE OF ORATORY.—Knowles.

THE principal means of communicating our ideas are two
—speech and writing. The former is the parent of the lat-

ter; it is the more important, and its highest efforts are called —Oratory.

If we consider the very early period at which we begin to exercise the faculty of speech, and the frequency with which we exercise it, it must be a subject of surprise that so few excel in Oratory. In any enlightened community, you will find numbers who are highly skilled in some particular art, or science, to the study of which they did not apply themselves, till they had almost arrived at the stage of manhood. Yet, with regard to the powers of speech—those powers which the very second year of our existence generally calls into action, the exercise of which goes on at our sports, our studies, our walks, our very meals; and which is never long suspended, except at the hour of refreshing sleep—with regard to those powers, how few surpass their fellow-creatures of common information and modern attainments! How very few deserve distinction! How rarely does one attain to eminence!

Oratory is highly useful to him that excels in it. In common conversation, observe the advantages which the fluent speaker enjoys over the man that hesitates, and stumbles in discourse. With half his information, he has twice his importance; he commands the respect of his auditors; he instructs and gratifies them. In the general transactions of business, the same superiority attends them. He communicates his views with clearness, precision and effect; he carries his point by his mere readiness; he concludes his treaty before another kind of man would have well set about it. Does he plead the cause of friendship?—How happy is his friend! Of charity? How fortunate is the distressed! Should he enter the legislature of his country, he approves himself the people's bulwark!

LESSON CXXIII.

THE BEAUTIES OF CREATION.—Heber.

I PRAISED the earth, in beauty seen,
With garlands gay of various green;
I praised the sea whose ample field
Shone glorious as a silver shield:
And earth and ocean seemed to say
"Our beauties are but for a day!"

I praised the sun, whose chariot rolled
On wheels of amber and of gold;
I praised the moon, whose softer eye
Gleamed sweetly through the summer sky!
And moon and sun in answer said,
"Our days of light are numbered!"

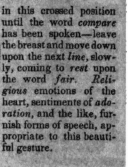

THIS Figure exhibits another chaste *devotional* attitude. The hands thus placed upon the breast, are said to be *crossed.* In the example selected for illustration, the *course* of the gesture begins at the letter *O;* the *stroke,* made by the pressure of the hands, comes upon the word *God;* and the hands—being suspended in this crossed position until the word *compare* has been spoken—leave the breast and move down upon the next *line*, slowly, coming to *rest* upon the word *fair. Religious* emotions of the heart, sentiments of *adoration,* and the like, furnish forms of speech, appropriate to this beautiful gesture.

|O *God!* O good beyond compare!
If thus thy meaner works are fair,)
If thus thy bounties gild the span
Of ruined earth and sinful man,
How glorious must the mansion be,
Where thy redeemed shall dwell with thee.

LESSON CXXIV.

CASABIANCA.—MRS. HEMANS.

YOUNG Casabianca, a boy about thirteen years old, son to the Admiral of the Orient, remained at his post in the battle of the Nile, after the ship had taken fire, and all the guns had been abandoned, and perished in the explosion of the vessel, when the flames had reached the powder.

THE boy stood on the burning deck,
Whence all but him had fled;
The flame that lit the battle's wreck,
Shone round him o'er the dead.

Yet beautiful and bright he stood,
　As born to rule the storm ;
A creature of heroic blood,
　A proud, though child-like form.

The flames rolled on—he would not go,
　Without his Father's word;
That Father faint in death below,
　His voice no longer heard.

He called aloud :—"say, Father, say,
　If yet my task is done ?"
He knew not that the chieftain lay
　Unconscious of his son.

"Speak, Father !" once again he cried,
　"If I may yet be gone !
And"—but the booming shots replied,
　And fast the flames rolled on.

Upon his brow he felt their breath,
　And in his waving hair,
And looked from that lone post of death,
　In still, yet brave despair—

And shouted but once more aloud,
　"My Father ! must I stay ?"
While o'er him fast, through sail and shroud,
　The wreathing fires made way.

They wrapt the ship in splendor wild,
　They caught the flag on high,
And streamed above the gallant child,
　Like banners in the sky.

There came a burst of thunder sound—
　The boy—oh ! where was he ?
Ask of the winds that far around
　With fragments strewed the sea.

With mast, and helm, and pennon fair,
　That well had borne their part—
But the noblest thing which perished there,
　Was that young faithful heart !

LESSON CXXV.

THE SHIP.—Anonymous.

THE summer sun is on the wave,
    The zephyr seeks the sea,
And ripples, dancing round her, lave
    The bulwark of the free.

THIS Figure exhibits an attitude of *discovery* mingled with *admiration.* The *course* of the gesture begins at the word *how;* the *stroke* comes upon the word *beautiful,* and the hands—being suspended through the rest of the line—commence their *downward* course upon the word *the,* and come to *rest* upon the word *swell.—* The pupil will notice that the position of the *feet* is quite *extended,* the right hand well *elevated,* with the middle and little fingers *curved* considerably inward; the left hand has the palm *downward.* The right foot is *firmly* planted, and the knee well *braced.* Emotions of *friendship,* of *warm salutation, applause,* and the like, or the issuing of directions *to* or *concerning* a distant *person* or *object,* may employ this form of action.

|How *beautiful* and brave a thing !
    The rising swell) she rides,
While sun and shade, uniting, fling
    Their colors on her sides.

Her decks on which the sun beams play,
    Are girt by many a gun,
That guard our fame by night and day,
    Where laurels green are won.
And ever may she lift on high
    The banner of our glory,
Bearing in every azure sky
    The stars that tell our story.

And though the tempest clouds may lower
    Above the angry deep,
And storms, with wild convulsive power,
    Around that vessel sweep,

While yet there is one shattered sail
  To flutter in the blast,
Oh may she bear through gloom and gale,
  That banner to the last.

LESSON CXXVI.

THE SNOW! THE SNOW!—Knight.

The snow, the snow! I love the snow,
  With its wild and frantic curl,
As it dances along on the frigid blast,
That flings it about as it whistles past,
  In many an eddying whirl!
    O give me the snow, the white-winged snow,
      That falls from the wintry sky,
    That robes the earth in a vest of white,
    And sparkles and shines in the sun's rich light,
      Like the starry arch on high!

The snow, the snow! I love the snow,
  'Tis ever dear to me!
With the gladsome cry of the bright-cheek'd boy,
Who hails its flight with a shout of joy—
  With a shout *so* full of glee!
    Then give me the snow, the white-winged snow,
      That falls from the wintry sky,
    That robes the earth in a vest of white,
    And sparkles and shines in the sun's rich light,
      Like the starry arch on high!

LESSON CXXVII.

OLD IRONSIDES.—Holmes.

The United States frigate Constitution is meant by *Old Ironsides*.
She was a noble ship of war, and after waging many victorious battles, was
condemned to be broken up. The indignant tone of public sentiment may
be inferred from the following spirited verses.

Ay, tear her tattered ensign down!
  Long has it waved on high,
15*

And many an eye has danced to see
    That banner in the sky;
Beneath it rang the battle shout,
    And burst the cannon's roar;
The meteor of the ocean air
    Shall sweep the clouds no more!

Her deck, once red with heroes' blood,
    Where knelt the vanquished foe,
When winds were hurrying o'er the flood,
    And waves were white below,
No more shall feel the victor's tread,
    No more the conquered knee;
The harpies of the shore shall pluck
    The eagle of the sea.

Oh! better that her shattered hulk
    Should sink beneath the wave:—
Her thunders shook the mighty deep,
    And there should be her grave!
Nail to the mast her holy flag,
    Set every threadbare sail,
And give her to the god of storms,—

THE *course* of this gesture *begins* at the word *the;* the hand passes up *instantly* to the word *lightning*, making its *stroke* there, with *spread* fingers; it falls to *rest* at the word *gale*. With the *beginning* of the gesture, the speaker slides into the *second* right position; as represented in the figure,—and with the *termination* of it, he comes again into the *first* right. This gesture, as here applied, if well executed, is *appropriate* and *impressive.* I have seen small boys, in reciting the admirable poem of Marco Bozzaris,—see *U. S. Speaker*, page 316,— make quite a point with it, upon the expression,— " As *lightnings* from the mountain cloud." It is proper to language of *sudden alarm, fearful emergency,*— wherever, indeed, the speaker designs to give force to a *startling idea.*

|The *lightning*, and the gale!)

LESSON CXXVIII.

SURVIVORS OF THE REVOLUTION.—Webster.

Venerable Men! you have come down to us from a former generation. Heaven has bounteously lengthened out your lives, that you might behold this joyous day. You are now, where you stood, fifty years ago, this very hour, with your brothers, and your neighbors, shoulder to shoulder, in the strife for your country. Behold, how altered! The same heavens are indeed over your heads ; the same ocean rolls at your feet ; but all else, how changed! You hear now no roar of hostile cannon, you see no mixed volumes of smoke and flame rising from burning Charlestown. The ground strewed with the dead and the dying ; the impetuous charge ; the steady and successful repulse ; the loud call to repeated assault; the summoning of all that is manly to repeated resistance ; a thousand bosoms freely and fearlessly bared in an instant to whatever of terror there may be in war and death ;—all these you have witnessed, but you witness them no more. All is peace; and God has granted you the sight of your country's happiness, ere you slumber in the grave forever. He has allowed you to behold and to partake the reward of your patriotic toils ; and he has allowed us, your sons and countrymen, to meet you here, and in the name of the present generation, in the name of your country, in the name of liberty, to thank you! May the Father of all mercies smile upon your declining years, and bless them! And when you shall here have exchanged your embraces ; when you shall once more have pressed the hands which have been so often extended to give succor in adversity, or grasped in the exultation of victory ; then look abroad into this lovely land, which your young valor defended, and mark the happiness with which it is filled ; yea, look abroad into the whole earth, and see what a name you have contributed to give to your country, and what a praise you have added to freedom, and then rejoice in the sympathy and gratitude, which beam upon your last days from the improved condition of mankind.

LESSON CXXIX.

INTEMPERANCE.—Anonymous.

Oh! take the maddening bowl away;
  Remove the poisonous cup!
My soul is sick—its burning ray
  Hath drunk my spirit up:
Take—take it from my loathing lip,
  Ere madness fires my brain;|

This Figure exhibits an attitude of *aversion* mingled with *fear*.—The *course* of the gesture begins immediately after the word *brain*; at the same instant the *head* turns from the object of dislike, the feet change from the *first right* to the *first left* position, and the arms *dart out* with the hands *up*—as seen in the picture — making the *stroke* upon the word *take;* the *first right* position is resumed, as before, on the word *its,* and the hands come to *rest* upon the word *liquid.* Sentiments of *disgust, hate, abhorrence,* and the like, are appropriate to this form of action.

Take—take it hence, nor let me sip
  Its liquid) death again.

Oh! dash it on the thirsty earth,
  For I will drink no more:
It cannot cheer the heart with mirth
  That grief hath wounded sore;
For serpents wreath its sparkling brim,
  And adders lurk below;
It hath no soothing charm for him
  Who sinks oppressed with wo.

Then, hence! away, thou deadly foe—
  I scorn thy base control:
Away, away!—I fear thy blow,
  Thou palsy of the soul!
Henceforth I drink no more of thee,
  Thou bane of Adam's race,
But to a heavenly fountain flee,
  And drink the *dews of grace.*

LESSON CXXX.

THE STORM.—Anonymous.

The storm is dreadful. The heavens are one vast black cloud. The sheated rain comes down in torrents. The fair earth is deluged. The sea, the broad breasted sea, is tossed in terrible commotion, and the whole round world seems wrapt in eternal midnight.—God reigns! let all the earth stand in awe of him;—Hark! it is his voice, the rolling thunder!—See! it is his eye, the fearful lightning! the smit rock declares his power, and the monarch oak, rent from the adamantine hills.

Alas!—on such a night—for the poor sea-boy. No friendly star lights his dread course. The wind spirit howls. Wild raves the maddened ocean. The demons of the storm make merry at his fate. Look! now tossed on mountain billows—now sunk to the lowest depths,—"a thing of elemental sport"—the frail bark hurries to destruction.—O God! have mercy on the poor sea-boy!—Hark! he shrieks—"help—help," he cries, "help!"—but ah! no help is nigh. The monsters of the deep stand ready for their prey, and the victim in despair awaits his awful fate. The booming gun, and the shriek of human agony are vain. He who rules the storm, permits the destiny, and the doomed ship strikes on the fatal rock.

"Oh! sailor boy! woe to thy dreams of delight!
    In darkness dissolves the gay frost-work of bliss—
Oh! where is the picture that fancy touched bright
    Thy father's fond pressure—thy mother's fond kiss!
Oh! sailor boy! sailor boy! never again
    Shall home, friends or kindred thy wishes repay;
Beloved and lamented—down deep in the main,
    Full many a score fathom, thy frame shall decay.
On beds of green sea-flowers, thy limbs shall be laid;
    Around thy white bones, the red coral shall grow;
Of thy fair yellow locks threads of amber be made,
    And every part suit to thy mansion below.
Days, months, years and ages, shall circle away,
    And still the vast waters above thee shall roll—
Earth loses thy pattern for ever and aye—
    Oh! sailor boy! sailor boy! peace to thy soul."

LESSON CXXXI.

THE FLIGHT OF THE MUSKOGEE INDIAN.—Anonymous.

On the shore of Carolina an Indian warrior stood,
A captive of the Shawanees and reddened with their blood;
Strange arts of varied torture, his conquerors tried in vain,
Like a rock that stands the billows he dashed them off again.

He shouted, and the echoes returned the lengthened shriek,
"I have rent you as the eagle rends the dove within his beak,
And ye give me women's tortures ; see, I lightly cast them by,
As the Spirit of the storm-cloud throws the vapor from the
    sky."

"Ye are women!" the wild echo came wilder on the air—
"*I* will show a worthy trial for a Muskogee to bear ;
Let me grasp a heated gun in this raw and bloody hand,
And ye shall not see an eyelash move to shame my father-land.

They gave the glowing steel. He took it with a smile,
And held it as a plaything ;—they stood in awe the while ;
Then, springing like an antelope, he brandished it around,
And toward the beetling eminence upstarted with a bound.

This Figure exhibits an attitude of *painful observation and surprise*. On the phrase—"*One leap and he is over !*"—the speaker inclines intensely forward, gazing, as it were, after the *escaping Indian;* immediately after the word *over* is pronounced, the *course* of the gesture *begins*, the *second right* position is assumed, the hands are *elevated* and *drawn back*, with the fingers *spread*, — as seen in the picture —making the *stroke* upon the word *fierce;* the speaker returns to the *first* right position on the word *massy,* and the hands fall to *rest* at the word *form*. This gesture may be applied to the language of *astonishment, simple affright, alarmed compassion*, and the like.

One leap and he is over ! | *fierce*, dashing through the stream,
And his massy form) lies floating 'neath the clear and sunny
    beam ;

A hundred arrows sped at once, but missed that warrior bold,
And his mangled arms, ere set of sun, his little ones enfold.

LESSON CXXXII.

NATIONAL CHARACTER.—Maxcy.

THE loss of a firm national character, or the degradation
of a nation's honor, is the inevitable prelude to her destruction. Behold the once proud fabric of a Roman Empire—
an empire carrying its arts and arms into every part of the
eastern continent; the monarchs of mighty kingdoms dragged at the wheels of her triumphal chariots; her eagle
waving over the ruins of desolated countries. Where is her
splendor, her wealth, her power, her glory? Extinguished
forever. Her mouldering temples, the mournful vestiges
of her former grandeur, afford a shelter to her muttering
Monks. Where are her statesmen, her sages, her philoso-
phers, her orators, her generals? Go to their solitary tombs
and inquire. She lost her national character and her destruction followed. The ramparts of her national pride were
broken down, and Vandalism desolated her classic fields.

Such—the warning voice of antiquity, the example of all
republics proclaim may be our fate. But let us no longer
indulge these gloomy anticipations. The commencement of
our liberty presages the dawn of a brighter period to the
world. That bold, enterprising spirit which conducted our
heroes to peace and safety, and gave us a lofty rank amid
the empires of the world, still animates the bosoms of their
descendants. Look back to that moment when they unbarred
the dungeons of the slave and dashed his fetters to the earth,
when the sword of a Washington leapt from its scabbard to
revenge the slaughter of our countrymen. Place their example before you. Let the sparks of their veteran wisdom
flash across your minds, and the sacred altars of your liberty,
crowned with immortal honors, rise before you. Relying on
the virtue, the courage, the patriotism, and the strength of our
country, we may expect our national character will become
more energetic, our citizens more enlightened, and may hail
the age as not far distant, when will be heard, as the proudest exclamation of man :—I am an American !

LESSON CXXXIII.

I'LL DRINK NO MORE.

No, no; I'll drink no more,
The witching spell is o'er;
The cup was sparkling bright,
And thrilled with wild delight;

This Figure exhibits an attitude expressive of *wildness*, or *distress of mind*. The *course* of the gesture *begins* at the word *soon*, and the hands —with the fingers *spread* —come to the *forehead*, making the *stroke* upon the word *brain*; the fingers *press* with energy, and—upon the *second* word *brain*—coming closer together, are *drawn* slowly toward the *temples*, indicative of mental anguish; the hands, then, in a *curve*, make a *downward horizontal stroke*, upon the word *burnt*, and fall to *rest* upon the word *maniac*. Much of the effect of this and similar gestures, depends upon the *skill* with which it is executed. Good taste and practice, however, render them impressive and beautiful. *Mental agony, despair, fear of apprehended evil*, and the like, are illustrated by this form of action.

But |soon my *brain*, my brain,
Had burnt with maniac) pain.

No, no; I'll drink no more—
'Twas foolish, mad before,
But now 'twere damning sin,
To let the tempter in;
For now I *know* his cup
With death is brimming up.

No, no; I'll drink no more,
The hellish dream is o'er;
I wake, I wake to bliss,
Oh, God! I'm sure of this;
And shall I lift the bowl,
And wreck my Heaven-bound soul?

No, no; I'll drink no more,
Though golden goblet pour

The ruby tide in showers,
In pleasure's brightest bowers;—
The Circean spell is o'er,
I'll drink, I'll drink no more.

LESSON CXXXIV.

UNION—LIBERTY.—Anonymous.

Hail, our country's natal morn,
Hail, our spreading kindred born,
Hail, thou banner not yet torn,
    Waving o'er the free !
While, this day, in festal throng,
Millions swell the patriot song
Shall not we thy notes prolong,
    Hallowed Jubilee ?

Who would sever Freedom's shrine ?
Who would draw the invidious line ?—
Though by birth, one spot be mine,
    Dear is all the rest :
Dear to me the South's fair land,
Dear, the central Mountain-band,
Dear, New England's rocky strand,
    Dear the prairied West.

By our altars, pure and free,
By our Law's deep rooted tree,
By the past's dread memory,
    By our Washington ;
By our common parent tongue,
By our hopes, bright, buoyant, young,
By the tie of country strong,—
    We will still be *one*.

Fathers ! have ye bled in vain ?
Ages ! must ye droop again ?
Maker ! shall we rashly stain
    Blessings sent by Thee ?
No ! receive our solemn vow,
While before thy throne we bow,
Ever to maintain as now,
    " Union—Liberty."

16

LESSON CXXXV.

PATIENCE RECOMMENDED.—BOLINGBROKE.

THE darts of adverse fortune are always leveled at our heads. Some reach *us* and some fly to wound our neighbors. Let us, therefore, impose an equal temper on our minds, and pay, without murmuring, the tribute which we owe to humanity. The winter brings cold, and we must freeze. The summer returns with heat, and we must melt. The inclemency of the air disorders our health, and we must be sick. This established course of things it is not in our power to change, but it is in our power to assume such a greatness of mind as becomes the wise and virtuous, and enables them to encounter the accidents of life with fortitude. Let us address ourselves to God who governs all, as Cleanthes did in those admirable verses—

> Parent of Nature! Master of the world,
> Where'er thy Providence directs, behold
> My steps with cheerful resignation turn;
> Fate leads the willing, drags the backward on;
> Why should I grieve, when grieving I must bear,
> Or take with guilt, what guiltless I must share?

THESE Figures, and those which follow, in this part of the book, exhibit examples of *continuous* gesture. The pupil is to understand that the Figures represent *but one person*. In the present example, the first Figure shows the *first* gesture. It is made with the *index finger*. The *course* is *upward* upon the word *thus*, and *downward* upon the words *let us*, the *stroke* coming upon the word *speak*.

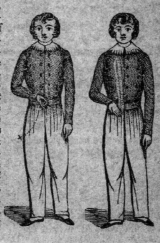

The second Figure exhibits the *continuous* gesture. The hand *opens* upon the word *and*, and so *ascends* upon the word *thus, descending* upon the words *let us*, and making the *stroke* upon the word *act;* it makes a *curve* upon the word *resignation* and there comes to *rest*. This form of action is called *noting*, and it is used to *particularize*, to *enumerate*, to *discriminate*, and the like.

| Thus let us *speak*, and | thus let us *act*. Resignation) to the will of God is true magnanimity. But the sure mark of

a feeble and pusillanimous spirit, is to struggle against, to censure the order of Providence, and, instead of mending our own conduct, to set up for correcting that of our Maker.

LESSON CXXXVI.

THE INQUIRY.—Anonymous.

Tell me, ye winged winds,
That round my pathway roar,
Do ye not know some spot
Where mortals weep no more?
Some lone and pleasant dell,
Some valley in the west,
Where, free from toil and pain,
The weary soul may rest?
The loud wind dwindled to a whisper low,
And sighed for pity, as it answered, " No!"

Tell me, thou mighty deep,
Whose billows round me play,
Knowest thou some favored spot,
Some island far away,
Where weary man may find
The bliss for which he sighs,
Where sorrow never lives,
And friendship never dies?
The loud waves rolling in perpetual flow,
Stopped for a while, and sighed to answer, "No!"

And thou, serenest moon,
That with such holy face
Dost look down upon the earth
Asleep in night's embrace—
Tell me, in all thy round,
Hast thou not seen some spot,
Where miserable man
Might find a happier lot?
Behind a cloud the moon withdrew in woe,
And a sweet voice, but sad, responded, " No!"

Tell me, my sacred soul;
Oh! tell me, hope and faith,
Is there no resting-place
From sorrow, sin, and death?
Is there no happy spot
Where mortals may be blessed,

Where grief may find a balm,
And weariness a rest ?
Faith, hope, and love, best boons to mortals given,
Waved their bright wings, and answered, "Yes, *in
heaven.*"

LESSON CXXXVII.

THE VOICE OF THE PEOPLE.—KNOWLES.

THE gentleman, Sir, has brought forward a very curious
argument, for the purpose of proving, that the Romans were
incapable of being a free people ; namely, that their magis-
trates were the mere echoes of the people. He adverts, I
suppose, to what were called the tribunes of the people—
officers that acted particularly for the plebeian orders, and
were generally chosen from their body. But those magis-
trates, or tribunes, were, it seems, the mere voices of the
people, and that circumstance rendered the people incapable
of being free ! To me, at least, this is a paradox. Who
elected these tribunes ?—The people. What were they ?—
The representatives of the people. Whose affairs did they
manage ?—The affairs of the people. To whom were they
responsible ?—The people. What should they have been,
then, but the voices, or as the gentleman has expressed it,
the echoes of the people ? But this circumstance rendered

THE *first* gesture is made with the *right index finger* in the *left open hand,* as seen in the first Figure ; the *continuous* gesture, with the *right open hand,* in the *left open hand,* as seen in the second Figure. The *course* of the *first* begins at the word *did,* rising gradually till it reaches its *height* upon the word *them;* it then descends in the same manner, making its *stroke* upon the word *tribunes.* The *course* of the *continuous* is the same as that of the *first,* making the *stroke* upon the word *measures.* The hands now move outward in a *curve,* with some *emphasis* upon the word *bondage,* and gradually come to *rest* at the word *affairs.*—This is another example of *noting.*

the Roman people incapable of being free ! |Did it shackle
them to have a control over their *tribunes* ? |Did it enslave
them to have a voice in their own *measures* ? Did it sell
them into bondage to have the disposal of their own *affairs* ?)

If it did, I should advise you, Sir, not to meddle with that
honest man, your steward. Bid him let what farms he
pleases; demand what fines he pleases; cultivate what land
he pleases; fell what timber he pleases; keep what accounts
he pleases; and make what returns he pleases; lest, by
impertinently meddling with your servant, in your own
affairs, you rob yourself—ruin your estate—become in-
volved in debt—and end your days in prison!

LESSON CXXXVIII.

TAKE HEED.—Anonymous.

I knew him when a little child,
   As opening rosebud fair;
He seemed an angel when he smiled,
   So pure a light was there.

I knew him when a brave, bright boy,
   With spirit like a bird's;
His heart a gushing fount of joy,
   And music all his words.

I knew him when a noble youth,
   With fame-aspiring eye;
His very look was that of truth—
   The truth beyond the sky.

I knew him when young manhood came—
   How proud the wreath he wore;
To every heart his gifted name
   Virtue's bright promise bore.

I knew him when his youthful bride,
   Joyous he came to wed;
The country's flower, the country's pride,—
   "God bless them!" thousands said.

I knew him when he stooped to kiss—
   How sweet that kiss must be!—
The pledges of his wedded bliss,
   Bright, blessed cherubs three.

16*

I knew him at the holy shrine—
   The altar of his God;
I saw him take the bread and wine,
   And pure the path he trod.

I knew him this—I knew him all
   The fondest heart could crave;
I knew—yet, God! his blackened pall,
   Covers a *drunkard's grave!*

LESSON CXXXIX.

WAR-SONG OF THE GREEKS.—PROCTOR.

AWAKE! 'tis the terror of war,
   The Crescent is tossed on the wind;
But our flag flies on high, like the perilous star

THESE Figures exhibit an example of what is sometimes called *alternate* gesture. The *second right hand gesture, palm up,* is made upon the word *before,* and the *second left hand gesture, palm up off,* upon the word *behind.* The *left* hand *commences* its action, precisely as the *right* hand *begins* to come to *rest,* upon the word *and.*

Of the battle. {*Before* and *behind,*
Wherever } it glitters, it darts
Bright death into tyrannous hearts.

Who are they that now bid us be slaves?
   They are foes to the good and the free;
Go bid them first fetter the might of the waves;
   The sea may be conquered,—but we
Have spirits untamable still,
And the strength to be free,—and the will.

Shall we—shall we die in our chains,
   Who once were as free as the wind?
Who is it that threatens,—who is it arraigns?
   Are they princes of Europe or Ind?
Are they kings to the uttermost pole?
They are *dogs*, with a taint on their soul!

LESSON CXL.

BIRTH-DAY OF WASHINGTON.—Webster.

WHEN sublime virtues cease to be abstractions—when they become imbodied in human character, and exemplified in human conduct, we should be false to our own nature, if we did not indulge in the spontaneous effusions of our gratitude and our admiration. A true lover of the virtue of patriotism delights to contemplate its purest models; and that love of country may be well suspected, which affects to soar so high into the regions of sentiment as to be lost and absorbed in the abstract feeling, and becomes too elevated, or too refined, to glow with fervor in the commendation or the love of individual benefactors. All this is unnatural. It is as if one should be so enthusiastic a lover of poetry as to care nothing for Homer or Milton; so passionately attached to eloquence as to be indifferent to Tully and Chatham; or such a devotee to the arts, in such an ecstacy with the elements of beauty, proportion, and expression, as to regard the master-pieces of Raphael and Michael Angelo with coldness or contempt. We may be assured, gentlemen, that he who really loves the thing itself, loves its finest exhibitions. A true friend of his country loves her friends and benefactors, and thinks it no degradation to commend and commemorate them. The voluntary outpouring of the public feeling made to-day from the north to the south, and from the east to the west, proves this sentiment to be both just and natural. In the cities and in the villages, in the public temples and in the family circles, among all ages and sexes, gladdened voices, to-day, bespeak grateful hearts and a freshened recollection of the virtues of the Father of his Country. And it will be so, in all time to come, so long as public virtue is itself an object of regard. The ingenuous youth of America will hold up to themselves the bright model of Washington's example, and study to be what they behold; they will contemplate his character till all his virtues spread out and display themselves to their delighted vision; as the earliest astronomers, the shepherds on the plains of Babylon, gazed at the stars till they saw them form into clusters and constellations, overpowering at length the eyes of the beholders with the united blaze of a thousand lights.

LESSON CXLI.

OLD WINTER.—MOORE.

OLD Winter is coming again—alack!
   How icy and cold is he!
He cares not a pin for a shivering back—
He's a saucy old chap to white and black—
He whistles his chills with a wonderful knack,
   For he comes from a cold country!

A witty old fellow this Winter is—
   A mighty old fellow for glee!
He cracks his jokes on the pretty sweet Miss—
The wrinkled old maiden unfit to kiss—
And freezes the dew of their lips—for this
   Is the way with such fellows as he!

Old Winter 's a frolicksome blade, I wot—
   He is wild in his humor, and free!
He 'll whistle along for the " want of his thought,"
And set all the warmth of our furs at naught,
And ruffle the laces by pretty girls bought,
   For a frolicksome fellow is he.

Old Winter is blowing his gusts along,
   And merrily shaking the tree!
From morning till night he will sing his song,

Now moaning and short—now howling and long—
His voice is loud, for his lungs are strong;
   A merry old fellow is he!

Old Winter's a wicked old chap I ween—
   As wicked as ever you see;
He withers the flowers so fresh and green—
And bites the pert nose of the miss of sixteen,
As she trippingly walks in maidenly sheen;
   A wicked old fellow is he!

Old Winter's a tough old fellow for blows,
   As tough as ever you see!
He will trip up our trotters and rend our clothes,
And stiffen our limbs from fingers to toes;
He minds not the cries of his friends or his foes—
   A tough old fellow is he!

A cunning old fellow is Winter, they say,
   A cunning old fellow is he!
He peeps in the crevices day by day,
To see how we're passing our time away,
And marks all our doings from grave to gay:
   I'm afraid he is peeping at me!

LESSON CXLII.

THE LAND OF OUR BIRTH.—Anonymous.

THERE is not a spot in this wide-peopled earth
So dear to the heart as the land of our birth;
'Tis the home of our childhood! the beautiful spot
Which memory retains when all else is forgot:
     May the blessings of God
     Ever hallow the sod,
And its valleys and hills by our children be trod.

Can the language of strangers in accents unknown,
Send a thrill to our bosom like that of our own?
The face may be fair, and the smile may be bland,
But it breathes not the tones of our dear native land!
     There's no spot on earth
     Like the land of our birth,
Where heroes keep guard o'er the altar and hearth!

How sweet is the language which taught us to blend
The dear name of parent, of husband and friend;
Which taught us to lisp on our mother's soft breast,
The ballads she sung as she rocked us to rest.
        May the blessings of God
        Ever hallow the sod,

THE *course* of the *first* gesture begins at the word *and*, its *stroke* coming upon the word *valleys;* it is the *first double gesture, palms up.* The *continuous* gesture *commences* where the first *ends,* its *stroke* coming upon the word *hills;* it is the *third double gesture, palms up;* the hands descend to the *second double gesture, palms up,* upon the word *children,* and come to rest upon the word *trod.*

|And its *valleys* |and *hills* by our children be trod!)

LESSON CXLIII.

THE WIND IN A FROLIC.—Howitt.

THE wind one morning sprung up from sleep,
Saying, "Now for a frolic! now for a leap!
Now for a mad-cap galloping chase!
I'll make a commotion in every place!"
So it swept with a bustle right through a great town,
Creaking the signs, and scattering down
Shutters; and whisking with merciless squalls,
Old women's bonnets, and gingerbread stalls;

There never was heard a much lustier shout,
As the apples and oranges tumbled about,
And the urchins, that stand with their thievish eyes
For ever on watch, ran off each with a prize.
Then away to the field it went blustering and humming,
And the cattle all wondered whatever was coming;
It plucked by their tails the grave matronly cows,
And tossed the colts' manes all about their brows,
Till, offended at such a familiar salute,
They all turned their backs and stood silently mute.
So on it went capering and playing its pranks,
Whistling with reeds on the broad river's banks;
Puffing the birds as they sat on the spray,
Or the traveler grave, on the king's highway.
It was not too nice to hustle the bags
Of the beggar, and flutter his dirty rags;
'Twas so bold that it feared not to play its joke
With the doctor's wig, and the gentleman's cloak.
Through the forest it roared, and cried gaily, "Now,
You sturdy old oaks, I'll make you bow!"
And it made them bow without more ado,
And cracked their great branches through and through.
Then it rushed like a monster on cottage and farm,
Striking their dwellers with sudden alarm,
And they ran out like bees in a mid-summer swarm.
There were dames with their 'kerchiefs tied over their caps,
To see if their poultry were free from mishaps.
The turkies they gobbled, the geese screamed aloud,
And the hens crept to roost in a terrified crowd;
There was rearing of ladders, and logs laying on,
Where the thatch from the roof threatened soon to be gone.
But the wind had passed on, and had met in a lane
With a school-boy, who panted and struggled in vain;
For it tossed him, and twirled him, then passed, and he
    stood
With his hat in a pool, and his shoe in the mud.

LESSON CXLIV.

THE RAINBOW.—Amelia.

I sometimes have thought, in my loneliest hours,

THE *first* gesture is made by bringing the *open hand* to the breast; its *course* begins at the word *that*, and its *stroke* comes upon the word *heart*. The *continuous* gesture is the *first right hand gesture, palm down*; its *course* begins at the word *like*, descending from the *breast*, and its *stroke* comes upon the word *dew*; the hand falls to *rest* on the word *flowers*.

|That lie on my *heart* |like the *dew* on the flowers,)
Of a ramble I took one bright afternoon,
When my spirit was light as a blossom in June;
The green earth was moist with the late fallen showers—
The breeze fluttered down and blew open the flowers—
While a single white cloud to its haven of rest,
On the white wing of peace floated off in the west.

As I threw back my forehead to catch the cool breeze,
That scattered the rain drops and dimpled the seas,
Far up the blue sky a fair rainbow unrolled
Its soft-tinted pinions of purple and gold;
'Twas born in a moment, yet quick as its birth,
It had stretched to the uttermost ends of the earth,
And fair as an angel, it floated all free,
With a wing on the earth and a wing on the sea.

How wide was the sweep of its beautiful wings!
How boundless its circle! how radiant its rings!
If I looked on the sky 'twas suspended in air,
If I looked on the ocean the rainbow was there;

Thus forming a girdle as brilliant and whole
As the thoughts of the rainbow that circled my soul;
Like the wing of the Deity, calmly unfurled,
It bent from the cloud and encircled the world.

LESSON CXLV.

PARENTAL RESPONSIBILITY.—ANONYMOUS.

THE intrinsic value of every child, invests the parental relation with surpassing interest. Immortality is the birthright of every child; and it is a birthright of which he can never be defrauded. Man can make him a cripple; a lunatic; a slave; a corpse; but in his nobler nature, he can never make him mortal.

Yonder tree has stood in the forest since the days of the flood, and drank its nourishment from the dust of a thousand generations; but the hand of death is on it, and the next blast will bring it to the earth. And those stars, "scattered like flowers through the blue fields of heaven," which bloomed and gladdened us so long—they, too, must fade, and droop, and fall. And that great king of day, who has looked down so long upon our sorrows and our joys—his eyes must grow dim, his hour must come—death shall cast a pall over his burnished throne. But the *soul*—when shall *that* die—when shall it be carried to the tomb? After ages have passed away, countless as the leaves of the forest, countless as the sands on the shores of eternity, *that boy* will still be alive—a seraph or a fiend, a glorified saint or a wretched spirit. My soul is overwhelmed within me, when I think of the height of glory, or the depth of shame, to which each child in every family is destined. Take a child from a hovel, and put him on a throne; and how greatly have you exalted him! How wonderful a change! You can only stand still and lift your hands in dumb astonishment. And yet, what have you done for him? Will he weep less than other men? Will he suffer less? Will he live longer than other men? Crowns that can keep away neither sorrow, nor pain, nor death—those may have them who want them. But that *boy* —Oh! that boy shall be a priest and prince, where tears, and groans, and knells are not known. The crown which he shall wear, will be an eternal diadem. That boy may be

a king—ah! he may be a fiend! His career may end in
heaven—alas! it may end in hell! Instead of robes he may
be wrapped in flames! Instead of a crown, he may pillow
his naked head on the rocks of perdition! And, father,
mother, much of the responsibility of this alternative is cast
on you.

LESSON CXLVI.

THE LITTLE SHROUD.—Miss Landon.

She put him on a snow-white shroud,
  A chaplet on his head;
And gathered early primroses
  To scatter o'er the dead.

She laid him in his little grave—
  'Twas hard to lay him there,
When spring was putting forth its flowers,
  And every thing was fair.

She had lost many children—now
  The last of them was gone;
And day and night she sat and wept
  Beside the funeral stone.

One midnight, while her constant tears
  Were falling with the dew,
She heard a voice, and lo! her child
  Stood by her, weeping too!

His shroud was damp, his face was white;
  He said—"I cannot sleep,
Your tears have made my shroud so wet;
  Oh, mother, do not weep!"

Oh, love is strong!—the mother's heart
  Was filled with tender fears;
Oh, love is strong!—and for her child
  Her grief restrained its tears.

One eve a light shone round her bed,
  And there she saw him stand—

Her infant, in his little shroud,
    A taper in his hand.

" Lo ! mother, see my shroud is dry,
    And I can sleep once more !"
And beautiful the parting smile
    The little infant wore.

And down within the silent grave
    He laid his weary head ;
And soon the early violets
    Grew o'er his grassy bed.

The mother went her house-hold ways—
    Again she knelt in prayer,
And only asked of Heaven its aid,
    Her heavy lot to bear.

LESSON CXLVII.

WINGS.—Hervey.

Oh ! for the wings we used to wear,
When the heart was like a bird,
And floated still through summer air,
And painted all it looked on fair,
And sung to all it heard !
When fancy put the seal of truth
On all the promises of youth.

It may not—oh, it may not be !
I cannot soar on fancy's wing ;
And hope has been,—like thee, like thee !—
These many weary years, to me
A lost and perished thing !
Are there no pinions left, to bear
Me where the good and gentle are !

Yes !—rise upon the morning's wing,
And, far beyond the farthest sea,
Where autumn is the mate of spring,
And winter comes not withering,
There is a home for thee !—

THE *first* gesture is made upon the first word *away;* it is the *second left hand gesture, palm up off,* as seen in the first Figure. The *continuous* gesture is made upon the second word *away,* and is the *third left hand gesture, palm up off,* as seen in the second Figure; the *star* marks the point from which the hand ascends in its *continuous* course. The pupil must keep in mind that the *two* Figures represent but *one* person. The hand descends *slowly* after the word *head,* and comes to *rest* upon the word *valley.*

|*Away*—|*away!* and lay thy head
In the low valley) of the dead!

LESSON CXLVIII.

ADAMS AND JEFFERSON.—Everett.

THEY have gone to the companions of their cares, of their toils. It is well with them. The treasures of America are now in Heaven. How long the list of our good and wise and brave assembled there! how few remain with us! There is our Washington; and those who followed him in their country's confidence, are now met together with him, and all that illustrious company. The faithful marble may preserve their image; the engraven brass may proclaim their worth; but the humblest sod of Independent America, with nothing but the dew-drops of the morning to gild it, is a prouder mausoleum than kings or conquerors can boast. The country is their monument. Its independence is their epitaph.

But not to their country is their praise limited. The whole earth is the monument of illustrious men. Wherever an agonizing people shall perish, in a generous convulsion, for want of a valiant arm and a fearless heart, they will cry, in the last accents of despair, Oh, for a Washington, an Adams, a Jefferson! Wherever a regenerated nation, starting up in its might, shall burst the links of steel that enchain it, the praise of our fathers shall be the prelude of their triumphal song.

The contemporary and successive generations of men will disappear. In the long lapse of ages, the tribes of America, like those of Greece and Rome, may pass away. The fabric of American Freedom, like all things human, however firm and fair, may crumble into dust. But the cause in which these our fathers shone, is immortal. They did that, to which no age, no people of reasoning men, can be indifferent.

Their eulogy will be uttered in other languages, when those we speak, like us who speak them, shall all be forgotten. And when the great account of humanity shall be closed at the throne of God, in the bright list of his children, who best adorned and served it, shall be found the names of our Adams and our Jefferson.

LESSON CXLIX.

PLEA OF THE RED INDIAN.—Anonymous.

Oh! why should the white man hang on my path,
  Like the hound on the tiger's track?
Does the flesh of my dark cheek waken his wrath?
  Does he covet the bow at my back?

He has rivers and seas, where the billow and breeze
  Bear riches for him alone;
And the sons of the wood never plunge in the flood
  That the white man calls his own.

Then why should he covet the streams where none
  But the red skin dare to swim?
Oh! why should he wrong the hunter, one
  Who never did harm to him?

The Father above thought fit to give
  To the white man corn and wine;
There are golden fields where he may live—
  But the forest wilds are mine.

17*

The eagle has its place of rest—
   The wild horse where to dwell ;
And the Spirit who gave the bird its nest,
   Made me a home as well.

THE *first* of these figures exhibits a beautiful *suspending* gesture made upon the first word *back*, by bringing the hands up *rapidly* and *crossed*, with *spread* fingers. The *second* Figure, an *emphatic*, *significant* gesture, made upon the second word *back*, by striking out the hands, spiritedly, in nearly a *horizontal* line; the hands come to *rest* after the word *red*.

Then |*back*, go |*back*, from the red) skin's track,
   For the hunter's eye grows dim,
To find that the white man wrongs the one
   Who never did harm to him.

————

LESSON CL.

ENCOURAGE EMIGRATION.—HENRY.

CAST your eyes, Sir, over this extensive country—observe the salubrity of your climate, the variety and fertility of your soil—and see that soil intersected in every quarter by bold, navigable streams flowing to the east and to the west, as if the finger of Heaven were marking out the course of your settlements, inviting you to enterprise, and pointing the way to wealth. Sir, you are destined, at some time or other, to become a great agricultural and commercial people; the only question is, whether you choose to reach this point by slow gradations, and at some distant period—lingering on through a long and sickly minority, subjected, meanwhile, to the machinations, insults, and oppressions of enemies, foreign and domestic, without sufficient strength to resist and chastise them—or whether you choose rather to rush at once, as it were, to the full enjoyment of those high destinies, and be able to cope, single-handed, with the proudest oppressor of the old world.

If you prefer the latter course, as I trust you do, encourage emigration—encourage the husbandman, the mechanics, the merchants of the old world, to come and settle in this land of promise—make it the home of the skillful, the industrious, the fortunate and happy, as well as the asylum of the distressed—fill up the measure of your population as speedily as you can, by the means which Heaven hath placed in your power—and I venture to prophesy there are those now living who will see this favored land among the most powerful on earth—able, Sir, to take care of herself, without resorting to that policy which is always so dangerous, though sometimes unavoidable, of calling in foreign aid. Yes, Sir—they will see her great in arts and in arms—her golden harvests waving over fields of immeasurable extent—her commerce penetrating the most distant seas, and her cannon silencing the vain boasts of those who now proudly affect to rule the waves.

But gentlemen object to any accession from Great Britain —and particularly to the return of the British refugees. Sir, I feel no objection to the return of those deluded people. I have no fear of any mischief that they can do us. Afraid of them!—what, Sir, shall we, who have laid the proud British lion at our feet, now be afraid of his whelps?

LESSON CLI.

CHRISTMAS TIMES.—Moore.

'Twas the night before Christmas, when all through the
    house
Not a creature was stirring, not even a mouse ;
The stockings were hung by the chimney with care,
In the hope that St. Nicholas* soon would be there.

* Santa Claus.

The children were nestled all snug in their beds,
While visions of sugar-plums danced in their heads;
And mamma in her 'kerchief, and I in my cap,
Had just settled our brains for a long winter's nap;
When out on the lawn there rose such a clatter,
I sprang from my bed to see what was the matter.
Away to the window I flew like a flash,
Tore open the shutters, and threw up the sash.
The moon on the breast of the new-fallen snow,
Gave the lustre of midday to objects below;
When what to my wondering eyes should appear,
But a miniature sleigh, and eight tiny rein-deer,
With a little old driver so lively and quick,
I knew in a moment it must be St. Nick.
More rapid than eagles his coursers they came,
And he whistled, and shouted, and called them by name;
" Now, Dasher! now, Dancer! now, Prancer! now, Vixen!
On, Comet! on, Cupid! on, Dunder and Blixen!
To the top of the porch! to the top of the wall!
Now dash away! dash away! dash away all!"
As dry leaves before the wild hurricane fly,
When they meet with an obstacle mount to the sky,
So up to the house-top the coursers they flew,
With the sleigh full of toys—and St. Nicholas too.
And then, in a twinkling, I heard on the roof,
The prancing and pawing of each little hoof;
As I drew in my head, and was turning around,
Down the chimney St. Nicholas came with a bound.
He was dressed all in fur from his head to his foot,
And his clothes were all tarnished with ashes and soot;
A bundle of toys were flung on his back,
And he looked like a pedler just opening his pack;
His eyes—how they twinkled! his dimples how merry!
His cheeks were like roses, his-nose like a cherry;
His droll little mouth was drawn up like a bow,
And the beard of his chin was as white as the snow;
The stump of a pipe he held tight in his teeth,
And the smoke it encircled his head like a wreath;
He had a broad face, and a little round belly,
That shook when he laughed like a bowl full of jelly;
He was chubby and plump, a right jolly old elf,
And I laughed when I saw him in spite of myself.
A wink of his eye and a twist of his head,
Soon gave me to know I had nothing to dread;

He spoke not a word, but went straight to his work,
And filled all his stockings ; then turned with a jerk,
And laying his finger aside of his nose,
And giving a nod, up the chimney he rose.
He sprang to his sleigh, to his team gave a whistle,
And away they all flew like the down of a thistle ;
But I heard him exclaim, ere he drove out of sight,
" Merry Christmas to all, and to all a good night."

LESSON CLII.

THE COUNTRY OF WASHINGTON.—WEBSTER.

GENTLEMEN, the spirit of human liberty and of free government, nurtured and grown into strength and beauty in America, has stretched its course into the midst of the nations. Like an emanation from heaven, it has gone forth, and it will not return void. It must change, it is fast changing, the face of the earth. Our great, our high duty, is to show, in our own examples, that this spirit is a spirit of health as well as a spirit of power ; that its benignity is as great as its strength ; that its efficiency to secure individual rights, social relations, and moral order, is equal to the irresistible force with which it prostrates principalities and powers. The world, at this moment, is regarding us with a willing, but something of a fearful admiration. Its deep and awful anxiety is to learn, whether free states may be stable as well as free ; whether popular power may be trusted as well as feared ; in short, whether wise, regular, and virtuous self-government is a vision, for the contemplation of theorists, or a truth established, illustrated, and brought into practice, in the country of Washington.

Gentlemen, for the earth which we inhabit, and the whole circle of the sun, for all the unborn races of mankind, we seem to hold in our hands, for their weal or woe, the fate of this experiment. If we fail, who shall venture the repetition? If our example shall prove to be one, not of encouragement, but of terror—not fit to be imitated, but fit only to be shunned—where else shall the world look for free models? If this great *Western Sun* be struck out of the firmament, at what other fountain shall the lamp of Liberty hereafter be lighted? What other orb shall emit a ray to glimmer, even, on the darkness of the world?

Gentlemen, there is no danger of our overrating, or over-stating, the important part which we are now acting in human affairs. It should not flatter our personal self-respect, but it should re-animate our patriotic virtues, and inspire us with a deeper and more solemn sense, both of our privileges and of our duties. We cannot wish better for our country, nor for the world, than that the same spirit which influenced Washington, may influence all who succeed him; and that that same blessing from above, which attended his efforts, may also attend theirs.

LESSON CLIII.

ON THE DEATH OF A BOY.—Anonymous.

No more on earth that little hand
    With brother's love shall clasp mine own;—
Like bird to a far-distant land,
    That voice—to *me* so sweet—is flown.

A fibre from my heart is riven!
    A life-drop from my heart is shed!

The *course* of the *first* gesture begins at the word *thy*, its *stroke* coming upon the word *spirit*. There are *two continuous* gestures in this example; the *course* and *stroke* of the *first* are upon the word *that's*, the hands being *suspended* till the utterance of the word *Heaven;* the *course* of the *other* begins at the word *'tis*, its *stroke* comes upon the word *dust*, and the hand falls to *rest* on the word *that's*.

Ay! but |thy *spirit*—|*that's* in Heaven—
    |'Tis but the *dust* that's) with the dead!

I'll gaze on yon bright star, and see
　　The home where thou art dwelling now—
Methinks soft wings are fanning me—
　　They soothe, they cool, my fevered brow !

I'll listen to the wind's soft swell,
　　And fancy thine the gentle sounds ;
They sigh not forth a sad farewell—
Thus in my ear the murmurs dwell,
　" We'll meet where endless love abounds !"

————

LESSON CLIV.

THE AWAKENING OF THE WIND.—Anonymous.

Hurrah! the wind ! the mighty wind,
　　Like lion from his lair upsprung,
Hath left his Arctic home behind,
　　And off his slumbers flung;
While over lake and peaceful sea,
With track of crested foam sweeps he.

Hurrah ! the wind, the mighty wind,
　　Hath o'er the deep his chariot driven,
Whose waters, that in peace reclined,
　　Uplash the roof of heaven;
Then on the quaking cliff-bound shore,
They foaming dash with deafening roar.

The ship loomed on the waveless sea,
　　Her form was imaged in its breast,
And beauteous of proportion she,
　　As ever billow prest ;
And graceful there as stately palm,
　　She towered amid the sultry calm .

Her flag hung moveless by the mast,
　　Her sails drooped breezeless and unbent
And oft the seaman's glance was cast
　　Along the firmament,
To note if there he might descry
The wakening gale approaching nigh.

On came the wind, the reckless wind,
  Fast sweeping on his furious way,
His tempest rushing pinions brined
  In wrathful ocean's spray:
On came the wind, and, as he past,
The shriek of death was in the blast!

The tall ship by the shrouds he took,
  To shivering shreds her canvas rent,
Then like a reed her mast he shook,
  And by the board it went;
While yawned the deep with hideous din,
As if prepared to gulf her in.

With fruitless effort on she reels,
  The giant wind is in her wake,
The mountain billow's coil she feels
  Around her like a snake:
Locked in that unrelenting grasp,
She struggling sinks with stifled gasp.

Hurrah! hurrah! the victor wind
  Hath swept the ocean rover down,
And left a shipless sea behind,
  With many a corse bestrewn;
And swift, unfettered, strong and free,
Like eagle on his path, speeds he!

LESSON CLV.

A DEATH BED.—J. ALDRICH.

HER suffering ended with the day,
  Yet liv'd she at its close,
And breathed the long, long night away,
  In statue-like repose.

But when the sun, in all his state,
  Illumed the eastern skies,
She passed through Glory's morning gate,
  And walked in Paradise!

THE YOUNG SPEAKER.

PART FOURTH.

LESSONS EXCLUSIVELY FOR READING.

THE *older* pupils should hold the book in the *left* hand, after the manner of the above Figure. Its position should be just opposite the *centre* of the breast. It should have an easy *slope* from the reader. It should never be permitted to obscure the expression of the face, nor obstruct the sound of the voice. The *thumb* should be placed on the *left hand* page, and the *little finger* on the *right hand* page ; the *forefinger* will come on the *left lid*, near the *back* of the book, and the *remaining two fingers* on the *right lid*. The *bottom* part of the book should be about *six inches* from the body. The *right* hand being at liberty, may be used, as occasion requires, *in turning over the leaves*, or in *keeping the place*, while the eye is directed from the book to the audience. By accomplished readers, it may also be employed, sparingly, in suitable gesticulation.

18

LESSON I.

A NOONDAY WALK.—BARBAULD.

COME, let us go into the thick shade, for it is the noonday, and the summer sun beats hot upon our heads.

The shade is pleasant and cool ; the branches meet above our heads, and shut out the sun as with a green curtain ; the grass is soft to our feet, and the clear brook washes the roots of the trees.

The sloping bank is covered with flowers ; let us lie down upon it ; let us throw our limbs on the fresh grass and sleep ; for all things are still and we are quite alone.

The cattle can lie down to sleep in the cool shade, but we can do what is better ; we can praise the great God who made us. He made the warm sun, and the cool shade ; the trees that grow upward, and the brooks that run murmuring along. All the things that we see are His work.

Can we raise our voices up to the high heaven ? Can we make Him to hear who is above the stars ? We need not raise our voices to the stars, for He heareth us when we only whisper, when we breathe our words softly with a low voice. He that filleth the heavens is here also.

The buds spread into leaves, and the blossoms swell to fruit, but they know not how they grow, nor who caused them to spring up from the bosom of the earth. Ask them if they will tell thee ; bid them break forth into singing, and fill the air with pleasant sounds.

They smell sweet ; they look beautiful ; but they are quite silent ; no sound is in the still air, no murmur of voices among the green leaves.

The plants and the trees are made to give fruit to man, but *man* is made to praise God who made him.

We love to praise Him, because he loveth to bless us ; we thank him for life, because it is a pleasant thing to be alive.

We love God who hath created all things ; we love all beings, because they are the creatures of God.

We cannot do good, as God does, to all persons every where ; but we can rejoice that every where there is a God to do them good.

We will think of God when we play, and when we work ; when we walk out, and when we come in ; when we sleep, and when we wake ; His praise shall dwell continually upon our lips.

LESSON II.

CHARITY.—Testament.

Though I speak with the tongues of men and of angels, and have not charity, I am become as sounding brass, or a tinkling cymbal.

And though I have the gift of prophecy, and understand all mysteries and all knowledge, and though I have all faith, so that I could remove mountains, and have not charity, I am nothing.

And though I bestow all my goods to feed the poor, and though I give my body to be burned, and have not charity, it profiteth me nothing.

Charity suffereth long, and is kind; charity envieth not; charity vaunteth not itself, is not puffed up,

Doth not behave itself unseemly, seeketh not her own, is not easily provoked, thinketh no evil:

Rejoiceth not in iniquity, but rejoiceth in the truth;

Beareth all things, believeth all things, hopeth all things, endureth all things.

Charity never faileth: but whether there be prophecies, they shall fail; whether there be tongues, they shall cease; whether there be knowledge, it shall vanish away.

For we know in part, and we prophecy in part.

But when that which is perfect is come, then that which is in part shall be done away.

When I was a child, I spake as a child, I understood as a child, I thought as a child; but when I became a man, I put away childish things.

For now we see through a glass darkly; but then we shall see face to face; now I know in part; but then shall I know even also as I am known.

And now abideth faith, hope, charity, these three; but the greatest of these is *charity*.

LESSON III.

THE RAINBOW.—Sturm.

When the sun reflects its rays on drops of water which fall from the clouds, and we are placed with our backs to the sun, and with the clouds opposite to us, we observe a rainbow. We may consider the drops of rain as little transparent balls, on which the rays fall and are refracted. From thence proceed the colors in the rainbow. They are seven in number; and in the following order: red, orange, yellow, green, blue, purple and violet. These colors appear so much the more lively, according as the cloud behind is darker, and the drops of rain fall the closer. The drops falling continually, produce a new rainbow every moment, and as each spectator has his particular situation, from whence he observes this phenomenon, it so happens, that two men cannot, properly speaking, see the same rainbow. This meteor can only last while the rain continues to fall. To consider a rainbow merely as a phenomenon of nature, it is one of the finest sights imaginable. It is a picture the most beautifully colored of any the Creator has given us. There cannot be a rainbow when it rains over the whole horizon. Every time, then, that this beautiful meteor appears, we may be certain that we have no deluge to apprehend, as in a deluge it must rain violently from every part of the sky. Thus when the sky is only covered with clouds on one side, and the sun appears on the other, it is a sign that these dark clouds will disperse, and that the sky will soon become serene. This is also the reason why we cannot see a rainbow unless the sun is behind us, and the rain opposite to us.

The sun and the rain must appear at the same time, to form a rainbow. No colors would be seen if the sky was too light; therefore, where it appears, the horizon must be covered with dark clouds. Neither could the colors of the rainbow exist without the refraction of the rays of the sun upon it.

LESSON IV.

NIGHT'S LESSONS.—Mrs. Sigourney.

Night's lessons! What are they? My son, one of these, you may learn in a moment. Did you say, that all will soon be sleeping? No. There is one Eye, that never slumbers. He who made all the people, keepeth watch above the everlasting hills. Commit yourself to His care.

Now, will you learn with me, the second lesson of the night? Lift your eyes to yon glorious canopy. Seest thou not there, a sentinel, set by the Eternal, at the northern gate of heaven? The pole-star!

The pole-star! Blessings are breathed upon it, by the weary caravan, fearing the poisonous wind of the desert,—by the red forest-children, seeking their home, beyond the far western prairies,—and by the lonely mariner, upon the pathless ocean.

The stars! See them! The oil in their lamps never burns out. These glorious constellations, wheel their mighty course unchanged, while man dieth and wasteth away; man giveth up the ghost, and where is he?

These brilliant orbs maintain their places, while countless generations pass away, and nations disappear and are forgotten. Let us bow in humility before Him, who " bringeth out their host by number, who calleth them all by name, through the greatness of his might, for that He is strong in power, not one faileth."

Thirteen times in the year, Night, the Teacher, gives extra lessons. Will you be there, to learn them?

First, she hangs up a pale crescent in the west. The ancient Jews hailed its infant beam, and answering fires of joy were kindled on the hills of Palestine.

Next, she summons forth a rounded orb, clad in full effulgence, and commits to it the regency, when the sun retires. Lastly, a slender, waning crescent appears nightly, like an aged man, ready to descend into the night of the tomb.

> " Soon as the evening shades prevail,
>   The moon takes up the wondrous tale,
>   And nightly to the listening earth,
>   Repeats the story of her birth:
>   While all the stars that round her burn,
>   And all the planets in their turn,
>   Confirm the tidings as they roll,
>   And spread the truth from pole to pole."

These are some of Night's lessons. Are you tired of them? Or will you learn one more? Lift up your heart to Him who has given you the past day, with thanks for its blessings,—with penitence for its faults,—with supplication for strength and wisdom, for the time that is to come.

"Day unto day uttereth speech, and night unto night,

showeth knowledge of God." Thus meekly and faithfully
studying Night's lessons, may we find,
        "That darkness shows us worlds of light,
        We never saw by day."

LESSON V.

THE BLESSEDNESS OF HEAVEN.—BARBAULD.

THE rose is sweet, but it is surrounded with thorns: the
lily of the valley is fragrant, but it springeth up among the
brambles.

The spring is pleasant, but it is soon past; the summer is
bright, but the winter destroyeth the beauty thereof.

The rainbow is very glorious, but it soon vanisheth away;
life is good, but it is quickly swallowed up in death.

There is a land where the roses are without thorns, where
the flowers are not mixed with brambles. In that land there
is eternal spring, and light without any cloud.

The tree of life groweth in the midst thereof; rivers of
pleasure are there, and flowers that never fade.

Myriads of happy spirits are there, and surround the
throne of God with a perpetual hymn.

The angels, with their golden harps, sing praises continually, and the cherubims fly on wings of fire!

This country is heaven, it is the country of those that are
good, and nothing that is wicked must inhabit there.

This earth is pleasant, for it is God's earth, and it is filled
with many delightful things.

But that country is far better; there we shall not grieve
any more, nor be sick any more, nor do wrong any more;
there the cold of winter shall not wither us, nor the heats of
summer scorch us.

In that country there are no wars nor quarrels, but all
love one another with dear love.

When our parents and friends die, and are laid in the cold
ground, we see them here no more; but there we shall embrace them again, and live with them, and be separated no
more.

There we shall meet all good men, whom we read of in
holy books.

There we shall see Abraham the called of God, the father

of the faithful ; and Moses, after his long wandering in the Arabian desert ; and Elijah, the prophet of God ; and Daniel, who escaped the lion's den ; and the son of Jesse, the shepherd king, the sweet singer of Israel.

They loved God on earth ; they praised Him on earth ; but in that country they will praise Him better, and love Him more.

There we shall see Jesus, who is gone before us, to that happy place ; and there we shall behold the glory of the High God.

We cannot see him here, but we will love Him here ; we must now be on earth, but we will often think on heaven.

That happy land is our home ; we are to be here but for a little while, and there forever, even for ages of eternal years.

LESSON VI.

PROFANE SWEARING.—Wood.

Of all the vicious habits to which children are liable, in common with those of more advanced years, that of profane swearing is, at once, one of the most impious and daring— the most low and degrading—the most senseless and inexcusable. Yet, in walking our streets, how often, alas! are our ears assailed with this most profane and disgusting language. Surely a single moment's reflection ought to be sufficient to convince even the youngest, and most thoughtless and inconsiderate offender of this description, of the heavy guilt, as well as extreme folly of such conduct. It is a vice obviously directed against the Majesty of Heaven itself—against that High and Holy Being, who hath himself given us his most positive commandment to swear not at all, neither by heaven, neither by the earth, neither by any other oath ; and hath at the same time given us his most solemn warning, that he will not hold him guiltless that taketh his name in vain, and that for every idle word which we shall speak, he will call us into judgment. And while the language in question is thus highly offensive to God, it is, at the same time, most disgusting to every well-regulated mind. Those even, who themselves are addicted to this most degrading vice, are not always the last to feel horror and disgust when they hear the

same, or similar language in the lips of an associate. It is
the habitual language only of the profligate and the abandoned—the language of those lawless bands who set God
and man alike at defiance. In many it is a habit acquired
from evil company in early youth, which has grown with
their growth, and strengthened with their strength. Let this
be an additional inducement to children, to be ever upon
their guard against the first inroads of this pernicious habit,
which, when it has acquired the ascendency, they may not
in mature years, find it so easy to shake off, even when beheld in all its hideous deformity.

LESSON VII.

THE HORSE.—Anonymous.

Horses are so extremely useful to mankind, that they are
naturally objects of great interest to us.

Of all quadruped animals, the horse is the most beautiful;
but to judge fairly of the graceful ease of his motions, we
should view this animal in those wild countries where nature
placed him, and where he bounds across the plains unfettered
by bit or bridle.

Horses, in their wild state, are very inoffensive, and do not
make war against any other race of animals; they are found
in various parts of Africa, particularly the southern part,
near the Cape of Good Hope. The most beautiful horses
come from Arabia.

There are very extensive plains in South America, called
the Pampas, where there are large troops of wild Horses.
The inhabitants of these plains are capital horsemen; the
children are accustomed to ride as early as four years old.

They generally perform their journeys on horseback, and
if the uorse on which they are mounted is tired, they catch
a fresh one from the troops around. This is done by means
of a *lasso*, a long piece of rope made of strips of leather,
with a loop or noose at the end, which they throw over the
animal's head: the noose is made with a slip-knot, which
becomes tighter when the horse struggles for liberty. The
horses when first mounted, always kick at any one who goes
behind them, and it is sometimes very difficult to fasten a
saddle and bridle on them. When properly broken in, they

are not vicious, and will allow children to mount by climbing up their tails. Though endowed with very great strength, the disposition of this noble animal is so mild and gentle, that he rarely uses his strength to his master's prejudice; on the contrary, he will endure fatigue, and even death itself, for the benefit of those who have treated them kindly.

The following story, showing what exertion the horse is capable of undergoing, would be almost incredible, were it not well authenticated.

Many years ago, a violent gale of wind setting in from north-northwest, a vessel in the road at the Cape of Good Hope dragged her anchors, was forced on the rocks, and bilged; and while the greater part of the crew fell an immediate sacrifice to the waves, the remainder were seen from the shore, struggling for their lives, by clinging to the different pieces of the wreck. The sea ran dreadfully high, and broke over the sailors with such amazing fury, that no boat whatever could venture off to their assistance.

Meanwhile, a planter, considerably advanced in life, had come on horseback from his farm to be a spectator of the shipwreck. His heart was melted at the sight of the unhappy seamen, and knowing the bold and enterprising spirit of his horse, and his particular excellence as a swimmer, he instantly determined to make a desperate effort for their deliverance.

He alighted and blew a little brandy into his horse's nostrils, when, again seating himself in the saddle, he instantly pushed into the midst of the breakers. At first both disappeared, but it was not long before they floated on the surface and swam up to the wreck; when, taking with him two men, each of whom held by one of his boots, the planter brought them safe to shore.

This perilous expedition he repeated seven times, and saved fourteen lives. But on his return the eighth time, his horse being much fatigued, and meeting a most formidable wave, he lost his balance, and was overwhelmed in a moment. The horse swam safely to the shore, but his gallant rider was no more!

LESSON VIII.

HUMANITY.—Anonymous.

During the retreat of the famous king Alfred at Athelney, in Somersetshire, after the defeat of his forces by the Danes, the following circumstance happened, which shows the extremities to which that great man was reduced, and gives a striking proof of his pious and benevolent disposition. A beggar came to his little castle, and requested alms. His queen informed him that they had only one small loaf remaining, which was insufficient for themselves and their friends, who were gone abroad in quest of food, though with little hopes of success. But the king replied, "Give the poor Christian the one-half of the loaf. He that could feed five thousand with five loaves and two fishes, can certainly make that half of the loaf suffice for more than our necessities." Accordingly the poor man was relieved; and this noble act of charity was soon recompensed by a providential store of fresh provisions, with which his people returned.

Sir Philip Sidney, at the battle near Zutphen, displayed the most undaunted courage. He had two horses killed under him; and while mounting a third, was wounded by a musket-shot out of the trenches, which broke the bone of his thigh. He returned about a mile and a half on horseback to the camp; and being faint with the loss of blood, and parched with thirst through the heat of the weather, he called for drink. It was presently brought him; but as he was putting the vessel to his mouth, a poor wounded soldier, who happened to be carried along at that instant, looked up to it with wishful eyes. The gallant and generous Sidney took the flagon from his lips, just when he was going to drink, and delivered it to the soldier, saying, "Thy necessity is greater than mine."

Frederick, king of Prussia, one day rang his bell, and nobody answered; on which he opened his door, and found his page fast asleep in an elbow-chair. He advanced toward him, and was going to awaken him, when he perceived a letter hanging out of his pocket. His curiosity prompting to know what it was, he took it out and read it. It was a letter from this young man's mother, in which she thanked him for having sent her part of his wages to relieve her in her misery, and finished with telling him that God would reward him for his dutiful affection. The king, after having read it, went back softly into his chamber, took a bag full of ducats, and slipped it with the letter into the page's pocket. Returning to his chamber, he rang the bell so violently that he awakened the page, who instantly made his appearance. "You have had a sound sleep," said the king. The page was at a loss how to excuse himself, and, putting his hand into his pocket by chance, to his utter astonishment he there found a purse of ducats. He took it out, turned pale, and looking at the bag, burst into tears, without being able to utter a single word. "What is that?" said the king; "what is the matter?" "Ah, Sire!" said the young man, throwing himself on his knees, "somebody seeks my ruin! I know nothing of this money which I have just found in my pocket!"

"My young friend," replied Frederick, "God often does great things for us even in our sleep. Send that to your mother, salute her on my part, and assure her that I will take care of both her and you."

LESSON IX.

IMPROVE THE INTELLECT.—BARBAULD.

Look at that spreading oak, the pride of the village green! its trunk is massy, its branches are strong. Its roots, like crooked fangs, strike deep into the soil, and support its huge bulk. The birds build among the boughs; the cattle repose beneath its shade; the neighbors form groups beneath the shelter of its green canopy. The old men point it out to their children, but they themselves remember not its growth; generations of men, one after another, have been born and died, and this son of the forest has remained the same, defying the storms of two hundred winters.

Yet this large tree was once a little acorn; small in size, insignificant in appearance; such as you are now picking up upon the grass beneath it.

Such an acorn, whose cup can only contain a drop or two of dew, contained the whole oak. All its massy trunk, all its knotted branches, all its multitude of leaves were in that acorn; it grew, it spread, it unfolded itself by degrees, it received nourishment from the rain, and the dews, and the well adapted soil, but it was all there. Rain, and dews, and soil, could not raise an oak without the acorn; nor could they make the acorn any thing but an oak.

The mind of a child is like the acorn; its powers are folded up, they do not yet appear, but they are all there. The memory, the judgment, the invention, the feeling of right and wrong, are all in the mind of a child; of a little infant just born; but they are not expanded, you cannot perceive them.

Think of the wisest man you ever knew or heard of; think of the greatest man; think of the most learned man, who speaks a number of languages, and can find out hidden things; think of a man who stands like that tree, sheltering and protecting a number of his fellow men, and then say to yourself, the mind of that man was once like mine—his thoughts were childish like my thoughts, nay, he was like the babe just born, which knows nothing, remembers nothing, which cannot distinguish good from evil, nor truth from falsehood.

If you had only seen an acorn, you could never guess at the form and size of an oak; if you had never conversed with a wise man, you could form no idea of him from the mute and helpless infant.

Instruction is the food of the mind; it is like the dew and the rain and the rich soil. As the soil and the rain and the dew cause the tree to swell and put forth its tender shoots, so do books and study and discourse feed the mind, and make it unfold its hidden powers.

Reverence therefore your own mind; receive the nurture of instruction, that the man within you may grow and flourish. You cannot guess how excellent he may become.

It was long before this oak showed its greatness; year after year passed away, and it had only shot a little way above the ground; a child might have plucked it up with his little hands; it was long before any one called it a tree; and it is long before the child becomes a man.

The acorn might have perished in the ground, the young tree might have been shorn of its graceful boughs, the twig might have bent, and the tree would have been crooked, but if it grew at all, it could have been nothing but an oak, it would not have been grass or flowers, which live their season, and then perish from the face of the earth.

The child may be a foolish man, he may be a wicked man, but he must be a man; his nature is not that of any inferior creature, his soul is not akin to the beasts which perish.

O, cherish then this precious mind, feed it with truth, nourish it with knowledge; it comes from God, it is made in his image; the oak will last for centuries of years, but the mind of man is made for immortality.

Respect in the infant the future man. Destroy not in the man the rudiments of an angel.

LESSON X.

DIFFERENCE BETWEEN MAN AND THE INFERIOR ANIMALS.—Taylor.

THE chief difference between man and the other animals consists in this, that the former has reason, whereas the latter have only instinct ; but in order to understand what we mean by the terms reason and instinct, it will be necessary to mention three things, in which the difference very distinctly appears.

Let us *first*, to bring the parties as near on a level as possible, consider man in a savage state, wholly occupied like the beasts of the field, in providing for the wants of his animal nature ; and here the first distinction that appears between him and the creatures around him is, *the use of implements.* When the savage provides himself with a hut, or a wigwam, for shelter, or that he may store up his provisions, he does no more than is done by the rabbit, the beaver, the bee, and birds of every species. But the man cannot make any progress in this work without tools ; he must provide himself with an axe even before he can lop down a tree for its timber ; whereas these animals form their burrows, their cells, or their nests, with no other tools than those with which nature has provided them. In cultivating the ground, also, man can do nothing without a spade or a plow, nor can he reap what he has sown till he has shaped an implement with which to cut down his harvests. But the inferior animals provide for themselves and their young without any of these things.

Now for the *second* distinction. Man in all his operations *makes mistakes ;* animals make none. Did you ever hear of such a thing as a bird sitting disconsolate on a twig, lamenting over her half-finished nest, and puzzling her little poll to know how to complete it ? Or did you ever see the cells of a bee-hive in clumsy irregular shapes, or observe any thing like a discussion in the little community, as if there were a difference of opinion among the architects ?

The lower animals are even better physicians than we are ; for when they are ill, they will, many of them, seek out some particular herb which they do not use as food, and which possesses a medicinal quality exactly suited to the complaint ; whereas the whole college of physicians will dispute for a century about the virtues of a single drug.

Man undertakes nothing in which he is not more or less puzzled; he must try numberless experiments before he can bring his undertakings to any thing like perfection; even the simplest operations of domestic life are not well performed without some experience; and the term of man's life is half wasted before he has done with his *mistakes*, and begins to profit by his lessons.

The *third* distinction is, that animals make no *improvements;* while the knowledge, and the skill, and the success of man are perpetually on the increase. Animals, in all their operations, follow the first impulse of nature, or that instinct which God has implanted in them. In all they do undertake therefore, their works are more perfect and regular than those of men. But man, having been endowed with the faculty of thinking or reasoning about what he does, is enabled by patience and industry to correct the mistakes into which he at first falls, and to go on constantly improving. A bird's nest is, indeed, a perfect and beautiful structure; yet the nest of a swallow of the nineteenth century is not at all more commodious or elegant than those that were built amid the rafters of Noah's ark. But if we compare the wigwam of the savage with the temples and palaces of ancient Greece and Rome, we shall then see to what man's mistakes, rectified and improved upon, conduct him.

LESSON XI.

THE APOSTLE PAUL'S DEFENSE.—Testament.

Then Agrippa said unto Paul, Thou art permitted to speak for thyself. Then Paul stretched forth the hand and answered for himself.

I think myself happy, king Agrippa, because I shall answer for myself this day before thee, touching all the things whereof I am accused of the Jews;

Especially, because I know thee to be expert in all customs and questions which are among the Jews: wherefore I beseech thee to hear me patiently.

My manner of life from my youth, which was at first among mine own nation at Jerusalem, know all the Jews;

Which knew me from the beginning, (if they would testify,) that, after the most rigid sect of our religion, I lived a Pharisee.

And now I stand and am judged for the hope of the promise made of God unto our fathers:

Unto which promise our twelve tribes, instantly serving God day and night, hope to come : for which hope's sake, king Agrippa, I am accused of the Jews.

Why should it be thought a thing incredible with you, that God should raise the dead ?

I verily thought with myself, that I ought to do many things contrary to the name of Jesus of Nazareth.

Which thing I also did in Jerusalem; and many of the saints did I shut up in prison, having received authority from the chief priests; and when they were put to death, I gave my voice against them.

And I punished them oft in every synagogue, and compelled them to blaspheme ; and, being exceedingly mad against them, I persecuted them even unto strange cities.

Whereupon, as I went to Damascus with authority and commission from the chief priests,

At mid-day, O king, I saw in the way a light from heaven, above the brightness of the sun, shining round about me, and them which journeyed with me.

And when we were fallen to the earth, I heard a voice speaking unto me, and saying in the Hebrew tongue, Saul, Saul, why persecutest thou me ? It is hard for thee to kick against the pricks.

And I said, Who art thou, Lord ? And he said, I am Jesus, whom thou persecutest.

But rise, and stand upon thy feet, for I have appeared unto thee for this purpose, to make thee a minister and a witness, both of these things which thou hast seen, and of those things in which I will appear unto thee,

Delivering thee from the people, and from the Gentiles, unto whom now I send thee,

To open their eyes, and to turn them from darkness to light, and from the power of Satan unto God, that they may receive forgiveness of sins, and inheritance among them which are sanctified by faith that is in me.

Whereupon, O king Agrippa, I was not disobedient unto the heavenly vision :

But shewed first unto them of Damascus, and at Jerusalem, and throughout all the coasts of Judea, and then to the Gentiles, that they should repent and turn to God, and do works meet for repentance.

For these causes the Jews caught me in the temple, and went about to kill me.

Having, therefore, obtained help of God, I continue unto this day, witnessing both to small and great, saying none other things than those which the prophets and Moses did say should come:

That Christ should suffer, and that he should be the first that should rise from the dead, and should show light unto the people, and to the Gentiles.

And as he thus spake for himself, Festus said with a loud voice, Paul, thou art beside thyself; much learning doth make thee mad.

But he said, I am not mad, most noble Festus; but speak forth the words of truth and soberness.

For the king knoweth of these things, before whom also I speak freely; for I am persuaded that none of these things are hidden from him; for this thing was not done in a corner.

King Agrippa, believest thou the prophets? I know that thou believest.

Then Agrippa said unto Paul, Almost thou persuadest me to be a Christian.

And Paul said, I would to God, that not only thou, but also all that hear me this day, were both almost and altogether such as I am, except these bonds.

And when he had thus spoken, the king rose up, and the governor, and Bernice, and they that sat with them.

And when they were gone aside, they talked between themselves, saying, This man doeth nothing worthy of death, or of bonds.

Then said Agrippa unto Festus, This man might have been set at liberty, if he had not appealed unto Cæsar.

LESSON XII.

LYING.—Wood.

It is of the utmost importance, my young friends, that you should always speak the truth. If you have the happiness to acquire this good habit now, while you are young, it will probably continue with you afterwards; but if at present you do not scruple to tell lies and to deceive, what can be expected, but that you will become more and more deceitful as you grow older? When you have done any wrong, you may perhaps be tempted to conceal it, by telling a lie to your parents or masters. But be on your guard against any such artifice. It would be adding one fault to another, and so your conduct would be worse than before. Besides, if you make an honest confession, it is probable that the less notice will be taken of your fault; whereas, if it be found that you have committed a fault, and have endeavored to conceal it by falsehood, your punishment ought to be, and probably will be the severer. If you wish to be free from the temptation to conceal your faults by falsehood, study to commit as few faults as you can. Be attentive to your lessons and to your work. Avoid mischievous tricks and disorderly behavior: and be careful to obey your parents and your masters. If your companions be bad and unprincipled, they will perhaps desire you to conceal their faults by telling lies; and, if you do not, they will reproach you, and call you *tell-tales*. It is, to be sure, very ill-natured, and very mean, to be always on the watch to discover faults, and, when they are discovered, to be eager to let them be known; but, when a question about the behavior of others is put to you, you should either be silent, or tell the plain and simple truth. In short, whatever be the circumstances that might tempt you to falsify, never yield to them. Falsehood is the mark of a mean and despicable spirit. If it should sometimes screen you from any inconvenience, and sometimes bring you a little gain, it would be an advantage not worth having; and you would not obtain even that advantage long. Persons who tell lies cannot fail to have their falsehood detected, and then nobody will believe them or trust them. Falsehood, besides, is the source of many other vices; it renders the character altogether hollow and heartless, and would at last sink you down in worthlessness and contempt. Consider, on the other hand, the advantages of truth. What think you of the satisfaction of your own minds? Will it not be very pleasant for you to reflect, that you have not descended to so mean a thing as falsehood? Is it not pleasant also to gain the esteem of others? And what is more estimable than truth? What can we say more honorable of any boy or girl, of any man or woman, than when we say, "This is one who may be trusted in every thing, and who scorns to deceive?" You are young, and perhaps you do not yet know the comforts and advantages of a good character; but believe me, if, by the blessing of God, the foundation be now laid of an upright and sincere character through life, you will all your days have cause to rejoice, that you were early taught to scorn a lie, and to love the truth. Above all, remember what is said

19*

respecting falsehood in the word of God. You are told in
the book of Proverbs, that lying lips are an abomination to
the Lord; and in the Book of Revelation, that whosoever
loveth and maketh a lie, cannot enter into heaven. Lay to
heart, my young friends, these impressive declarations, and
never forget, that, unless you love truth, and hate every false
way, you cannot please God, nor be received into his glorious
kingdom.

LESSON XIII.

LORD WILLIAM.—Southey.

No eye beheld when William plunged
  Young Edmund in the stream;
No human ear but William's heard
  Young Edmund's drowning scream.

Submissive all the vassals owned
  The murderer for their lord;
And he, as rightful heir, possessed
  The house of Erlingford.

The ancient house of Erlingford
  Stood in a fair domain;
And Severn's ample waters near,
  Rolled through the fertile plain.

But never could Lord William dare
  To gaze on Severn's stream;
In every wind that swept its waves
  He heard young Edmund's scream!

In vain, at midnight's silent hour,
  Sleep closed the murderer's eyes;
In every dream the murderer saw
  Young Edmund's form arise!

—Slow were the passing hours, yet swift
  The months appeared to roll;
And now the day returned, that shook
  With terror William's soul—

A day that William never felt
  Return without dismay ;
For well had conscience calendared
  Young Edmund's dying day.

A fearful day was that ! the rains
  Fell fast with tempest roar,
And the swollen tide of Severn spread
  Far on the level shore.

In vain Lord William sought the feast,
  In vain he quaffed the bowl,
And strove with noisy mirth to drown
  The anguish of his soul.

Reluctant now, as night came on,
  His lonely couch he pressed ;
And, wearied out, he sunk to sleep,—
  To sleep—but not to rest.

Beside that couch his brother's form,
  Lord Edmund, seemed to stand,—
Such, and so pale, as when in death
  He grasped his brother's hand ;

Such, and so pale his face, as when
  With faint and faltering tongue,
To William's care a dying charge,
  He left his orphan son.

" I bade thee with a father's love
  My orphan Edmund guard—
Well, William, hast thou kept thy charge !
  Now take thy due reward."

He started up, each limb convulsed
  With agonizing fear ;—
He only heard the storm of night,—
  'Twas music to his ear.

When lo ! the voice of loud alarm
  His inmost soul appals ;
" What, ho ! Lord William, rise in haste ;
  The water saps thy walls !"

He rose in haste,—beneath the walls
  He saw the flood appear ;
It hemmed him round,—'twas midnight now—
  No human aid was near.

He heard the shout of joy! for now
  A boat approached the wall ;
And eager to the welcome aid
  They crowd for safety all.

"My boat is small," the boatman cried,
  "'Twill bear but one away ;
Come in, Lord William, and do ye
  In God's protection stay."

The boatman plied the oar, the boat
  Went light along the stream ;
Sudden Lord William heard a cry
  Like Edmund's drowning scream.

The boatman paused,—"Methought I heard
  A child's distressful cry!"
"'Twas but the howling winds of night,"
  Lord William made reply.

"Haste!—haste!—ply swift and strong the oar!
  Haste!—haste across the stream!"
Again Lord William heard a cry
  Like Edmund's drowning scream.

"I heard a child's distressful scream,"
  The boatman cried again ;
"Nay, hasten on!—the night is dark—
  And we should search in vain.

"And, oh! Lord William dost thou know
  How dreadful 'tis to die?
And canst thou, without pitying, hear
  A child's expiring cry?

"How horrible it is to sink
  Beneath the chilly stream !
To stretch the powerless arms in vain !
  In vain for help to scream !"

The shriek again was heard. It came
  More deep, more piercing loud;—
That instant o'er the flood, the moon
  Shone through a broken cloud:

And near them they beheld a child;
  Upon a crag he stood—
A little crag, and all around
  Was spread the rising flood.

The boatman plied the oar, the boat
  Approached his resting-place :
The moonbeam shone upon the child,
  And showed how pale his face.

"Now reach thine hand !" the boatman cried,
  "Lord William, reach and save !"
The child stretched forth his little hands
  To grasp the hand he gave.

Then William shrieked ;—the hand he touched
  Was cold, and damp, and dead !
He felt young Edmund in his arms,
  A heavier weight than lead !

The boat sunk down—the murderer sunk
  Beneath th' avenging stream ;
He rose—he shrieked—no human ear
  Heard William's drowning scream.

LESSON XIV.

THE WAR OF THE REVOLUTION.

BEFORE the people who came from England landed here, this whole country was all a wilderness. No bridges were made over any of the streams ; no roads, nor any houses, except Indian wigwams. There was no plow, nor hoe, nor spinning-wheel, nor loom, nor saw-mill, nor grist-mill in this whole region.

Thousands of deer and bears, wolves, buffaloes, mooses, foxes, beavers, rabbits, and other animals, were running wild in the woods: but with all the fur in the country, the Indians did not know how to make a single hat.

They commonly settled near a river, for the sake of fish; or by the sea-shore, where they could catch lobsters, and oysters, and clams. All the hard work was done by their women. The men loved hunting, which they carried on with clubs, or bows and arrows.

Instead of living together like a band of brothers, through the whole country, they were divided into small tribes, engaged half the time in war, and murdering each other. They were as faithful to their friends as the best white people; but very cruel indeed to their enemies. As to reading and writing, these Indians did not know one letter from another; and so they were called savages.

Such was the condition of this country when the first ship-load of Englishmen came to Virginia, in 1607; and thirteen years afterward, another company to Plymouth, in Massachusetts. These people had to cut down trees, dig up stumps by the roots, and in a little time began to build themselves houses, and then churches and school-houses.

It was agreed that the king of England should be king of this country: but the people here were to worship God in their own way, and to be free. These conditions were written down on pieces of paper, with the king's name signed to them, and given to those who settled in different places here, in North America. These papers were called royal charters. The settlements made according to these charters, were called British colonies or provinces.

For about one hundred and fifty years the colonies continued in this way, working hard, and suffering many evils. One English king after another passed away, and a new king was seated on the throne. In these American colonies, the people grew old and died; their children became men and women, and took their places, under the same royal charters.

King George the Third received the crown of Great Britain, at the death of his grandfather. He had a set of men, called his ministers, or counsellors, to help him contrive plans, and govern his kingdom. They attempted to make the people of this country pay taxes to them. Many other acts they did contrary to the rights of our people.

This conduct dissatisfied the Americans. They said, "If King George can compel us, against our will, to use paper with his stamp upon it, and make us pay a tax for that stamp;

and if he can make us pay him three pence, sterling money, for each pound of tea we use, and which he has no right to; by the same rule he might take our cattle from us, or drive us from our farms."

They said, "the British government has no right to tax this country: we have a right to be free: we will be free; and we will not pay this tax."

When the king and his counsellors were told what the Americans had determined, they were greatly offended. The men called the Lords, and others called the Commons, five or six hundred of them in all, met with the ministers at the Parliament House, in London, and made a declaration, that they had a right to pass laws to compel the Americans to do whatever they said.

The news of this affair came across the Atlantic by the first ship to this country, and our people began to prepare for very serious difficulties. They chose their wisest men to meet and agree, in behalf of the people, on what was proper to be done.

These men wrote to the king, saying they thought that the persons about his palace, whom he listened to, did not know the particulars of our affairs, and were filling his ears with very wrong stories. At the same time, they also wrote letters to the inhabitants of England, Scotland, and Ireland, and said they hoped the people there would not help the king's bad advisers to practice their unjust and cruel schemes against the Americans.

But for fear of the worst, the colonists prepared, as well as they could, to take care of themselves. They collected powder and bullets, guns and swords, fifes and drums, so that if the king's armies should attempt to kill them, or chain them and make them slaves, they could defend themselves.

The king's officers and soldiers, with their red coats, came over in great numbers, to force us to submit. The British army took possession of Boston, and sent a party of soldiers out about twenty miles, to take the powder and other things which the Americans had collected at Concord.

By the way, they met with a company of American militia, at Lexington, paraded on the green, by the meeting-house. The British fired upon these, and killed eight men on the spot. A number of others were badly wounded. This affair happened the 19th of April, in the year 1775.

The war was now begun, and both parties exerted themselves with great vigor. Many bloody actions took place.

Our people again chose their ablest men to meet and devise
the best plans in their power to promote the American cause.
This meeting of wise and good men was called the Congress. The first important thing they did was to appoint that
most noble of men, George Washington, to be general-in-
chief of all the armies which could be raised to defend this
country.

After many battles and great sufferings, brought upon
these colonies by the British troops, the Congress, at Philadel-
phia, determined to make a bold stand in behalf of our countrymen, and to tell all the world what they meant to do.

They chose five of their best scholars to draw up a writing, on a large sheet of paper ; and, in that writing, they said
the king of England had done many wrongs toward the
Americans : he had reigned over them like a tyrant, and not
like a father ; and they could no longer bear such treatment.

They said that from that time, each of the thirteen colonies
should be a free state : they should be united to defend their
rights ; they should form a nation by themselves, and have a
government of their own, and make their own laws, and the
king of Great Britain should no longer be the king of this
country. They appealed to all nations, and to the God of
heaven and earth, for the justice of their cause.

Fifty-six members of Congress signed their names to this
paper, and pledged their lives, their fortunes, and sacred
honor, to make the proceeding stand good. This writing was
called the Declaration of American Independence. It was
dated the 4th day of July, in the year 1776.

The war now raged in a terrible manner, and vast numbers on both sides were slaughtered. The king of Great
Britain hired in Germany 17,000 soldiers, called the Hes-
sians, to come here and help his men to conquer this country.

Our people defended themselves with singular bravery ;
and in the year 1778, Dr. Franklin went to Paris and agreed
with Louis XVI, king of France, to send a French fleet and
army here, to assist in defending the United States.

At the same time a very noble and extraordinary young
man in France, by the name of La Fayette, hearing of the
sufferings of the people here, hired a brig, and came at the
risk of his life to save them from ruin. He was made a general in the American army, and passed through many dangers and hardships in our cause. He lived to be an old man,
and was remarkably beloved by all good people.

When the fighting had continued nearly eight years, and

two large British armies had been killed or taken prisoners by the Americans, King George concluded to give up the contest, and let the United States be a nation by themselves, as they had determined. This they called the war of the Revolution, because that by this war the government of the country was changed.

LESSON XV.

HUMMING BIRDS.—ANONYMOUS.

THESE little fairies of the feathered race—the smallest of birds, and perhaps the most brilliant—belong exclusively to our American continent and the adjacent islands. Most of them dwell in the warm climates, where flowers are ever in bloom, and where spring or summer hold perpetual sway. When flying in the sun, they look as if they were covered with gems and gold. The native American Indians, struck with the splendor of their hues, have called them " the hairs of the sun." One species alone visits our chill New England climate—the little fellow of the ruby throat. He comes to us in May, and makes himself familiar with our gardens and trellices, sports amid the flowers, and holds companionship only with the "flush and the fair." His stay is short, for early in September he is gone to more genial lands.

It is only in tropical countries that the several species of humming-birds are seen in their abundance, variety, and glory. The islands that stud the ocean between Florida and the main land of South America, literally swarm with them. In the wild and uncultivated parts, they inhabit the magnificent forests overhung with parasitical plants, whose blossoms hardly yield in beauty to the sparkling tints of these tenants of the air. In the cultivated portions, they abound in the gardens, and seem to delight in society, becoming familiar and destitute of fear, hovering often on one side of a shrub or plant, while the fruit is plucked on the other.

Lively, and full of energy, these winged gems are almost incessantly in the air, darting from one object to another, and displaying their gorgeous hues in the sunbeams. When performing a lengthened flight, as during migration, they pass through the air in long undulations, raising themselves
20

to a considerable height and, then falling in a curve. When feeding on a flower, they keep themselves poised in one position, as steadily, as if suspended on a bough—making a humming noise by the rapid motion of their wings.

In disposition, these creatures are intrepid; but, like some other little people, they are very quarrelsome. In defending their nests, they attack birds five times their size, and drive them off with ease. When angry, their motions are very violent and their flight as swift as an arrow. Often the eye is incapable of following them; and their shrill, piercing shriek alone announces their presence.

Among the most dazzling of this brilliant tribe is the bar-tailed humming-bird of Brazil. The tail is forked to the base, and consists of five feathers, graduated one above another at almost equal distances. Their color is of the richest flame, or orange-red, with a dazzling metallic burnish. The upper part of the body of the bird is golden green ; the lower is red, and the under surface of emerald-green.— Stoke's humming-bird may perhaps be cited as a rival of this little gem of beauty. The head and whole of the back is covered with scale-shaped feathers, those on the head being brilliant blue and changing to violet, those on the back being bright emerald-green. The cheeks are purplish-green, with small pink spots. Was there ever any lass at a fancy ball more gaily dressed ? Some of these beautiful creatures have splendid tufts on their heads. One has a crest of emerald-green ; another, of the brightest glossy blue ; another, a large cluster of violet plumes ; another has a gold tuft over each eye. There are more than a hundred kinds of this famous race, all noted for their littleness and their surpassing beauty. It is as if the flowers had taken wings, and life, and intelligence, and shared in the sports of animal life. And if we regard their beauty, the delicacy of their feathers, their energy and power compared with their size—if we consider the ingenious mechanism of their structure—can we sufficiently admire the Architect who made them and bade them go forth to add life, and beauty, and brilliancy to the landscape, while sharing themselves in the joys of existence?

Bright birds of the sun, how has every hue
Of the sky and the rainbow been lavished on you?
What are the robes that a monarch enfold,
Compared with your feathers of silver and gold ?
Ye are richly arrayed, without toil and care,

And the flower-bells furnish your daily fare;
A feast every morning before you is spread;
Ye are gloriously clothed, and luxuriously fed,
And ye drink the pure nectar, and cry *te-re*,
As ye fly from the flower to the blossoming tree.

Swift as an arrow ye hasten along:
Now ye are gleaming the lilies among;
Now through the gardens of roses you speed;
Now on the lofty magnolias you feed.
Gay birds of the sun! your plumes are as bright,
As if you had bathed in his fountain of light.
It is lovely indeed your wings to behold,
All gleaming and glistening with azure and gold.

LESSON XVI.

A WORTHY OF THE REVOLUTION.—Cardell.

In the afternoon, Solomon Belmot went with his young friend, Jack Halyard, to see the aged soldier, John Miller; because, said they, though the good old man is neglected by many, yet he has always borne an unspotted character; and though his purse is light, he has a noble soul.

He has read, said Solomon, the history of many nations, and thought much concerning their welfare. Once, too, he had a good house and farm; but he lost all, when this country was in its deepest trouble.

Mr. Miller had once been an orderly sergeant; this was many years ago; and some old people still called him sergeant Miller; but it was no matter what title he bore. He wanted no kingly patent of nobility. His heraldry was in his heart.

The aged patriot remembered Jack, with great affection, and received him with a most hearty welcome. The young men were much struck with his venerable appearance. His hair was white as silver; and when he began to speak of the war, he grew earnest, and they listened with deep attention, till he drew tears down their cheeks.

His musket lay on two wooden hooks, against the wall of the room. He took down this musket, which he had owned fifty years, and which, in all his distress, he would never

sell. Then moving himself to the table, he laid one of his
crutches upon it, and resting on the other, shouldered the
musket, striking it smartly with his right hand, to make the
bands rattle, as he used to do, when he was a young soldier
on the parade.

Suddenly he uttered a deep sigh, and his eyes glistened
with the starting tear. He stood for a short time perfectly
still, holding his musket at arm's length, and looking very
steadily upon it. He appeared to be thinking of the places
where he had been with that musket; for he had carried it
thousands of miles; and many friends dear to him, he had
seen fall, bleeding, around him, before his own leg was shot
off in battle.

Trembling with strong feeling, he wiped the tear from his
furrowed cheek. "O," said the aged man, "I have not
words to express my thoughts! The memory of past years
rushes like a flood, and hurries my mind away from this
little cottage that shelters me.

"I fancy myself standing on a high mountain, surveying
the grandest nation on which the sun ever shone. I behold
myriads of children, through a long train of generations,
thoughtlessly gay as the birds, and liable to go astray, because they know not their own blessings. O, that they
would listen to the warning of age, and be wise!

"If I could, I would speak to all the young people of
America at once. My voice should be heard from the shores
of Maine to the Rocky Mountains, and from the ocean to the
inland seas.

"I would lay the great cause of the country before them,
and call up every noble feeling in their bosoms. I would
put the question to their hearts, Can you content yourselves
to follow at a distance the slavish rules of foreign lands, instead of raising high the banner of your own freedom, as a
model for all nations?

"Have you read what your fathers have done? Have
you heard of the glory they gained? And do these things
seem like old fables, because they happened before you were
born? Go, then, my young friends, and view the fields they
trod; when the sun looked fiery and dim, through the smoke
of war, and stout hearts fainted; when widows and orphans
were multiplied as their defenders fell.

"Go, in the generous ardor of youth; trace on the frost-
bound earth, to Valley Forge, the honest farmers of our
land, by their footsteps marked in blood. Behold the suf-

fering band; some of your fathers among them; their anxious chief watching in his tent, through the silent hours of night, and learn of them to love your country.

"Go to Charlestown, wrapped in flames; to Flatbush, Guilford, Camden, Wilmington; see our brave men cut down on the battle plain, steeping the soil with their warm blood; breathing their prayers to Heaven, at once for their own parting souls, and their country's cause, and inquire of them, if what you enjoy was bought at a cheap rate.

"Go, where Europe has, for a hundred ages, swelled her domes, refined in vice, and strengthened her abuses; see there the pale victim of lawless power, in his lone dungeon, encircled by chains and torturing machines; wearing away his life by slow degrees; without hope of seeing, on earth, a helping hand, or pitying tear, and ask him, if freedom is a blessing of trifling value.

"O, my dear lads," said he to the young men, "you are just entering the stage of manhood; full of life, and heart-cheering hope; you see me poor and decrepid, drawing near to the grave, my resting place; but such as I am, I have always lived an honest life; I have abhorred fraud and falsehood; I have tried to be useful to my fellow-men.

"I can lay my hand on my heart, and look up with humble confidence to that Being who knows all my thoughts; and I would not change my situation, as a free American, with the proudest monarch of the globe. No, no: not all their glittering trappings; nor the bayonets of pampered guards; nor flattering tongues, can save them from a guilty conscience, and a dying bed."

"Ah," said Solomon to Jack, as they were returning, "what you and I have read of, this venerable man has seen, and acted, and felt. His reverend head, whitened by the frosts of so many winters, is a living record of the times he tells us of. We belong to a glorious empire. He was present when its foundations were laid."

"Any people," said Jack, "to be prosperous, must be united, wise, and good; and if these things are properly attended to here, we shall have the most splendid republic which the world has ever seen. This depends on the schools. I have read the opinions of eminent men, of different countries, respecting instruction.

"Mr. Beccaria says, in the book which he wrote about 'Crimes and Punishments,' that 'the most certain means of rendering a people free and happy, is to establish a perfect method of education.' It is impossible for a nation to be truly flourishing without good schools."

LESSON XVII.

DEATH OF A CONQUEROR.—Bible.

AND it shall come to pass in the day that the Lord shall give thee rest from thy sorrow, and from thy fear, and from thy hard bondage, wherein thou wast made to serve,

That thou shalt take up this proverb against the king of Babylon, and say,

How hath the oppressor ceased! The golden city ceases!

The Lord hath broken the staff of the wicked, and the sceptre of the rulers.

He who smote the people in wrath with a continual stroke, he that ruled the nations in anger, is persecuted, and none hindereth.

The whole earth is at rest, and is quiet; they break forth into singing.

Yea, the fir-trees rejoice at thee, and the cedars of Lebanon, saying, Since thou art laid down, no feller is come up against us.

The grave from beneath is moved for thee to meet thee at thy coming; it stirreth up the dead for thee, even all the chief ones of the earth; it hath raised up from their thrones all the kings of the nations.

All they shall speak and say unto thee,

Art thou also become weak as we? Art thou become like unto us?

Thy pomp is brought down to the grave, and the noise of thy viols; the worm is spread under thee, and the worms cover thee.

How art thou fallen from heaven, O Lucifer, son of the morning! how art thou cut down to the ground, which didst weaken the nations!

For thou hadst said in thine heart, I will ascend into heaven, I will exalt my throne above the stars of God: I will set also upon the mount of the congregation in the sides of the north:

I will ascend above the heights of the clouds; I will be like the Most High.

Yet thou shalt be brought down to the grave, to the sides of the pit.

They that see thee, shall narrowly look upon thee; and consider thee, saying, Is this the man that made the earth to tremble, that did shake kingdoms?

That made the world as a wilderness, and destroyed the cities thereof, that opened not the house of his prisoners?

LESSON XVIII.

THE GENEROUS RUSSIAN PEASANT.—Karamsin.

Let Virgil sing the praises of Augustus, genius celebrate merit, and flattery extol the talents of the great. The short and simple annals of the "poor" engross my pen; and while I record the history of Flor Silin's virtues, though I speak of a poor peasant, I shall describe a nobleman,—I ask no eloquence to assist me in the task,—modest worth rejects the aid of ornament to set it off.

It is impossible, even at this distant period, to reflect without horror on the miseries of that year, known in Lower Wolga by the name of the "*famine* year." I remember the summer, whose scorching heats had dried up all the fields, and the drought had no relief but from the tears of the ruined farmer;—I remember the cold comfortless autumn—and the despairing rustics, crowding round their empty farms, with folded arms and sorrowful countenances, pondering on their misery, instead of rejoicing, as usual, at the golden harvest;—I remember the winter which succeeded, and I reflect with agony on the miseries it brought with it,—whole families left their homes to become beggars on the highway. At night, the canopy of heaven served them as their only shelter from the piercing winds and bitter frost;—to describe these scenes would be to harm the feelings of my readers; therefore, to my tale.

In those days, I lived on an estate not far from Simbirsk; and, though but a child, I have not forgotten the impression made on my mind by the general calamity.

In a village adjoining, lived Flor Silin, a poor laboring peasant,—a man remarkable for his assiduity, and the skill and judgment with which he cultivated his lands. He was blessed with abundant crops, and his means being larger than his wants, his granaries, even at this time, were full of corn. The dry year coming on, had beggared all the village, except himself. Here was an opportunity to grow rich!—

Mark, how Flor Silin acted. Having called the poorest of his neighbors about him, he addressed them in the following manner :

"My friends, you want corn for your subsistence ;—God has blessed me with abundance—assist in thrashing out a quantity, and each of you take what he wants for his family."

The peasants were amazed at this unexampled generosity ; for sordid propensities exist in the village as well as in the populous city.

The fame of Flor Silin's benevolence having reached other villages, the famished inhabitants presented themselves before him, and begged for corn. This good creature received them as brothers ; and, while his store remained, afforded all relief.

At length, his wife, seeing no end to the generosity of his noble spirit, reminded him how necessary it would be to think on their own wants, and hold his lavish hand, before it was too late. "It is written in the Scripture," said he, "Give, and it shall be given unto you."

The following year Providence listened to the prayers of the poor, and the harvest was abundant. The peasants, who had been saved from starving by Flor Silin, now gathered around him.

"Behold," said they, "the corn you lent us. You saved our wives and children. We should have been famished but for you,—may God reward you,—he only can,—all we have to give, is our corn and grateful thanks." "I want no corn, at present, my good neighbors," said he ; "my harvest has exceeded all my expectations ; for the rest, thank Heaven, I have been but an humble instrument."

They urged him in vain. "No," said he, "I shall not accept your corn. If you have superfluities, share them among your poor neighbors, who, being unable to sow their fields last autumn, are still in want—let us assist them, my dear friends, the Almighty will bless us for it." "Yes," replied the grateful peasants, "our poor neighbors shall have this corn. They shall know that it is to you they owe this timely succor, and join to teach their children the debt of gratitude due to your benevolent heart."

Silin raised his tearful eye to heaven.—An angel might have envied him his feelings.

At another time, fourteen farm-houses were burnt down in an adjoining village—to each sufferer Silin sent two roubles and a scythe.

Sometime after, a like misfortune happened at another village—it was entirely consumed; and the inhabitants, reduced to the last degree of misery, had recourse to Silin; but his former benevolence had impoverished his means,—he had no money to help them,—what was to be done,—"Stop," said he, suddenly recollecting himself, "here is a horse—I do not actually want him—take and sell him."

He set at liberty two female slaves, whom he bought in the name of the lord of the manor, educated them as his own daughters, and when they married gave them a handsome dowry.

As long as thou continuest, noble Silin, to inhabit this world, so long will thy life be spent in acts of generosity and benevolence towards thy fellow creatures; and when thou hast exchanged this for a better life, the recording angel shall proclaim thy virtues in heaven; the Almighty will place thee high, above kings and princes, and thou wilt still be the friend of the comfortless, and a father to the poor and indigent on earth. If ever I revisit that country, whose ornament thou art, I shall approach thy cot with reverence, and pay homage to thy virtues: but, if the minister of peace hath removed thee into bliss, I will visit thy grave, sprinkle it with my tears, and place a stone upon the spot, on which, with my own hand, I will write—

Here rest the bones of a noble man!

LESSON XIX.

PARENTAL INSTRUCTION.—LAW.

PATERNUS had but one son, whom he educated himself. As they were sitting together in the garden, when the child was ten years old, Paternus thus addressed him:—Though you now think yourself so happy because you have hold of my hand, you are in the hands, and under the tender care of a much greater Father and Friend than I am, whose love to you is far greater than mine, and from whom you receive such blessings as no mortal can give.

You see, my son, this wide and large firmament over our heads, where the sun, and moon, and all the stars appear in their turns. If you were to be carried to any of these bodies, at this vast distance from us, you would still discover others as much above you, as the stars which you see here are above the earth. Were you to go up or down, east or west, north or south, you would find the same height without any top, and the same depth without any bottom.

Yet, so great is God, that all these bodies added together are only as a grain of sand in His sight. But you are as much the care of this great God and Father of all worlds, and all spirits, as if he had no son but you, or there were no creature for Him to love and protect but you alone. He numbers the hairs of your head, watches over you sleeping and waking, and has preserved you from a thousand dangers, unknown both to you and me.

Therefore, my child, fear, and worship, and love God. Your eyes indeed cannot yet see Him, but all things which you see, are so many marks of His power and presence, and He is nearer to you than any thing which you can see.

Take Him for your Lord, and Father, and Friend : look up unto Him as the fountain and cause of all the good which you have received from me, and reverence me only as the bearer and minister of God's good things to you. He that blessed my father before I was born, will bless you when I am dead.

As you have been used to look to me in all your actions, and have been afraid to do any thing, unless you first knew my will; so let it now be a rule of your life to look up to God in all your actions, to do every thing in His fear, and to abstain from every thing which is not according to His will.

Next to this, love mankind with such tenderness and affection, as you love yourself. Think how God loves all mankind, how merciful He is to them, how tender He is of them, how carefully He preserves them, and then strive to love the world as God loves it.

Do good, my son, first of all to those who most deserve it; but remember to do good to all. The greatest sinners receive daily instances of God's goodness towards them ; He nourishes and preserves them, that they may repent and return to Him; do you therefore imitate God, and think no one too bad to receive your relief and kindness, when you see that he wants it.

Let your dress be sober, clean, and modest—not to set off the beauty of your person, but to declare the sobriety of your mind, that your outward garb may resemble the inward plainness and simplicity of your heart. For it is highly reasonable that you should be one man, and appear outwardly such as you are inwardly.

In meat and drink, observe the rules of Christian temperance, and sobriety; consider your body only as the servant and minister of your soul; and only so nourish it, as it may best perform an humble and obedient service.

Love humility in all its instances, practice it in all its parts, for it is the noblest state of the soul of man; it will set your heart and affections right towards God, and fill you with whatever temper is tender and affectionate towards men. Let every day therefore be a day of humility; condescend to all the weakness and infirmities of your fellow-creatures; cover their frailties; love their excellencies; encourage their virtues; relieve their wants; rejoice in their prosperity; compassionate their distress; receive their friendship; overlook their unkindness; forgive their malice; be a servant of servants; and condescend to do the lowest offices for the lowest of mankind.

It seems but the other day since I received from my dear father, the same instructions which I am now leaving with you. And the God who gave me ears to hear, and a heart to receive, what my father enjoined on me, will, I hope, give you grace to love and follow the same instructions.

LESSON XX.

PICTURE OF A YOUTH.—Hardie.

Shall I relate to you the sad tale of corrupted virtue; the melancholy fate of him, whom the example of profligate companions has seduced from the maxims of prudence? The days were, when he was taught to tremble at the way of the wicked, and to lisp the prayer of infancy to Heaven. The days were, when he could boast of a mind unpolluted by the world, when he resisted the allurements of corruption, and was a joy to the hearts of his parents. As he rose in years, he rose in promise. His parents poured out their souls in gratitude to Heaven, who had given them such a reward for their toils and anxieties, and looked forward in rapturous anticipation to the time when he would be the pride and comfort of their declining age. But the day comes, when he must leave his home of peace and innocence. He must attempt his fortune in the walks of active life. He must brave the dangers and seductions of a deceitful world. He must go, and the best blessings of his father go with him. "Thou art young," says the aged father, "and it is a dark world thou art entering, but I trust that Providence will guide thee through its deceitful mazes. It has pleased God to deprive me of many children, and I bow under his dispensations. He has left thee for a staff and for a comforter. May his fear reign in thy heart, and may he preserve thee a joy and ornament to our family." He leaves them in tears and in silence. His heart swells with the purposes of virtue. He looks forward to the day, when he shall return to his mansion of piety; when his presence shall enliven the last days of a venerable father; when he shall weep over him in his dying hours, and close his eyes in peace. But, O Heaven! how mysterious are thy counsels! O man! how wretched the inconstancy of thy purposes! O example! how powerful and how fascinating thy seduction! For a while he firmly resists every allurement; he contemplates, in horror, the dark scenes with which he is surrounded; he turns, in disgust and indignation, from the corruption of his acquaintance, and sighs, in affectionate remembrance, over the temperance and simplicity of his father's house. But how shall the innocence of his youthful heart stand against the torrent of example? How can he resist that innumerable host of enemies, who conspire against his virtue? Here one practices his deceitful insinuations, and assures him, with a smiling countenance, that there is no harm. There, another turns against him the weapons of ridicule, and tries to laugh him out of his dull and spiritless sobriety. There, a third invites him to the repast of hospitality and friendship, only to expose his ears to the conversation of a licentious company. He at last falls a reluctant sacrifice to the arts of an unprincipled ingenuity. The disgusting features of vice soften down by the familiarity of habit. To shelter himself from the contempt and hostility of his acquaintance, he is forced to accommodate to their example. In the bowl of intoxication, he drowns the painful remembrance of a father's advice, and a father's anxiety. His soul maddens in the pursuit of pleasure, and he plunges headlong into all the infatuation of guilt.

Who can tell the sufferings of that hour, when the tidings of his fall reach the ears of an affectionate father; and when he hears, that the boy of his heart has been allured into the paths of destruction? The pillar of his hope is now overthrown, and he is left like a tree in a desert. He sinks to earth in deep and silent affliction. There is naught for him, but the gloom and desolation of age. He sighs that the grave may cover him, and that, in the tomb's peaceful retreat, he may forget the sufferings of his dreary pilgrimage. We have heard religion denounced for the hateful asperity of its aspect; but let us remember that it is the severity of benevolence. It is a flaming sword, to protect the weak and erring children of humanity, from the deceitful paths of licentiousness? Shall religion be denounced as hateful, because it lifts the voice of execration against the practices of an unfeeling depravity? Shall it be charged with the gloom and malignity of superstition, because it rises in all the thunder of resentment against the villainy of him, who can blast the hopes of an anxious and affectionate parent; who can spread the wiles of seduction, and trample, without a sigh, on the prostitution of youthful simplicity?

LESSON XXI.

DAMON AND PYTHIAS.—Brooke.

When Damon was sentenced by Dionysius, the tyrant of Syracuse, to die on a certain day, he prayed permission to retire, in the mean time, to his own country, to set the affairs of his disconsolate family in order. This the tyrant intended most peremptorily to refuse, by granting it, as he conceived, on the impossible condition of his procuring some one to remain as hostage for his return, under equal forfeiture of life. Pythias heard the condition, and did not wait for an application on the part of Damon. He instantly offered himself to confinement, in place of his friend, and Damon was accordingly set at liberty.

The king, and all his courtiers, were astonished at this action, as they could not account for it on any allowed principles. Self-interest, in their judgment, was the sole mover of human affairs; and they looked on virtue, friendship, benevolence, love of country, and the like, as terms invented by the wise to impose upon the weak. They, therefore, imputed this act of Pythias to the extravagance of his folly; to a defect of understanding, merely, and, no way, to any virtue or good quality of heart.

When the day of the destined execution drew near, the

tyrant had the curiosity to visit Pythias in his dungeon.
Having reproached him for the extravagance of his conduct,
and rallied him some time on his madness, in presuming that
Damon, by his return, would prove as romantic as himself—
"My lord," said Pythias, with a firm voice and noble aspect,
"I would it were possible, that I might suffer a thousand
deaths, rather than my friend should fail in any article of his
honor. He cannot fail therein, my lord. I am as confident
of his virtue, as I am of my own existence. But I pray, I
beseech the gods, to preserve the life and integrity of my
Damon together. Oppose him, ye winds! prevent the eager-
ness and impatience of his honorable endeavors; and suffer
him not to arrive, till, by my death, I have redeemed a life,
a thousand times of more consequence, of more estimation,
than my own; more estimable to his lovely wife, to his precious little innocents, to his friends, to his country. O!
leave me not to die the worst of deaths in my Damon." Dionysius was awed and confounded by the dignity of these
sentiments, and by the manner, still more affecting, in which
they were uttered. He felt his heart struck by a slight
sense of invading truth; but it served rather to perplex than
undeceive him. He hesitated. He would have spoken;
but he looked down, and retired in silence.

The fatal day arrived. Pythias was brought forth; and
walked, amidst the guard, with a serious but satisfied air, to
the place of execution. Dionysius was already there. He
was exalted on a moving throne drawn by six white horses,
and sat pensive and attentive to the demeanor of the prisoner.
Pythias came. He vaulted slightly on the scaffold, and, beholding for some time the apparatus of death, he turned, and,
with a pleasing countenance, thus addressed the assembly.
"My prayers are heard. The gods are propitious. You
know, my friends, that the winds have been contrary till
yesterday. Damon could not come; he could not conquer
impossibilities. He will be here to-morrow; and the blood
which is shed to-day, shall have ransomed the life of my
friend. O! could I erase from your bosoms every doubt,
every mean suspicion, of the honor of the man for whom I
am about to suffer, I should go to my death, even as I would
to my bridal. Be it sufficient, in the mean time, that my
friend will be found noble—that his truth is unimpeachable—
that he will speedily approve it—that he is now on his way,
hurrying on, accusing himself, the adverse elements, and the
gods. But I hasten to prevent his speed. Executioner, do

your office!". As he pronounced the last words, a buz began
to arise among the remotest of the people. A distant voice
was heard. The crowd caught the words; and, "Stop, stop
the execution!" was repeated by the whole assembly. A
man came at full speed. The throng gave way to his approach. He was mounted on a steed of foam. In an instant
he was off his horse, on the scaffold, and held Pythias straitly
embraced. "You are safe," he cried; "you are safe, my
friend, my beloved! the gods be praised, you are safe! I,
now, have nothing but death to suffer; and I am delivered
from the anguish of those reproaches, which I gave myself,
for having endangered a life so much dearer than my own."
Pale, and almost speechless, in the arms of his Damon,
Pythias replied, in broken accents, "Fatal haste!—Cruel
impatience! What envious powers have wrought impossibilities in your favor? But I will not be wholly disappointed.
Since I cannot die to save, I will not survive you."

Dionysius heard, beheld, and considered all, with astonishment. His heart was touched; his eyes were opened; and
he could no longer refuse his assent to truths, so incontesti-
bly proved by facts. He descended from his throne. He
ascended the scaffold. "Live, live, ye incomparable pair!"
he exclaimed. "Ye have borne unquestionable testimony
to the existence of virtue!—Live happy! live renowned!
And, O! form me by your precepts, as you have invited me
by your example, to be worthy of the participation of so
sacred a friendship."

LESSON XXII.

THE ALMIGHTY.—The Scriptures.

I WILL extol thee, my God, O King! and I will bless thy
name for ever and ever. I will speak of the glorious honor
of thy majesty, and of thy wondrous works; I will declare
thy greatness.

The Lord our God is one Lord:—the high and lofty One,
that inhabiteth eternity, whose name is Holy:—the King
eternal, immortal, invisible;—dwelling in the light which no
man can approach unto.

Honor and majesty are before him; strength and beauty

are in his sanctuary. He is clothed with majesty. His greatness is unsearchable.

Consider the wondrous works of God,—of him that is perfect in knowledge. The earth is full of the goodness of the Lord.

God formed the earth. He spake, and it was done; he commanded, and it stood fast. He hangeth the earth upon nothing. He hath established it; he created it not in vain; he formed it to be inhabited. God created *man* upon the earth. By him were *all* things created that are in the earth; all things were created *by* him, and *for* him.

He covereth the heavens with clouds; he prepareth rain for the earth,—the former and the latter rain in its season. He visiteth the earth, and watereth it; he maketh it soft with showers; he blesseth the springing thereof. He maketh grass to grow upon the mountains. The pastures are clothed with flocks; the valleys also are covered over with corn. He reserveth unto us the appointed weeks of the harvest.

He causeth the vapors to ascend from the ends of the earth. He divideth a way for the lightning with thunder. He maketh lightnings for the rain; he bringeth the wind out of his treasuries. He giveth snow like wool: he scattereth the hoar-frost like ashes. By the breath of his mouth frost is given:—who can stand before his cold?

Lift up your eyes on high. Behold the clouds which are higher than thou. Look unto the heavens and see. Behold the height of the stars. Tell the stars, if thou be able to number them. Behold, who hath created these things?

"*My* hands," saith God, "have stretched out the heavens, and all the host have I commanded. I form the light, and create darkness.

The heavens declare the *glory* of God, and the firmament sheweth his handywork. He telleth the number of the stars; He calleth them all by their names. He giveth the sun for a light by day, and the ordinances of the moon and of the stars for a light by night. His glory covereth the heavens, and the earth is full of his praise!

O Lord! how great are thy works! and thy thoughts are very deep! When I *consider* thy heavens, the work of thy fingers; the moon, and the stars, which thou hast ordained; —what is man that thou art mindful of him!—and the son of man that thou visitest him!

Thine, O Lord! is the greatness, and the power, and the glory, and the victory, and the majesty; for all that is in heaven and in earth is thine ; thine is the kingdom, O Lord !, and thou art exalted as head above all. Thou reignest over all, and in thine hand is power and might; and in thine hand it is to make great, and to give strength unto all.

The Lord killeth, and maketh alive ; the Lord maketh poor, and maketh rich ; he bringeth low, and lifteth up. He changeth the times and the seasons ; he removeth kings, and setteth up kings. He increaseth the nations, and destroyeth them ; he enlargeth the nations, and straiteneth them. All nations before him are as nothing ; and they are counted to him less than nothing, and vanity.

Lo, these are parts of his ways ; but how little a portion is heard of him !—the thunder of his power, who can understand ? Touching the Almighty, we cannot find him out. Great things doeth he which we cannot comprehend.

The eyes of the Lord are in every place, beholding the evil and the good. His eyes are upon the ways of man ; He seeth his going. All things are naked and opened unto the eyes of Him with whom we have to do.

Wo unto them that seek deep to hide counsel from the Lord ! and say—" Who seeth us ?" Shall the work say of him that made it,—" He made me not ?"—or shall the thing framed say of him that framed it, " He had no understanding ?" There is no wisdom, nor understanding, nor counsel against the Lord. Wo unto him that striveth with his Maker ! At his wrath the earth shall tremble ; and the nations shall not be able to abide his indignation. Our God is a consuming fire.

The Lord is good. Gracious is the Lord ; yea, our God is merciful. The Lord is nigh unto all them that call upon him, to all that call upon him in truth. He will fulfil the desire of them that fear him ; He also will hear their cry, and will save them. He preserveth all them that love him ; —but all the wicked will he destroy.

The Lord is righteous in all his ways, and holy in all his works. Righteousness and judgment are the habitation of his throne.—Shall not the judge of all the earth do right ?

Acquaint now thyself with him, and be at peace. Receive the law from his mouth, and lay up his words in thine heart. Then shalt thou have thy delight in the Almighty, and shall lift up thy face unto God. Happy is that people that is in such a case : yea, happy is that people whose God is the Lord !

LESSON XXIII.

MORTALITY.—Barbauld.

CHILD of mortality, whence comest thou? Why is thy countenance sad, and why are thine eyes red with weeping?

I have seen the rose in its beauty; it spread its leaves to the morning sun: I returned—it was dying upon its stalk; the grace of the form of it was gone; its loveliness was vanished away; the leaves thereof were scattered on the ground; and no one gathered them again.

A stately tree grew on the plain; its branches were covered with verdure; its boughs spread wide and made a goodly shadow; the trunk was like a strong pillar; the roots were like crooked fangs: I returned—the verdure was nipt by the east wind; the branches were lopt away by the axe; the worm had made its way into the trunk, and the heart thereof was decayed: it mouldered away, and fell to the ground.

I have seen the insects sporting in the sunshine, and darting along the streams; their wings glittered with gold and purple; their bodies shone like the green emerald; they were more numerous than I could count; their motions were quicker than my eye could glance: I returned—they were brushed into the pool; they were perishing with the evening breeze; the swallow had devoured them; the pike had seized them; there were none found of so great a multitude.

I have seen man in the pride of his strength; his cheeks glowed with beauty; his limbs were full of activity; he leaped; he walked; he ran; he rejoiced in that he was more excellent than those: I returned—he lay stiff and cold on the bare ground; his feet could no longer move, nor his hands stretch themselves out; his life was departed from him; and the breath out of his nostrils;—therefore do I weep, because Death is in the world: the spoiler is among the works of God; all that is made must be destroyed; all that is born must die; let me alone, for I will weep yet longer.

LESSON XXIV.

IMMORTALITY.—Barbauld.

I HAVE seen the flower withering on the stalk, and its bright leaves spread on the ground. I looked again and it sprung forth afresh; the stem was crowned with new buds, and the sweetness thereof filled the air.

I have seen the sun set in the west, and the shades of night shut in the wide horizon; there was no color, nor shape, nor beauty, nor music; gloom and darkness brooded around. I looked—the sun broke forth again from the east, he gilded the mountain tops; the lark rose to meet him from her low nest, and the shades of darkness fled away.

I have seen the insect, being come to its full size, languish and refuse to eat; it spun itself a tomb, and was shrouded in the silken cone; it lay without feet, or shape, or power to move. I looked again—it had burst its tomb; it was full of life, and sailed on colored wings through the soft air; it rejoiced in its new being.

Thus shall it be with thee, O man! and so shall thy life be renewed.

Beauty shall spring up out of ashes; and life out of the dust.

A little while shalt thou lie in the ground, as the seed lieth in the bosom of the earth; but thou shalt be raised again; and if thou art good, thou shalt never die any more.

Who is He that cometh to burst open the prison doors of the tomb; to bid the dead awake, and to gather His redeemed from the four winds of heaven?

He descendeth on a fiery cloud; the sound of a trumpet goeth before him; thousands of angels are on His right hand.

It is Jesus, the son of God; the Savior of men; the friend of the good.

He cometh in the glory of his Father; he hath received power from on high.

Mourn not, therefore, child of immortality;—for the spoiler, the cruel spoiler that laid waste the works of God, is subdued; Jesus hath conquered death; child of immortality! mourn no longer.

LESSON XXV.

INFLUENCE OF KNOWLEDGE.—J. KEESE.

WE observe the elevating influence of knowledge in all the various stages of advantageous industry. It ennobles the youth that is just entering the arena of manly care; wisdom

and diligence walk hand in hand to cheer the toil of the arti-
zan, embellish the fields of the agriculturist, enliven the pur-
suits of the tradesman, and adorn the chamber of commercial negociation, to spread taste and refinement through the
scenes of domestic life, and hang delightful mementoes in all
the pure bowers of retirement ; to connect the charms of poetry with severer intellectual exertion ; to guide the efforts
of reason in the pulpit, the forum and the legislative hall ; to
increase and beautify the fascinating influences of native eloquence, and impart sensibility and power where nature has
not profusely endowed.   The clown of yesterday is now the
philosopher ; the youth who was recently vulgar and ob-
scene, to-day is refined and distinguished ; the pence which
lately were the whole invoice of the merchant's capital, now
have attracted princely opulence to their society ; the boy
who recently toiled to learn the mysterious characters of the
alphabet, already surprises and delights by their wonderful
combinations.   We see an individual who was lately an
American schoolmaster, at present wearing the crown of
France ; we trace the career of our late Executive to a boyhood of penury ; from a similar origin we follow the present
Chief Magistrate of this great Republic to his exalted station,
while we remember that our eloquent Webster was but recently toiling in the fields of his paternal home ; and observe
the course of the graceful and impassioned Clay, from the
obscure scenes of indigence and virtue, whence, by the
magic force of genius and diligence, he has risen to the lofty
eminence where he now shines with dazzling, yet cheerful
effulgence, in the constellation of luminaries that enlighten
and guide the world.

From these familiar considerations we perchance may
gather some advantageous practical ideas.   We perceive the
truth of the ancient maxim, that knowledge is power.   We
learn that for brilliant results, judicious thought and patient,
skillful action should be associated ; we note the work of per-
severing energy ; we see that poverty and obscure parentage
cannot imprison the aspirings of virtuous and lofty ambition ;
we observe that suitable attention to ordinary duties need not
debar the intellectual from treading the walks of science and
seeking enjoyment in its refreshing groves ; that extensive
acquisitions in literature are compatible with sedulous activity for securing honorable fortunes ; that knowledge is chiefly
valuable when usefully applied, and that the practice of wisdom is its most essential part.   Will you ask, then, what

is knowledge worth?—Repair to Egypt, and Greece, and Rome; explore the literature of England, France, and Germany; recite the story of our youthful Republic; portray the march of improvement through the length and breadth of this goodly land; observe the immense conquests of art; survey all that is deemed necessary and desirable in the productions of human skill; let the sciences speak; consider the whole field of happiness that human wisdom cultivates; remember the constant progress of genius and industry, and then reply. What is the value of knowledge? Let poetry say; let reason answer; let each heart respond. What is knowledge worth indeed? What has it done?—the ocean, the air, the devouring elements; these it much controls and appropriates; the heavenly bodies, the wonders of the universe, these it opens to our scrutiny. Man! Man in degradation and sorrow! him it cheers, ennobles, and elevates.

LESSON XXVI.

A NOBLE BOY.—WILLIS.

THERE's something in a noble boy,
    A brave free-hearted careless one,
With his unchecked, unbidden joy,
    His dread of books and love of fun,
And in his clear and ready smile,
Unshaded by a thought of guile,
    And unrepressed by sadness—
Which brings me to my childhood back,
As if I trod its very track,
    And felt its very gladness.
And yet it is not in his play,
    When every trace of thought is lost,
And not when you would call him gay,
    That his bright presence thrills me most.
His shout may ring upon the hill,
    His voice be echoed in the hall,
His merry laugh like music trill,
    And I unheeding hear it all—
For like the wrinkles on my brow,
I scarcely notice such things now—

But when amid the earnest game,
He stops as if he music heard,
    And, heedless of his shouted name,
As of the carol of a bird,
Stands gazing on the empty air,
As if some dream were passing there—
'Tis then that on his face I look,
    His beautiful but thoughtful face,
And like a long forgotten book,
    Its sweet, familiar meanings trace—
Remembering a thousand things
Which passed me on those golden wings,
    Which time has fettered now—
Things that came o'er me with a thrill,
And left me silent, sad and still,
    And threw upon my brow
A holier and a gentler cast,
That was too innocent to last.

'Tis strange how thoughts upon a child
    Will, like a presence, sometimes press—
And when his pulse is beating wild,
    And life itself is in excess—
When foot and hand, and ear and eye,
Are all with ardor straining high—
    How in his heart will spring
A feeling, whose mysterious thrall
Is stronger, sweeter far than all;
    And on its silent wing,
How with the clouds he 'll float away,
As wandering and as lost as they !

LESSON XXVII.

INDIAN RESOLUTION.—IRVING.

No hero of ancient or modern days can surpass the Indian
in his lofty contempt of death, and the fortitude with which
he sustains its cruellest affliction. Indeed, we here behold
him rising superior to the white man, in consequence of his
peculiar education. The latter rushes to glorious death at
the cannon's mouth ; the former calmly contemplates its

approach, and triumphantly endures it, amidst the varied torments of surrounding foes and the protracted agonies of fire. He even takes a pride in taunting his persecutors, and provoking their ingenuity of torture; and as the devouring flames prey on his very vitals, and the flesh shrinks from the sinews, he raises his last song of triumph, breathing the defiance of an unconquered heart, and invoking the spirits of his fathers to witness that he dies without a groan.

In one of the homely narratives of the Indian wars in New-England, there is a touching account of the desolation carried into the tribe of the Pequot Indians. Humanity shrinks from the cold-blooded detail of indiscriminate butchery. In one place we read of the surprisal of an Indian fort in the night, when the wigwams were wrapped in flames, and the miserable inhabitants shot down and slain in attempting to escape, "all being dispatched and ended in the course of an hour." After a series of similar transactions, "our soldiers," as the historian piously observes, "being resolved, by God's assistance, to make a final destruction of them," the unhappy savages, being hunted from their homes and fortresses, and pursued with fire and sword, a scanty but gallant band, the sad remnant of the Pequot warriors, with their wives and children, took refuge in a swamp.

Burning with indignation, and rendered sullen by despair; with hearts bursting with grief at the destruction of their tribe, and spirits galled and sore at the fancied ignominy of their defeat, they refused to ask their lives at the hands of an insulting foe, and preferred death to submission.

As the night drew on, they were surrounded in their dismal retreat, so as to render escape impracticable. Thus situated, their enemy "plied them with shot all the time, by which means many were killed and buried in the mire." In the darkness and fog that preceded the dawn of day, some few broke through the besiegers and escaped into the woods: "the rest were left to the conquerors, of which many were killed in the swamp, like sullen dogs who would rather, in their self-willedness and madness, sit still and be shot through, or cut to pieces," than implore for mercy. When the day broke upon this handful of forlorn but dauntless spirits, the soldiers, we are told, entering the swamp, "saw several heaps of them sitting close together, upon whom they discharged their pieces, laden with ten or twelve pistol bullets, at a time; putting the muzzles of the pieces under the boughs, within a few yards of them; so as, besides those that were found dead, many more were killed and sunk into the mire, and never were minded more by friend or foe."

Can any one read this plain, unvarnished tale, without admiring the stern resolution, the unbending pride, the loftiness of spirit, that seemed to nerve the hearts of these self-taught heroes, and to raise them above the instinctive feelings of human nature? When the Gauls laid waste the city of Rome, they found the senators clothed in their robes, and seated with stern tranquillity in their circle chairs; in this manner they suffered death without resistance or even supplication. Such conduct was, in them, applauded as noble and magnaminous; in the hapless Indians it was reviled as obstinate and sullen. How truly are we the dupes of show and circumstance! How different is virtue, clothed in purple and enthroned in state, from virtue naked and destitute, and perishing obscurely in a wilderness!

LESSON XXVII.

WASHINGTON, A TEACHER TO THE YOUNG.—ANONYMOUS.

THERE is no name in the annals of any country more revered than that of George Washington. It is a matter of interest to inquire how he became so good and great, and how he obtained so desirable a reputation; how he was able to do so much good to his country, and to mankind; how he was qualified to leave behind him so excellent an example; how he acquired that great wisdom which guided him in life, and prepared him for death—which made him, like Moses in ancient days, the leader of a nation through a wilderness of trial, and suffering, and danger,—and now that he has been dead more than forty years, renders him still the teacher, not only of the United States, but all the civilized world.

It is a good plan for every one who wishes to be useful, good and happy, to study the story of Washington, and see how it was that he became so useful, so good, and so happy. It is only by study that we can gain knowledge; and the best way to find out the path of duty and of success, is carefully to read the history of those who have been successful.

George Washington was born in Virginia, on the 22d of February, 1732. His father was a wealthy planter; but he died in 1743, when George was eleven years old. He was, therefore, left to the care of his mother, who was a good and wise woman.

Now you must remember that when Washington was a boy, young people had not the advantages that they have now. In Virginia there were no academies, high-schools, or colleges. He had, therefore, only the privileges of a common school education, where writing, reading, arithmetic, and a little of geometry, were taught.

Now some boys with these simple helps had never been great; the reason why they were sufficient for Washington, I will tell you. In the first place, he had a good mother, who, like almost all good mothers, frequently counseled and advised her son to make the best use of his time at school; to pay attention to his lessons, to learn them well, and thus, not only to store his mind with knowledge, but to get into the habit of studying thoroughly, and of improving his mind. In the second place, *Washington had the good sense, the virtue, and the wisdom to mind his mother in these things.* These are the two great reasons why a common-school education was sufficient for so great a man, and they are the two chief reasons why he became so great.

Now this shows that the advantages a boy possesses are of less consequence than the way in which he improves them. A boy may be sent to a high-school, and go through college, and have good natural capacity, and yet turn out to be a useless, weak, and ignorant man. Merely going through a high-school, or an academy, or a college, cannot make a good, useful, or great man. In order to be good, useful, great, or even happy, it is necessary in youth to do as Washington did.

Another thing to be noticed here is, that Washington had none of that folly which some boys think smartness, or a mark of genius, or manliness—a disposition to disobey a mother or a schoolmaster. Washington was obedient to both of them. If, therefore, a boy wishes to be successful in life, let him cultivate obedience to parents and teachers.

One of the great advantages that followed from Washington's making the best of his school privileges was, his adopting good habits. *He got into the habit of doing everything thoroughly.* He was not willing to learn a lesson by halves, and when he came to recite, to guess and shuffle his way out. No, indeed! He did not leave a lesson till he had mastered it—till he knew all about it—till he had stamped it so firmly in his mind as to make the impression indelible.

22

The reason why habits are so important, is, that they hang about a person, and actually guide him through life. How important it is therefore that we form good habits.

If a boy gets the habit of studying in a half-way, slovenly, slip-shod manner, he is almost certain to be greatly injured thereby. If he goes to college, he there continues the same habit; when he comes out, he still carries it with him; when he enters upon business, it still hangs about him. He does nothing well, or thoroughly; he is careless and slovenly in all he does; there is imperfection and weakness in his career, and finally he turns out an unsuccessful man. If he is a merchant, he usually fails in business; if a lawyer, a physician, or minister, he is generally at the tail-end of his profession, poor, useless, and despised. Such is the mighty influence of our habits; and remember that they are formed in early life. Remember that every day feeds and fosters our habits.

It is interesting to trace the way that Washington's youthful habits operated upon him. Some of his early school-books are extant, and these show that he was very thorough in writing. He even took pains to write out, in a fine hand, the forms in which notes of hand, bills of exchange, receipts, bonds, deeds, wills, should be drawn. Thus he cultivated the habit of writing neatly, of being patient in copying papers, of being accurate in making copies; and at the same time made himself acquainted with the forms of drawing up business documents. In all this, we see the habit of doing things patiently, accurately, and thoroughly. We see that Washington had so trained himself, that he could sit down and do that which was mere toil, and which some boys would think stupid drudgery.

Another thing that is remarkable at this early period of Washington's life, is, that in writing he was careful to study neatness and mechanical precision. Several quires of his school-manuscripts remain, in which he worked out questions in arithmetic and mathematics. These manuscripts are very neatly executed; there are several long sums which are nicely done and beautifully arranged. There are, also, extensive columns of figures, and all set down with careful precision.

Another thing visible in these manuscripts, is, that Washington studied accuracy; his sums were all right. What a beautiful illustration of the great man's life! His youthful manuscripts show that he learned to render his school-boy pages fair; to work out all his sums right. Thus he started in life—and thus he became qualified to make the pages of his history glorious; the footing up of his great account such as the sentiment of justice throughout the world would approve!

Another thing that had great influence in the formation of Washington's character, and in securing success in life, was, that very early he adopted a code or system of rules of behavior. This was found among his papers after his death, in his own hand-writing, and written at the age of thirteen. I will give you a few extracts from this code of manners, or rules of conduct:

EXTRACTS.

Every action in company ought to be with some sign of respect to those present.

Be no flatterer, neither play with any one that delights not to be played with.

Read no letters, books, or papers in company.

Come not near the books or papers of another so as to read them.

Look not over another when he is writing a letter.

Let your countenance be cheerful, but in serious matters be grave.

Show not yourself glad at another's misfortune.

Let your discourse with others on matters of business be short.

It is good manners to let others speak first.

Strive not with your superiors in argument, but be modest.

When a man does all he can, do not blame him though he succeeds not well.

Take admonitions thankfully.

Be not hasty to believe flying reports to the injury of another.

In your dress, be modest, and consult your condition.

Play not the peacock, looking vainly at yourself.

It is better to be alone than in bad company.

Let your conversation be without malice or envy.

Urge not your friend to discover a secret.

Break not a jest where none take pleasure in mirth.

Speak not injurious words either in jest or earnest.

Gaze not on the blemishes of others.

When another speaks, be attentive.

Be not apt to relate news.

Be not curious to know the affairs of others.

Speak not evil of the absent.

When you speak of God, let it ever be with reverence.

Labor to keep alive in your heart that spark of heavenly fire called conscience.

Such are some of those rules that Washington wrote out in a fair hand at thirteen. Most of these rules turn on one great principle, which is, that you treat others with respect; that you are tender of the feelings, and rights, and characters of others; that you do to others as you would have others do to you.

But another thing, also, is to be considered, which is, that Washington not only had a set of good rules of behavior, all written out in a fair hand and committed to memory, but he was in the habit of observing them; and he not only observed them when a child, but after he became a man. He got into the habit of obeying every one of these rules, and thus it was that his manners were always so dignified, kind, and noble; thus it was that his character and conduct became so great and good.

Now, I would not have my readers suppose that Washington was always a man; on the contrary, when he was a boy, he loved fun as well as any body. He liked to run, to leap, to wrestle, and play at games. He had a soldierly turn, even in boyhood, and was fond of heading a troop of boys, and marching them about with a tin kettle for a drum.

Washington, too, was quick-tempered and passionate when a boy; but the beauty of his story in this point is, that by adopting good habits and principles he overcame these tendencies of his nature, and he showed that all quick-tempered boys can do the same, if they please. They can govern their tempers; they can adopt good rules of conduct; they can get into the habit of being calm, patient and just, and thus grow up to honor and usefulness.

There are many other traits of character belonging to Washington that are interesting and worthy of imitation. He was accurate and just in all his dealings; he was punctual in the performance of promises; he was a man of prayer, and an observer of the Sabbath. And the point here to be noticed by youth, is, that all these qualities which we have been noticing, appear to be the fruit of seed sown in his youth. They appear all to have taken root in one great principle—OBEDIENCE—obedience to his mother, obedience to his teachers—obedience to a sense of duty formed into habit in early life. This is the real source of Washington's greatness. He was not made greater or better than most others, but he adopted good habits, and under their influence he became great.

Another thing to be observed, is, that in adopting good habits, Washington rejected bad ones. He was guilty of no profanity; no rudeness or harshness of speech; he had no vulgar love of eccentricity; he affected not that kind of smartness which displays itself in irregularity or excess; he did not think it clever to disobey teachers or parents; he was no lover of scandal, or of profane and rude society.

The teaching, then, of Washington's example is this: study obedience, patience, industry, thoroughness, accuracy, neatness, respect to the rights and feelings of others, and make these things habitual—rail-tracks in the mind. The path of obedience is the path to glory; the path of disobedience is the path of failure and disappointment in the race of life.

LESSON XXVIII.

THE DUTIES OF SCHOOL-BOYS.—Rollin.

Almost all the duty of scholars has been included in this one piece of advice, To love those who teach them, as they love the knowledge which they derive from them; and to look upon them as fathers, from whom they derive, not the life of the body, but that instruction, which is, in a manner, the life of the soul. Indeed, this sentiment of affection and respect suffices to make them apt to learn during the time of their studies, and full of gratitude all the rest of their lives. It seems to me to include a great part of what is to be expected from them.—Docility, which consists in submitting to directions, in readily receiving the instructions of their masters, and reducing them to practice, is properly the virtue of scholars, as that of masters is to teach well. The one can do nothing without the other; and as it is not sufficient for a laborer to sow the seed, unless the earth, after having opened its bosom to receive it, in a manner hatches, warms, and moistens it; so likewise the good fruit of instruction depends upon a good correspondence between the masters and the scholars. Gratitude to those who have labored in our education, is the character of an honest man, and the mark of a good heart. Who is there among us, says an ancient orator, that has been instructed with any care, who is not highly delighted with the sight, or even the bare re- membrance of his teachers, and of the place where he was taught and brought up. An ancient philosopher exhorts young men to preserve always a great respect for their masters, to whose care they are indebted for the amendment of their faults, and for having imbibed sentiments of honor and probity. Their exactness and severity displeases some- times at an age, when we are not in a condition to judge of the obligations we owe to them ; but, when years have ripen- ed our understanding and judgment, we then discern, that what made us dislike them, is expressly the very thing which should make us esteem and love them.—Another em- inent writer of antiquity, after having noted the different characters of the mind in children, draws, in a few words, the image of what he judged to be a perfect scholar, and certainly it is a very amiable one. " For my part," says he, " I like a child who is encouraged by commendation, is animated by a sense of glory, and weeps when he is outdone. A noble emulation will always keep him in exercise, a rep- rimand will touch him to the quick, and honor will serve instead of a spur. We need not fear that such a scholar will ever give himself up to sullenness." How great a value soever this writer puts upon the talents of the mind, he es- teems those of the heart far beyond them, and looks upon the other as of no value without them. He declares, he should never have a good opinion of a child, who placed his study in occasioning laughter, by mimicking the behavior, mien, and faults of others. " A child," says he, cannot be truly ingenious, in my opinion, unless he be good and virtuous: I should rather choose to have him dull and heavy, than of a bad disposition."

THE YOUNG SPEAKER.

PART FIFTH.

DIALOGUES FOR SPEAKING OR READING.

THESE Figures represent two boys making their bows preparatory to speaking a *dialogue*. They should enter, if convenient, at opposite sides of the platform ; then, having placed themselves at a suitable distance from each other, and standing in a position directly front, one should bow to the *right*, and the other to the *left* portion of the audience. This arrangement will not only be pleasing to the eye, but indicate a sentiment of propriety and respect. The speaker on the *left* of the audience, should perform his bow precisely as directed on page 94 ; the one on the *right* will *deviate* in this particular,—he will *begin* by sliding out the *left* foot instead of the right. In other respects his bow is entirely similar to that of his companion.—Some dialogues do *not* admit of the bow ; as, for instance, where the parties are supposed to meet in *great haste*, or with *highly excited* feelings. In all cases where it is proper, however, it is certainly very becoming,—and the pupil will aim to do it well. Let him be in love with neatness and simplicity, and he can hardly fail to be correct and graceful.

LESSON I.

CHOICE OF HOURS.—Mrs. Gilman.

FIRST SPEAKER—SECOND SPEAKER.

First Speaker.

I LOVE to walk at twilight,
  When sunset nobly dies,
And see the parting splendor
  That lightens up the skies,
And call up old remembrances
  Deep, dim as evening gloom,
Or look to heaven's promises,
  Like star-light on a tomb.

Second Speaker.

I love the hour of darkness
  When I give myself to sleep,
And I think that holy angels
  Their watch around me keep.
My dreams are light and happy
  As I innocently lie,
For my mother's kiss is on my cheek,
  And my father's step is nigh.

LESSON II.

CONSCIENCE.—Anonymous.

YOUNGER BROTHER—ELDER BROTHER.

Younger Brother.

I HAVE a little voice within,
That always tells me when I sin ;
I'm sure I know not whence it came,
Pray, brother, tell me what's its name ?
There is no one however near,
Whispers so sternly in my ear ;
And often in my lively play,
If anything I do or say

That's wrong or wicked, then I hear
This gentle tapping in my ear.
I know it is not *mother's tone*,
Nor Father's, for when they are gone,
It keeps on prompting just the same,
If aught I do *that they would blame.*

Elder Brother.

And, brother, don't it always tell
In kindly notes when you v'e *done well ;*
Are not its whispers always mild,
When you have been a dutious child ?
God gave not to the *bud nor flower*,
This inward voice of wondrous power :
Ah, no, it only has its birth
In us, who perish not with earth ;
Its name is conscience, and 'twill be
A voice from which you cannot flee ;
It keeps a registry within,
Rebuking those who live in sin,
And utters words of softest tone,
To those who will its dictates own.

LESSON III.

FREEDOM'S JUBIELE.—Hewitt.

BOY—FATHER.

Boy.

Father, look up and see that flag,
How gracefully it flies—
Those pretty stripes—they seem to be
A rainbow in the skies.

Father.

It is your country's flag, my son,
And proudly drinks the light ;
O'er ocean's wave, in foreign climes,
A symbol of our might.

Boy.

Father, what fearful noise is that,
Like thundering in the clouds ?

Why do the people wave their hats,
    And rush along in crowds ?

Father.

It is the voice of cannonry—
    The glad shouts of the free ;
This is a day to memory dear—
    'Tis Freedom's Jubilee.

Boy.

I wish that I was now a MAN,
    I 'd fire my cannon too ;
And cheer as loudly as the rest—
    But, father, why don't you ?

Father.

I am getting old, and weak—but still
    My heart is big with joy;
I 've witnessed many a day like this—
    Shout you aloud my boy.

Boy.

Hurrah! for Freedom's Jubilee!
    God bless our native land !
And may I live to hold the boon
    Of Freedom in my hand!

Father.

Well done, my boy—grow up and love
    The land that gave you birth—
A land where freedom loves to dwell—
    A paradise on earth.

LESSON IV.

HOT COCKLES.—Anonymous.

HENRY—CHARLES.

Charles. Brother, all our friends have left us, and yet I
am still in a playful humor. What game shall we choose ?

Henry. There are only two of us, and I am afraid we
should not be much diverted.

Charles. Let us play at something, however.

Henry. But at what?

Charles. At blindman's-buff, for instance.

Henry. That is a game that would never end. It would not be as if there were a dozen, of which number some are generally off their guard; but where there are only two, I should not find it difficult to shun you, nor you me; and then when we had caught each other, we should know for certain who it was.

Charles. That is true, indeed. Well, then, what think you of hot cockles?

Henry. That would be the same, you know. We could not possibly guess wrong.

Charles. Perhaps we might. However, let us try.

Henry. With all my heart, if it please you. Look here, if you like it, I will be Hot Cockles first.

Charles. Do, brother. Put your right hand on the bottom of this chair. Now stoop down and lay your face close upon it, that you may not see. (*He does so.*) That is well; —and now your left hand on your back. Well master—but I hope your eyes are shut. (*Carefully looking round to see.*)

Henry. Yes, yes; do not be afraid.

Charles. Well, master, what have you to sell?

Henry. Hot cockles! hot!

Charles. (*Slapping him with his left hand.*) Who struck?

Henry. (*Getting up.*) Why, you, you little goose!

Charles. Yes, yes; but with which hand?

Henry. The—the right!

Charles. No, it was the left. Now you are the goose.

LESSON V.

THE CHILD'S FIRST GRIEF.—Mrs. Hemans.

CHILD—FATHER.

Child.

O, CALL my brother back to me,
    I cannot play alone;
The summer comes with flower and bee,—
    Where is my brother gone?

The butterfly is glancing bright
    Across the sunbeam's track;

I care not now to chase its flight—
O call my brother back!

The flowers run wild,—the flowers we sowed
Around our garden-tree;
Our vine is drooping with its load—
O call him back to me!

Father.

He would not hear my voice, fair child!
He may not come to thee;
The face that once, like spring-time smiled,
On earth no more thou'lt see.

The rose's brief, bright light of joy,
Such unto him was given;—
Go,—thou must play alone, my boy!
Thy brother is in heaven.

Child.

And has he left his bird and flowers?
And must I call in vain?
And through the long, long summer hours,
Will he not come again?

And by the brook, and in the glade,
Are all our wanderings o'er?
Oh! while my brother with me played,
Would I had loved him more!

LESSON VI.

CHILDREN'S WISHES.—Mrs. Gilman.

FIRST SPEAKER—SECOND SPEAKER—THIRD SPEAKER—FOURTH
SPEAKER.

First Speaker.

I wish I was a little bird,
Among the leaves to dwell;
To scale the sky in gladness
Or seek the lonely dell.

My matin song should celebrate
  The glory of the earth;
And my vesper hymn ring gladly,
  With the thrill of careless mirth.

Second Speaker.

I wish I were a floweret,
  To blossom in the grove;
I'd spread my opening leaflets
  Among the plants I love,—
No hand should roughly cull me,
  And bid my odors fly;
I silently would ope to life,
  And quietly would die.

Third Speaker.

I wish I was a gold fish,
  To seek the sunny wave,
To part the gentle ripple,
  And amid its coolness lave;
I'd glide through day delighted,
  Beneath the azure sky,
And when night came on in softness,
  Seek the star-light's milder eye.

Fourth Speaker.

Hush, hush, romantic prattlers,
  You know not what you say,
When *soul*, the crown of mortals,
  You would lightly throw away:
What is the songster's warble,
  And the floweret's blush refined,
To the noble thought of Deity,
  Within your opening mind?

LESSON VII.

THINGS BY THEIR RIGHT NAMES.

FATHER—CHARLES.

Charles. Papa, you grow very lazy I think. You used
to tell me a great many stories, but now you hardly ever tell
23

me any. I wish you would tell me a very pretty one, dear
papa.

Father. Well, with all my heart—what shall it be?

Charles. A bloody murder, papa!

Father. A bloody murder! Well then—Once upon a
time, some men, dressed all alike——

Charles. With black crape over their faces?

Father. No; they had steel caps on:—having crossed a
dark heath, wound cautiously along the skirts of a deep forest——

Charles. They were ill-looking fellows, I dare say.

Father. I cannot say so; on the contrary, they were tall
personable men, as most, one shall see:—leaving on their
right hand an old ruined tower on the hill——

Charles. At midnight, just as the clock struck twelve;
was it not, papa?

Father. No, really; it was on a fine balmy summer's
morning:—and moved forward, one behind another——

Charles. As still as death, creeping along under the
hedges.

Father. On the contrary—they walked remarkably upright; and so far from endeavoring to be hushed and still,
they made a loud noise as they came along, with several
sorts of instruments.

Charles. But, papa, they would be found out immediately.

Father. They did not seem to wish to conceal themselves;
on the contrary, they gloried in what they were about.—They
moved forward, I say, to a large plain, where stood a neat
pretty village, which they set on fire——

Charles. Set a village on fire? wicked wretches!

Father. And while it was burning, they murdered twenty
thousand men.

Charles. O fie! papa! you do not intend I should believe
this; I thought all along you were making up a tale, as you
often do; but you shall not catch me this time. What! they
lay still, I suppose, and let these fellows cut their throats!

Father. No, truly, they resisted as long as they could.

Charles. How should these men kill twenty thousand
people, pray?

Father. Why not? the *murderers* were thirty thousand.

Charles. O, now I have found you out—I understand
you! You mean a battle.

Father. Indeed I do. I do not know of any *murderers*
half so bloody.

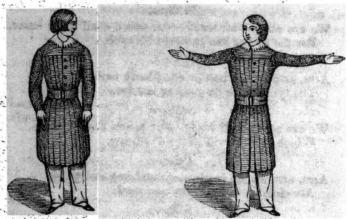

These Figures represent *two* boys in the act of speaking a dialogue. The one *addressed* is in the *second* position; it is not necessary, nor, perhaps, proper, to keep in this position *all* the time the other speaker is declaiming, but it will be well, in general, to assume it, at least before the *reply* is made. It will enable the respondent to come into the *first* position as he begins, and thus impart life and beauty to his action. Whether he change or not, however, must depend somewhat upon the style of the composition and the spirit of his part. The pupil will notice, particularly, that the breast of each Figure is *full front* to the audience. This is a point of considerable importance. Whether the speakers be *two* or a *greater number*, each must stand in such a manner, that the language of his *countenance* shall be as distinct to the *eye*, as that of his *voice* is to the *ear*. The dialogue is *between the speakers*, but it is intended for the *amusement* or *gratification* of the *audience*. How ill-bred it appears when we see boys thus engaged, standing directly face to face, and almost turning their backs to those who have kindly assembled to witness their juvenile performances, in an art, which more than almost any other, perhaps, demands of its votaries, taste, skill, and propriety of deportment.

LESSON VIII.

WAR SONG OF THE REVOLUTION.—Anonymous.

OFFICERS—SOLDIERS.

This is a good selection for class or concert speaking—the officers should be six, or any other reasonable number, arranged on one side, and the soldiers twenty or more.

Officers.

Arm, arm for the battle—Invasion has come—
    His shadow has darkened our soil.

Soldiers.

We are ready—all ready—our sword shall strike home,
  Ere the robber has gathered his spoil.

Officers.

Arm, arm for the battle—'tis liberty calls,
  The tyrants are leagued as her foe.

Soldiers.

We are ready—all ready—our hearts are her walls,
  Which tyrants will never o'erthrow.

Officers.

Arm, arm for the battle—our children and wives
  Are sinking with terrors oppressed.

Soldiers.

We are ready—all ready—and pledged are our lives,
  That these dear ones in safety shall rest.

Officers.

Arm, arm for the battle—and cowards may fly—
  The foe like a torrent sweeps on.

Soldiers.

We are ready—all ready—we'll shout ere we die—
  Hurrah! for the battle is won.

LESSON IX.

WINTER.—Anonymous.

FIRST SPEAKER—SECOND SPEAKER.

First Speaker.

How dreary is winter! how sad is the hour
When the bleak winds have scattered the leaves from the
    bower,
  And the snow on the meadow lies cold!

Second Speaker.

How pleasant is winter, how sweet is the day,
When blessed with the warmth of the fire's cheering ray,
  With our friends sweet communion we hold.

First Speaker.

The voice of the songsters can cheer us no more,
Their days of rejoicing and pleasure are o'er—
  To the southward they 've taken their way.

Second Speaker.

'Tis the time for reflection, when winter appears,
When our thoughts may ascend from this valley of tears,
  To the regions of infinite day.

First Speaker.

'Tis an emblem of life, when the spring time is past,
And dreary old age is approaching at last,
  And the sun is unclouded no more.

Second Speaker.

'Tis an emblem of purity, free from a stain,
Of such as in Heaven forever shall reign,
  When the tempests of life-time are o'er.

LESSON X.

THE CHILDREN'S CHOICE.—Mrs. Gilman.

MOTHER, (OR FATHER,)—JOHN—WILLIAM.

John.

I MEAN to be a soldier,
  With uniform quite new,
I wish they 'd let me have a drum,
  And be a captain too,—
I would go amid the battle,
  With my broad sword in my hand,
And hear the cannon rattle,
  And the music all so grand.

Mother, (or Father.)

My son! my son! what if that sword
  Should strike a noble heart,
And bid some loving father
  From his little ones depart?
What comfort would your waving plumes,
  And brilliant dress bestow,

23*

When you thought upon his widow's tears
And her orphan's cry of woe.

William.

I mean to be a President,
    And rule each rising state,
And hold my levees once a week,
    For all the gay and great:
I'll be a king, except a crown,
    For that they won't allow,
And I'll find out what the tariff is,
    That puzzles me so now.

Mother, (or Father.)

My son! my son! the cares of state,
    Are thorns upon the breast,
That ever pierce the good man's heart,
    And rob him of his rest:
The great and gay to him appear,
    As trifling as the dust,
For he knows how little they are worth,
    How faithless is their trust.
Oh! children, sad it makes my soul
    To hear your playful strain;
I cannot bear to chill your path
    With images of pain—
Yet humbly take what God bestows,
    And, like his own fair flowers,
Look up in sunshine with a smile,
    And gently bend in showers.

LESSON XI.

LIFE, DEATH, AND ETERNITY.—ANONYMOUS.

FIRST SPEAKER—SECOND SPEAKER—THIRD SPEAKER.

First Speaker.

A SHADOW moving by one's side,
    That would a substance seem,
That is, yet is not,—though descried,—
    Like skies beneath the stream:

A tree that's ever in the bloom,
  Whose fruit is never ripe ;
A wish for joys that never come,—
  Such are the hopes of Life.

    Second Speaker.

A dark, inevitable night,
  A blank that will remain ;
A waiting for the morning light,
  When waiting is in vain ;
A gulf where pathway never led,
  To show the deep beneath ;
A thing we know not, yet we dread,—
  That dreaded thing is Death.

    Third Speaker.

The vaulted void of purple sky,
  That every where extends,
That stretches from the dazzled eye,
  In space that never ends ;
A morning whose uprisen sun
  No setting e'er shall see ;
A day that comes without a noon,—
  Such is Eternity.

LESSON XII.

THE WORLD.—ANONYMOUS.

FIRST CHILD—SECOND CHILD.

First Child. How beautiful the world is ! The green earth covered with flowers—the trees laden with rich blossoms—the blue sky, the bright water, and the golden sunshine. The world is, indeed, beautiful, and He who made it must be beautiful.

Second Child. It is a happy world. Hark ! how the merry birds sing—and the young lambs—see ! how they gambol on the hill-side. Even the trees wave and the brooks ripple in gladness. Yon Eagle !—Ah ! how joyously he soars up to the glorious heavens—the bird of liberty, the bird of America.

First Child. Yes ;

" His throne is on the mountain top ;
    His fields the boundless air ;
And hoary peaks, that proudly prop
    The skies—his dwellings are.

" He rises like a thing of light,
    Amid the noontide blaze ;
The midway sun is clear and bright—
    It cannot dim his gaze "

Second Child. It is happy—I see it and hear it all about me—nay, I feel it—here, in the glow, the eloquent glow of my own heart. He who made it must be happy.

First Child. It is a great world. Look off to the mighty ocean when the storm is upon it ; to the huge mountain, when the thunder and the lightnings play over it ; to the vast forest—the interminable waste,—the sun, the moon, and the myriads of fair stars, countless as the sands upon the sea-shore. It is a great, a magnificent world,—and He who made it,—Oh ! He is the perfection of all loveliness, all goodness, all greatness, all gloriousness !

LESSON XIII.

THE LAND OF THE BLEST.—Mrs. Abdy.

FATHER—CHILD.

Child.

Dear Father, I ask for my mother in vain,
Has she sought some far country her health to regain ;
Has she left our cold climate of frost and of snow,
For some warm sunny land where the soft breezes blow ?

Father.

Yes, yes, gentle boy, thy loved mother has gone
To a climate where sorrow and pains are unknown ;
Her spirit is strengthened, her frame is at rest,
There is health, there is peace, in the Land of the Blest.

Child.

Is that land, my dear Father, more lovely than ours—
Are the rivers more clear, and more blooming the flowers ;

Does Summer shine over it all the year long—
Is it cheered by the glad sounds of music and song?

Father.

Yes, the flowers are despoiled not by winter or night,
The well-springs of life are exhaustless and bright;
And by exquisite voices sweet hymns are addressed
To the Lord who reigns over the Land of the Blest.

Child.

Yet that land to my mother will lonely appear,
She shrunk from the glance of a stranger, while here;
From her foreign companions I know she will flee,
And sigh, dearest Father, for you and for me.

Father.

My darling, thy mother rejoices to gaze
On the long severed friends of her earliest days;
Her parents have there found a mansion of rest,
And they welcome their child to the Land of the Blest.

Child.

How I long to partake of such meetings of bliss,
That land must be surely more happy than this;
On you, my kind Father, the journey depends,—
Let us go to my mother, her kindred, and friends.

Father.

Not on me, love; I trust I may reach that bright clime,
But in patience I stay till the Lord's chosen time,
And must strive while awaiting his gracious behest,
To guide thy young steps to the Land of the Blest.

Thou must toil through a world full of dangers, my boy,
Thy peace it may blight and thy virtue destroy;
Nor wilt thou, alas! be withheld from its snares
By a mother's fond counsels, a mother's fond prayers.

Yet fear not—the God whose direction we crave,
Is mighty to strengthen, to shield, and to save;
And his hand may yet lead thee, a glorified guest,
To the home of thy mother, the Land of the Blest.

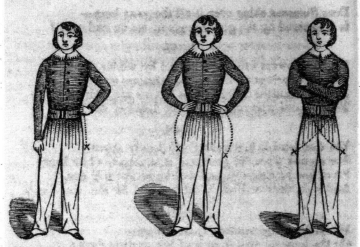

THESE Figures are designed to exhibit positions of the hands and arms which a boy may very properly assume, when he is the *addressed* or *listening* party in a dialogue. To stand, when not speaking, *always with the hands down by the side,* after the manner of the *first* Figure, on page 267, however easily and neatly managed, could not produce other than a monotonous and unpolished effect.—The first of the three Figures is represented with the *left* arm a *kimbo,* the hand resting on the belt at the point of the *hip,* with the fingers pressed inward upon the palm ; the *second* has *both* arms a kimbo, with the hands clasping the hips, having the fingers in *front;* the *third* Figure presents the arms *folded,*—the arms are crossed and enclose each other, the fingers of the *right hand,* holding the *left arm,* and the *left* hand passing under the *right* arm. This arrangement of the arms may be *reversed* at the pleasure of the speaker. These positions should not be *assumed* or *changed* without *discretion;* directed by *propriety,* they are becoming and graceful ; they do *not* give to the speaker an air of false consequence, or *affectation*—they are appropriate and manly.

LESSON XIV.

MAN AND WOMAN.—MONTGOMERY.

FIRST SPEAKER—SECOND SPEAKER.

First Speaker.

MAN is the proud and lofty pine,
That frowns on many a wave-beat shore ;

Second Speaker.

Woman, the young and tender vine,
Whose curling tendrils round it twine,
And deck its rough bark sweetly o'er.

First Speaker.

Man is the rock, whose towering crest
Nods o'er the mountain's barren side;

Second Speaker.

Woman, the soft and mossy vest,
That loves to clasp its sterile breast,
And wreathe its brow with verdant pride.

First Speaker.

Man is the cloud of coming storm,
Dark as the raven's murky plume,

Second Speaker.

Save where the sun-beam, light and warm,
Of woman's soul—of woman's form,
Gleams brightly through the gathering gloom.

First Speaker.

Yes, 'tis to lovely woman given,
To soothe our griefs, our woes allay—
To heal the heart by misery riven—
Change earth into an embryo heaven,—
And drive life's fiercest cares away.

LESSON XV.

STRANGER AND CHILD.—Mrs. Hemans.

Stranger.

Why wouldest thou leave me, oh! gentle child?
Thy home on the mountain is bleak and wild,
A straw-roofed cabin with lowly wall—
Mine is a fair and pillared hall,
Where many an image of marble gleams,
And the sunshine of picture forever streams.

Child.

Oh! green is the turf where my brothers play,
Through the long bright hours of the summer day ;
They find the red cup-moss where they climb,
And they chase the bee o'er the scented thyme,
And the rocks where the heath-flower blooms they know—
Stranger! kind stranger! oh! let me go.

Stranger.

Content thee, boy! in my bower to dwell,
There are sweet sounds which thou lovest well ;
Flutes on the air in the stilly noon,
Harps which the wandering breezes tune ;
And the silvery wood-note of many a bird,
Whose voice was ne'er in thy mountains heard.

Child.

Oh! my mother sings at the twilight's fall,
A song of the hills far more sweet than all ;
She sings it under our own green tree,
To the babe half-slumbering on her knee ;
I dreamed last night of that music low—
Stranger! kind stranger! oh! let me go.

Stranger.

Thy mother is gone from her cares to rest,
She hath taken the babe on her quiet breast ;
Thou wouldest meet her footstep, my boy, no more,
Nor hear her song at the cabin door.
Come thou with me to the vineyards nigh,
And we'll pluck the grapes of the richest dye.

Child.

Is my mother gone from her home away ?—
But I know that my brothers are there at play ;
I know they are gathering the fox-glove's bell,
Or the long fern-leaves of the sparkling well,
Or they launch their boats where the bright streams flow,—
Stranger! kind stranger! oh! let me go.

Stranger.

Fair child, thy brothers are wanderers now,
They sport no more on the mountain's brow ;
They have left the fern by the spring's green side,

And the streams where the fairy barks were tried.
Be thou at peace in thy brighter lot,
For thy cabin-home is a lonely spot.

Child.

Are they gone, all gone from the sunny hill?
But the bird and the blue-fly rove o'er it still;
And the red deer bound in their gladness free;
And the heath is bent by the singing bee;
And the waters leap, and the fresh winds blow,—
Stranger! kind stranger! oh! let me go.

LESSON XVI.

CANUTE'S REPROOF.—Aikin.

Canute, *King of England*—Oswald, Offa, *Courtiers.*

Scene—*The sea-side, near Southampton, the tide coming in.*

Canute. Is it true, my friends, what you have so often told me, that I am the greatest of monarchs?

Offa. It is true, my liege; you are the most powerful of all kings.

Oswald. We are all your slaves; we kiss the dust of your feet.

Offa. Not only we, but even the elements, are your slaves. The land obeys you from shore to shore; and the sea obeys you.

Canute. Does the sea, with its loud boisterous waves, obey me? Will that terrible element be still at my bidding?

Offa. Yes, the sea is yours; it was made to bear your ships upon its bosom, and to pour the treasures of the world at your royal feet. It is boisterous to your enemies, but it knows you to be its sovereign.

Canute. Is not the tide coming up?

Oswald. Yes, my liege; you may perceive the swell already.

Canute. Bring me a chair, then; set it here upon the sands.

Offa. Where the tide is coming up, my gracious lord?

Canute. Yes, set it just here. (*Places himself in the chair.*)

24

Oswald. (*Aside.*) I wonder what he is going to do!

Offa. (*Aside.*) Surely he is not such a fool as to believe us!

Canute. O, mighty Ocean! thou art my subject; my courtiers tell me so; and it is thy bounden duty to obey me. Thus, then, I stretch my sceptre over thee, and command thee to retire. Roll back thy swelling waves, nor let them presume to wet the feet of me, thy royal master.

Oswald. (*Aside.*) I believe the sea will pay very little regard to his royal commands.

Offa. See how fast the tide rises!

Oswald. The next wave will come up to the chair. It is folly to stay; we shall be covered with salt water.

Canute. Well, does the sea obey my commands? If it be my subject, it is a very rebellious subject. See how it swells, and dashes the angry foam and salt spray over my sacred person. (*Rises.*) Vile sycophants! did you think I was the dupe of your base lies? that I believed your abject flatteries? Know, there is only one being whom the sea will obey. He is Sovereign of heaven and earth, King of kings, and Lord of lords. It is only he who can say to the ocean, "Thus far shalt thou go, but no farther, and here shall thy proud waves be stayed." A king is but a man; and man is but a worm. Shall a worm assume the power of the great God, and think the elements will obey him? Take away this crown, I will never wear it more. May kings learn to be humble from my example, and courtiers learn truth from your disgrace!

LESSON XVII.

THE BROTHERS.—Sprague.

FIRST BOY—SECOND BOY.

First Boy.

We are but two—the others sleep
Through death's untroubled night;
We are but two—Oh let us keep
The link that binds us bright.

Second Boy.

Heart leaps to heart—the sacred flood
That warms us is the same;

That good old man—his honest blood
  Alike we fondly claim.

First Boy.

We in one mother's arms were locked,
  Long be her love repaid ;
In the same cradle we were rocked,
  Round the same hearth we played.

Second Boy.

Our boyish sports were all the same,
  Each little joy and woe ;
Let manhood keep alive the flame
  Lit up so long ago.

Both.

We are but two—be that the band
  To hold us till we die ;

THE boy on the *left* —from the audience— takes the hand of the boy on the *right*, each, at the same time, passing his arm affectionately round the neck of the other, as will be seen by the *hands* on the up- per part of the shoulders. The arm of the boy on the right, passes *under* that of the boy on the left. The placing of the *feet*, seen in the picture, needs no explanation.

Shoulder to shoulder let us stand,
  Till side by side we lie.

LESSON XVIII.

INDIAN CHANT.—Schoolcraft.

FIRST INDIAN—SECOND INDIAN—THIRD INDIAN—FOURTH INDI-
  AN—FIFTH INDIAN—SIXTH INDIAN.

First Indian.

THE eagles scream on high,
  They whet their forked beaks :

Raise—raise the battle cry,
'Tis fame our leader seeks.

Second Indian.

'Tis fame my soul desires,
By deeds of martial strife:
Give—give me warlike fires,
Or take—ah take my life.

Third Indian.

The deer awhile may go
Unhunted o'er the heath,
For now I seek a nobler foe,
And prize a nobler death.

Fourth Indian.

Lance and quiver, club and bow,
Now alone attract my sight;
I will go where warriors go,
I will fight where warriors fight.

Fifth Indian.

Now my heart with valor burns,
I my lance in fury shake;
He who falters, he who turns,
Give him fagot, fire and stake.

Sixth Indian.

See my visage scarred and red—
See my brows with trophies bright—
Such the brows that warriors dread—
Such the trophies of the fight.

LESSON XIX.

PATRIOTISM.—BRETSON.

FIRST SPEAKER—SECOND SPEAKER.

First Speaker.

POOR is his triumph, and disgraced his name,
Who draws the sword for empire, wealth, and fame;

For him, though wealth be blown on every wind,
Though fame announce him mightiest of mankind,
Though twice ten nations crouch beneath his blade,
Virtue disowns him, and his glories fade;
For him no prayers are poured, no pæans sung;
No blessings chanted from a nation's tongue:
Blood marks the path to his untimely bier;
The curse of widows, and the orphan's tear,
Cry high to heaven for vengeance on his head:
Alive detested, and accurst when dead;
Indignant of his deeds, the muse who sings
Th' undaunted truth, and scorns to flatter kings,
Shall show the monster in his hideous form,
And mark him as an earthquake or a storm.

Second Speaker.

Not so, the patriot chief, who dared withstand
The base invaders of his native land;
Who made her weal his noblest, only end;
Ruled but to serve her; fought but to defend;
Who firmly virtuous, and severely brave,
Sunk with the freedom that he could not save,
On worth like his the muse delights to wait;
Reveres alike in triumph or defeat;
Crowns with true glory, and with spotless fame,
And honors Pæoli's more than Frederick's name.

LESSON XX.

THE CHAMBER OF SICKNESS.—Colton.

FIRST VOICE—SECOND VOICE.

First Voice.

How awful the place—how gloomy—how chill!
Where the pangs of disease are lingering still,
    And the life-pulse is fluttering in death.

Second Voice.

How delightful the place—how peaceful—how bright;
There, calmly, and sweetly, the taper's soft light,
    Shines—an image of man's fleeting breath.

24*

First Voice.

There the angel of death on the vitals is preying,
While beauty and loveliness fast are decaying,
And life's joys are all fading away.

Second Voice.

There the spirits of mercy round the pillow are flying,
As the angel-smile plays on the lips of the dying,
And hope cheers the soul with her ray.

First Voice.

How the spirit is pained, e'en when loved ones are near,
Or sympathy bathes its lone couch with a tear;
Its hopes are all dead—its joy is despair.

Second Voice.

How the holiest endearments that kindred souls cherish,
Though the mortal decay and its graces all perish,
Are perfected and purified there.

First Voice.

How ghastly the visage of death doth appear,
How frightful the thought of the shroud and the bier,
And the blood-crested worm how vile!

Second Voice.

How friendly the hand that faith is now lending,
How benignant her look o'er the pillow while bending,
How sweet, how assuring her smile!

First Voice.

There, in triumph, the death-knell is fitfully pealing,
While the shivering chill to the cold heart is stealing,
And the life-current warms—no—never.

Second Voice.

Hear the joy-speaking voice of some angel calling—
As the visions of heaven, on the rapt soul are falling,
And hope—is fruition for ever.

LESSON XXI.

FATHER'S BIRTH-DAY.—Edgeworth.

CHERRY—PHILIP.

A new mown field.—Cherry and Philip carrying a large basket of green boughs and flowers.

Cherry. Here, Philip, let us set it down here, for I am quite tired.

Philip. Tired! but you must not be tired, Cherry; consider that this is our father's birth-day, and we have a great, great deal to do! to make his room into a bower with these green branches and honey-suckles. Oh, it will be beautiful, with roses here and there, in garlands; and then we must make nosegays for papa and mamma, and aunts, and have a green bough for every house in the village. Oh! Cherry, indeed you must not say you are tired.

Cherry. Well I will not: but I may say I am hot, may I not?

Philip. Hot, are you? well, so I am, I must confess, hot enough, if that's all: but push your hat back as I do—off with this frilikin ruff, that you have about your neck. There, now, sit down comfortably, and I will fan you with this great green fan. (*Fans her with a green bough.*) Is not that pleasant, Cherry?

Cherry. Very pleasant, only I think it makes me hotter afterwards; besides, it must make you all the time so very hot, doing it. Now, Philip, let us make our nosegays; that will cool us best. Here, this moss-rose bud, I'll have for mamma.

Philip. But it is not her birth-day.

Cherry. But she may have a rose for all that, may not she? Here, Philip, is a beautiful blush-rose for papa.

Philip. Mamma should have the blush-rose, because she is a woman, and blushes. But I will tell you what, Cherry, it will not be right to give papa a red, and mamma a white rose.

Cherry. Why?

Philip. Because it would seem as if they had quarreled.

Cherry. (*Laughing.*) Quarreled!

Philip. (*Gravely.*) I assure you it is no laughing matter, as you would know if you had read the history of England, as I have. A great while ago, in the dark ages, the houses of York and Lancaster—but you are not old enough to understand me.

Cherry. But I know *what* I am old enough to understand, and something that you don't know, Philip.

Philip. What?

Cherry. Oh! that is a secret.

Philip. A secret! and you will not tell it to Philip!

Cherry. No, not to Philip, or anybody; for I was desired not.

Philip. By whom?

Cherry. Oh! by somebody; but that's a secret too, and I have promised not to tell till the time comes, and the time will come this evening, this very evening—after dinner—after tea, you will see!—you will be very much surprised; and you will be very happy; and you will then know all.

Philip. I know all now, Cherry.

Cherry. Oh! no, indeed, Philip, you do not know about Edwin.

Philip. Yes, but I do.

Cherry. And about the play?

Philip. Oh! hush! take care—you promised not to tell.

Cherry. But since you know it——

Philip. But how do you know that I know it?

Cherry. My dear! did you not say so?

Philip. But you might tell me by accident more than I know; and I should be very sorry for that, because it would not be right.

Cherry. Then the best way is for you to tell me, Philip, all that you know.

Philip. All that I know is, that my brother Edwin has written a little play, for my father's birth-day.

Cherry. Ah! but I know the name.

Philip. So do I. But come, we must go along.

LESSON XXII.

KING ALFRED AND THE PEASANT.—Knowles.

ALFRED—EDWIN.

Scene—*The inside of Edwin's Hut.*

Edwin. How feel you now?

Alfred. As one that hath escaped
With a rich gem he feared he should be stripped of.

Edwin. Nay, give not over yet—although the fare

I guess is poor to what the board provides,
You're wont to sit at.

Alfred. Rich!—Was never meat
Served up at banquet with its seasoning.
'Tis hunger makes a feast! No spicery
Like that of its rare dish! All else is tasteless!
Plain dressing, which the sated palate heeds not!

Edwin. How long were you bewildered in the forest?

Alfred. Since yesternight.

Edwin. So, we have lost the day?

Alfred. We have.

Edwin. And do you think the country's lost?

Alfred. Not lost.

Edwin. You say her bands are all dispersed?

Alfred. They may collect again.

Edwin. The king, you say,
Survived the battle.

Alfred. Yes.

Edwin. (*After a pause.*) The country lives
If the king lives! The people love the king.
The present panic o'er, his banner yet
Would rally them. Believe you he is safe?

Alfred. I hope he is.

Edwin. No Saxon but hopes that.

Alfred. Of this be sure—the storm that sweeps the land
Blows not aloof from him; nor long as e'er
The meanest head's exposed, will he remain
Content with shelter!

Edwin. Happy were the head
That by its self-exposing, sheltered him.

Alfred. You love the king?

Edwin. Who does not love the king?
You're sure he left the field with life?

Alfred. He did.

Edwin. Unhurt?

Alfred. Unhurt.

Edwin. Thank Heaven!—Did many men
Of note escape along with him?

Alfred. There did.

Edwin. He's guarded then?

Alfred. No!

Edwin. No! how's that?

Alfred. They were commanded from him.

Edwin. They were traitors
That did obey.

Alfred. Would'st have them disobey
The king?
  Edwin. For the king's sake.
  Alfred. For the king's sake,
They left him.
  Edwin. How?
  Alfred. To speed them to their holds,
And ward them for the king, till he should find
As many backers as would warrant him
To take the field again.
  Edwin. He wanders then,
Perhaps alone.—Perhaps no better furnished
Than thou hast been.—No charger to assist
His flight.—No larder to supply him food.
The leafy penthouse of the forest tree
Perhaps his roof at night,—its knotted root
His pillow,—or, at best, he lodges in
Some sorry shed like this that shelters thee;
With such another pallet as hard need
Will make thee bear to stretch thy limbs upon.
  Alfred. Even so.
  Edwin. Even so? Why, hast thou e'er shed tears
To say it with dry eyes, while mine do rain
That only echo thee? Would I could find
My king!
  Alfred. He's nearer than thou thinkest.
  Edwin. How!—What!
  Alfred. He grasps thee by the hand, and thanks thee for
His life.

This posture not unfrequently, becomes necessary, in the exercises of school exhibitions, and the pupil is sometimes troubled to know *how* to assume it; he has but to recollect, however, that he should kneel upon the knee *farthest from* the party addressed, and the difficulty is over. Young children and rustics, generally fall upon *both* knees.

Edwin. (*Kneeling.*) My king! My king! Sure Providence

With its own hand has led thee to my hut.
I am thy neat-herd, though thou knowest me not.
Thou art my master, well as king, although
Before this hour I ne'er set eyes upon thee!
  Alfred. So near my castle! Show me to it.
  Edwin. Not to-night.
  Alfred. Why not?
  Edwin. Delay till morning! Not
To-night for any cause! 'Twill be a storm—
The wind is rising—and as we came in
I felt a thunder drop.

LESSON XXIII.

AMERICAN BOY AND ENGLISH BOY.

MRS. GILMAN AND MRS. HEMANS.

American Boy speaks.

Look from the ancient mountains down,
  My noble English boy!
Thy country's fields around thee gleam,
  In sunlight and in joy.

Ages have rolled since foeman's march
  Passed o'er that old firm sod ;
For well the land hath fealty held
  To freedom and to God!

Gaze proudly on, my English boy!
  And let thy kindling mind
Drink in the spirit of high thought,
  From every chainless wind.

Gaze proudly on—gaze further yet,
  My gallant English boy!
Yon blue seas bear thy country's flag,
  The billow's pride and joy.

Those waves in many a fight have closed
  Above her faithful dead ;
That red cross flag victoriously
  Has floated o'er their bed.

Lift up thy heart, my English boy !
  And pray like them to stand,
Should God so summon thee, to guard
  The altars of the land.

English Boy speaks.

And thou, my young American,
  Stand firmly on the earth,
Where noble deeds and mental power
  Yield titles over birth.

A hallowed land thou claimest, my boy,
  By early stuggles bought ;
Heaped up with noble memories,
  And wide,—aye, wide as thought.

What, though you boast no ancient towers,
  Where ivied streamers twine ?
The laurel lives upon your soil—
  The laurel, boy, is thine.

And who shall gaze on yon *blue sea,*
  If thou must turn away,
When thy brave country's stripes and stars,
  Are floating in the day ?

Thine is a land for patriot thought ;
  There sleep the good and brave ;
There kneel, my boy, and altars raise
  Above the martyr's grave.

And when thou r't told of knighthoods shields,
  And English battles won—
Look up, my boy, and breathe one word—
  The name of WASHINGTON.

LESSON XXIV.

CHOICE OF COUNTRIES.—Mrs. GILMAN.

FIRST SPEAKER—SECOND SPEAKER—THIRD SPEAKER—FOURTH
SPEAKER.

First Speaker.

I WOULD cross the wide Atlantic,
  And the cliffs of England hail,

For there my country's fathers
  First set their western sail.
I would view its domes and palaces,
  And tread each learned hall,
And on the soil where Newton trod,
  My foot should proudly fall.
I would gaze upon its landscapes,
  The dell and sunny glade,
And tread with awe the cloistered aisle,
  Where Addison is laid.

Second Speaker.

I would seek the Indian Ocean,
  Where the sea-shell loves to grow,
Where the tints upon its bosom,
  In gorgeous beauty glow.
I would chase the parting billow
  For treasures new and rare,
And with wreaths of blushing coral
  Entwine my waving hair.

Third Speaker.

I would be a ship's commander,
  And find the northern pole,
While o'er untraveled oceans
  My venturous bark should roll.
Or I'd seek untrodden islands,
  Amid Antarctic seas,
And the standard of my country,
  Plant first before the breeze.

Fourth Speaker.

The whole broad earth is beautiful
  To minds attuned aright,
And whereso'er my feet have turned,
  A smile has met my sight.
The city, with its bustling walk,
  Its splendor, wealth, and power,—
A ramble by the river side,—
  A passing summer flower;
The meadow green, the ocean's swell,
  The forest waving free,
Are gifts of God, and speak in tones
  Of kindliness to me.

25

And oh, where'er my lot is cast,
Where'er my footsteps roam,
If those I love are near to me,
I feel that spot my home.

LESSON XXV.

THE TWO ROBBERS.—AIKIN.

ALEXANDER—ROBBER—SOLDIERS.

SCENE—*Alexander the Great, in his tent.—Guards.—A man with a fierce countenance, chained and fettered, brought before him.*

Alexander. What, art thou the Thracian robber, of whose exploits I have heard so much?

Robber. I am a Thracian, and a soldier.

Alexander. A soldier!—a thief, a plunderer, an assassin! the pest of the country! I could honor thy courage, but I must detest and punish thy crimes.

Robber. What have I done of which *you* can complain?

Alexander. Hast thou not set at defiance my authority, violated the public peace, and passed thy life in injuring the persons and properties of thy fellow-subjects?

Robber. Alexander! I am your captive—I must hear what you please to say, and endure what you please to inflict. But my soul is unconquered; and if I reply at all to your reproaches, I will reply like a free man.

Alexander. Speak freely. Far be it from me to take the advantage of my power to silence those with whom I deign to converse!

Robber. I must then answer your question by another. How have *you* passed your life?

Alexander. Like a hero. Ask Fame, and she will tell you. Among the brave I have been the bravest: among sovereigns, the noblest: among conquerors, the mightiest.

Robber. And does not Fame speak of me, too? Was there ever a bolder captain of a more valiant band? Was there ever—But I scorn to boast. You yourself know that I have not been easily subdued.

Alexander. Still, what are you but a *robber*—a base, dishonest *robber?*

Robber. And what is a *conqueror?* Have not you, too, gone about the earth like an evil genius, blasting the fair fruits of peace and industry;—plundering, ravaging, killing, without law, without justice, merely to gratify an insatiable lust for dominion? All that I have done to a single district with a hundred followers, you have done to whole nations with a hundred thousand. If I have stripped individuals, you have ruined kings and princes. If I have burned a few hamlets, you have desolated the most flourishing kingdoms and cities of the earth. What is then the difference, but that as you were born a king, and I a private man, you have been able to become a mightier *robber* than I?

Alexander. But if I have taken like a king, I have given like a king. If I have subverted empires, I have founded greater. I have cherished arts, commerce, and philosophy.

Robber. I, too, have freely given to the poor what I took from the rich. I have established order and discipline among the most ferocious of mankind ; and have stretched out my protecting arm over the oppressed. I know, indeed, little of the philosophy you talk of ; but I believe neither you nor I shall ever repay to the world the mischiefs we have done it.

Alexander. Leave me—take off his chains, and use him well. (*Exit Robber.*)—Are we then so much alike ?—Alexander to a robber ?—Let me reflect.

LESSON XXVI.

TELL'S MEETING WITH HIS PATRIOT FRIENDS.—Knowles.

TELL—ERNI—VERNER—FURST.

Scene—*A Lake and Mountains.*

Tell. Ye crags and peaks, I 'm with you once again!
I hold to you the hands ye first beheld,
To show they still are free. Methinks I hear
A spirit in your echoes answer me,
And bid your tenant welcome to his home
Again!—O, sacred forms, how proud you look!
How high you lift your heads into the sky!
How huge you are! how mighty, and how free!
Ye are the things that tower, that shine—whose smile

Makes glad—whose frown is terrible—whose forms,
Robed or unrobed, do all the impress wear.
Of awe divine. Ye guards of liberty,
I'm with you once again! I call to you
With all my voice!—I hold my hands to you
To show they still are free. I rush to you.
As though I could embrace you!

Erni. (*Without.*) William! William!
Tell. Here, Erni, here!

Erni enters.

Erni. You're sure to keep the time
That comes before the hour.
Tell. The hour
Will soon be here. O when will liberty
Be here, my Erni? That's my thought, which still
I find beside. Scaling yonder peak,
I saw an eagle wheeling near its brow
O'er the abyss:—his broad-expanded wings
Lay calm and motionless upon the air,
As if he floated there without their aid,
By the sole act of his unlorded will,
That buoyed him proudly up. Instinctively
I bent my bow; yet kept he rounding still
His airy circle, as in the delight
Of measuring the ample range beneath,
And round about absorbed, he heeded not
The death that threatened him.—I could not shoot!
'Twas liberty!—I turned my bow aside,
And let him soar away!

Enter Verner and Furst.

Tell. Here, friends!—Well met!—Do we go on?
Verner. We do.
Tell. Then you can count upon the friends you named?
Verner. On every man of them.
Furst. And I on mine.
Erni. Not one I sounded, but doth count his blood
As water in the cause! Then fix the day
Before we part.
Verner. No, Erni; rather wait
For some new outrage to amaze and rouse
The common mind, which does not brood so much
On wrongs gone by, as it doth quiver with
The sense of present ones.

Tell. (*To Verner.*) I wish with Erni,
But think with thee. Yet when I ask myself
On whom the wrongs shall light for which we wait—
Whose vineyard they'll uproot—whose flocks they'll ravage—
Whose threshold they'll profane—whose hearth pollute—
Whose roof they'll fire ?—When this I ask myself,
And think upon the blood of pious sons,
The tears of venerable fathers, and
The shrieks of mothers, fluttering round their spoiled,
And nestless young—I almost take the part
Of generous indignation, that doth blush
At such expense to wait on sober prudence.
     Furst. Yet it is best.
     Tell. On that we're all agreed !
Who fears the issue when the day shall come ?
     Verner. Not I !
     Furst. Nor I !
     Erni. Nor I !
     Tell. I'm not the man
To mar this harmony. Nor I, no more
Than any of you ! You commit to me
The warning of the rest. Remember, then,
My dagger sent to any one of you,
As time may press, is word enough : the others
I'll see myself. Our course is clear—
When next we meet upon this theme,
All Switzerland shall witness what we do !

LESSON XXVII.

THE LITTLE REBELS.—Anonymous.

Founded on Fact.

GEN. HOWE—HIS AID—SENTINEL—GEORGE—JAMES—BOYS.

Scene 1—*Boston Common.—A crowd of Boys assembled near the Skating Pond.*

George. Here it is again, boys. The ice is all broken in by the red-coats. We shall have no fun to-day.
James. I wish we were not boys. If I were big enough to carry a sword and a musket, I would drive 'em out of the
25*

land, faster than neighbor Tuft's dog ever went out of father's store.

George. And what if we are boys? I, for one, have no mind to bear this treatment any longer.

All. Right, George, right!

James. But what can we do, boys?

George. I'll tell you. Form a line of march, and with drum, and fife, and colors, wait upon General Howe, at his tent, and tell him we will not be insulted by British soldiers, nor any other soldiers.

All. Hurra! Hurra! Hurra! (*Exeunt.*) (*A short pause, and then again ringing without.*) Hurra! Hurra! Hurra!

SCENE 2.—*General Howe's Head Quarters.—A sentinel pacing before the door with a musket over his shoulder.—Noise of fife and drum at a distance.*

Sentinel. What in the name of wonder can that be? Are they up in arms again in this rascally town? A troop of a hundred boys, as I live. An Indian painted on their flag, and no sign of the English Cross. Oh; the land is full of rebellion. It is full of it, and running over. (*The boys halt in front of the tent, and George approaches the sentinel, with the standard in his hand.*)

George. Is General Howe at home?

Sentinel. Who are you?

George. We are Boston boys, Sir.

Sentinel. And what do you want here?

George. We come for our rights; and we wish to speak to the British general.

Sentinel. The British general has better business than listening to a parcel of ragamuffin little rebels; I shall do none of your messages.

George. As you please, Sir; but here we wait till we see General Howe. We *will* see him; and he *shall* do us justice.

All. Hurra! Hurra! Hurra!

Sentinel. That, you little rascals, would be to hang you and your cowardly countrymen. I suppose you are making all this fuss about the little dirty pond on the common, that don't at the best hold water enough to fill a sizeable Dutch milk pan.

All. Cowards, do you call us! Say it again if you dare. (*General Howe and one of his aids step out.*)

General. What is the matter here? why is this disturbance?

George. General Howe, we come to complain of the insults and the outrages of your soldiers. They break our kite strings, ruin our skating pond, and steal our drums from us. We have spoken more than once, to no purpose; and now we have come to say, that we cannot, and we will not endure it any longer.

General. (*Aside to his Aid.*) Good Heavens! liberty is in the very air, and the boys breathe it. (*To the Boys.*) Go my brave lads; you have the word of General Howe that your sports shall never be disturbed again, without punishment to the offender. Does that satisfy you?

George. Yes, General Howe; and in the name of my country I present you thanks.

General. No thanks; you are brave boys, you are English boys; I see plainly, you are English boys.

All. No Sir, Yankees—Yankees—Yankee boys, Sir. Hurra! Hurra! (*The drum strikes up, and the little band march off with flying colors.*)

LESSON XXVIII.

ALFRED THE GREAT.—AIKIN.

ALFRED, *King of England.*—GUBBA, *a Farmer.*—GANDELIN, *his Wife.*—ELLA, *an Officer of Alfred.*—SOLDIERS.

SCENE 1—*The Isle of Athelney.*

Alfred. How retired and quiet is every thing in this little spot! The river winds its silent waters round this retreat; and the tangled bushes of the thicket, fence it in from the attack of an enemy. The bloody Danes have not yet pierced into this wild solitude. I believe I am safe from their pursuit. But I hope I shall find some inhabitants here, otherwise I shall die of hunger.—Ha! here is a narrow path through the wood; and I think I see the smoke of a cottage rising between the trees. I will bend my steps thither. (*Going.*)

Gubba. (*Enters.*) Holloa! Holloa! Stranger!

Alfred. Good even to you, good man; do you live near?

Gubba. I do.

Alfred. Are you disposed to show hospitality to a poor traveler?

Gubba. Why truly there are so many poor travelers now-a-days, that if we entertain them all, we shall have nothing left for ourselves. However, come along to my wife, and we will see what can be done for you—come along.

WHEN a number of characters appear at the same time, it is important that they should be properly and tastefully grouped. The arrangement should be, at once, natural and picturesque. In the above example, Alfred, the person of greatest consequence, occupies a *central* position; next in rank, Ella, his faithful officer, is placed on the *right*; while the cottagers, Gubba and his wife, have their station on the *left*; the soldiers fill up the *back-ground*. The characters immediately in front, should stand in a line *not straight*, but somewhat *circular*. The *distances* between them should also be well preserved, leaving the hero of the scene and the other important personages, as conspicuous as possible. Alfred, inspirited by the news brought by Ella, has *thrown off his disguise*, and stands before the astonished and affrighted peasants, in all the dignity and distinction of their *king*. This attitude is appropriate to the last two lines of the piece—

> "Till dove-like peace return to England's shore,
> And war and slaughter vex the land no more."

SCENE 2—*Inside the Cottage.*

(*Gandelin busy in preparing cakes for Breakfast.—Enter Gubba and Alfred.*)

Gubba. Wife, I am very weary; I have been chopping wood all day.

Gandelin. You are always ready for your supper, but it is not ready for you, I assure you; the cakes will take an hour to bake, and the sun is yet high; it has not yet dipped behind the old barn. But who can you have with you, I trow?

Alfred. Good mother, I am a stranger, and entreat you to afford me food and shelter.

Gandelin. Good mother, quotha! Good wife, if you please, and welcome. But I do not love strangers, and the land has no reason to love them. It has never been a merry day for Old England since strangers came into it.

Alfred. I am not a stranger in England, though I am a stranger here; I am a true born Englishman.

Gubba. And do you hate those wicked Danes, that eat us up, and burn our houses, and drive away our cattle?

Alfred. I do hate them.

Gandelin. Heartily! He does not speak heartily, husband.

Alfred. Heartily I hate them; most heartily.

Gubba. Give me thy hand then; thou art an honest fellow.

Alfred. I was with king Alfred in the last battle he fought.

Gandelin. With king Alfred? Heaven bless him!

Gubba. What is become of our good king?

Alfred. Did you love him, then?

Gubba. Yes, as much as a poor man may love a king; and kneeled down and prayed for him every night, that he might conquer those Danish wolves: but it was not to be so.

Alfred. You could not love Alfred better than I did.

Gubba. But what has become of him?

Alfred. He is thought to be dead.

Gubba. Well, these are sad times; Heaven help us! Come, you shall be welcome to share the brown loaf with us; I suppose you are too sharp set to be nice.

Gandelin. Ay, come with us; you shall be as welcome as a prince! But hark ye, husband; though I am very willing to be charitable to this stranger,—it would be a sin to be otherwise,—yet there is no reason he should not do something to maintain himself: he looks strong and capable.

Gubba. Why that's true. What can you do, friend?

Alfred. I am very willing to help you in anything you choose to set me about. It will please me best to earn my bread before I eat it.

Gubba. Let me see. Can you tie up fagots neatly?

Alfred. I have not been used to it. I am afraid I should be awkward.

Gubba. Can you thatch? There is a piece blown off the cow-house yonder.

Alfred. Alas, I cannot thatch.

Gandelin. Ask him if he can weave rushes; we want some new baskets.

Alfred. I have never learned.

Gubba. Can you stack hay?

Alfred. No.

Gubba. Why, here's a fellow! and yet he hath as many pair of hands as his neighbors. Dame, can you employ him in the house? He might lay wood on the fire, and rub the tables.

Gandelin. Nay let him watch the cakes then, at the fire. I must go and milk the kine.

Gubba. And I'll go and stack the wood, since supper is not ready.

Gandelin. But pray observe, friend! do not let the cakes burn; turn them often on the hearth.

Alfred. I shall observe your directions. (*Exeunt Gubba and Gandelin.*)

Alfred. For myself, I could bear it; but England, my bleeding country, for thee my heart is wrung with bitter anguish!—From the Humber to the Thames, the rivers are stained with blood! My brave soldiers cut to pieces!—My poor people—some massacred, others driven from their warm homes, stripped, abused, insulted:—and I, whom Heaven appointed their sheperd, unable to rescue my defenseless flock from the ravenous jaws of these devourers!—Gracious Heaven! if I am not worthy to save this land from the Danish sword, raise up some other hero to fight with more success than I have done, and let me spend my life in this obscure cottage, in these servile offices; I shall be content, if England is happy. Oh! here come my blunt host and hostess.

Enter Gubba and Gandelin, with a pail of milk borne on her head.

Gandelin. Help me down with the pail, husband. This new milk, with the cakes, will make an excellent supper.

(*Goes to the fire for the cakes.*) (*Returning.*)

Gandelin. Mercy on us, how they are burnt! black as my shoe; they have not once been turned; you oaf, you lubber, you lazy loon——

Alfred. Indeed, dame, I am sorry for it; but my mind was full of sad thoughts.

Gubba. Come, wife, you must forgive him; perhaps he is in love. I remember when I was in love with thee——

Gandelin. You remember!

Gubba. Yes, dame, I do remember it, though it is many a long year since; my mother was making a kettle of furmety——

Gandelin. Pry'thee, hold thy silly tongue, and let us eat

our suppers; come, friend, sit down. (*They sit. Gandelin distributes the basins, cakes, &c. They eat a short time in silence.*)

Alfred. How refreshing is this new milk, and this wholesome bread.

Gubba. Eat heartily, friend. Where shall we lodge him, Gandelin?

Gandelin. We have but one bed, you know; but there is fresh straw in the barn.

Alfred. (*Aside.*) If I shall not lodge like a king, at least I shall lodge like a soldier. Alas! how many of my poor soldiers are stretched on the bare ground!

Gandelin. What noise do I hear? It is the trampling of horses. Good husband, go and see what is the matter.

Alfred. Heaven forbid my misfortunes should bring destruction on this simple family! I had rather have perished in the wood.

Gubba returns, followed by Ella, with his sword drawn, and Soldiers.

Gandelin. Mercy defend us—a sword!

Gubba. The Danes! The Danes! O do not kill us.

Ella. (*Kneeling.*) My liege, my lord, my sovereign; have I found you?

Alfred. (*Embracing him.*) My brave Ella!

Ella. I bring you good news, my sovereign; your troops that were shut up in Kinwith castle, made a desperate sally. The Danes were slaughtered. The fierce Hubba lies gasping on the plain.

Alfred. Is it possible! Am I yet a king?

Gubba and Gandelin. The king!

Ella. Their famous standard, the Danish raven, is taken; their troops are panic-struck; the English soldiers call aloud for Alfred. Here is a letter which will inform you of more particulars. (*Gives a letter.*)

Gubba. (*Aside.*) What will become of us! Ah dame, that tongue of thine, that tongue of thine has undone us!

Gandelin. O, my poor dear husband! we shall all be hanged, that's certain. But who could have thought it was the king?

Gubba. Why, Gandelin, do you see, we might have guessed he was born to be a king, or some such great man, because, you know, he was fit for nothing else.

Alfred. (*Coming forward.*) God be praised for these tidings! Hope is sprung up out of the depths of despair. O, my friend! shall I again shine in arms,—again fight at the head of my brave Englishmen,—lead them on to victory. Our friends shall now lift their heads again.

Gandelin. Ah, husband, what will become of us!

Ella. Yes, you have many friends, who have long been obliged, like their master, to skulk in deserts and caves, and wander from cottage to cottage. When they hear you are alive, and in arms again, they will leave their fastnesses, and flock to your standard.

Alfred. I am impatient to meet them; my people shall be revenged.

Gubba and Gandelin. (*Throwing themselves on their knees at the feet of Alfred.*) O, my lord——

Gandelin. We hope your Majesty will put us to a merciful death. Indeed, we did not know your Majesty's grace.

Gubba. If your Majesty could but pardon my wife's tongue: she means no harm, poor woman!

Alfred. Pardon you, good people! I not only pardon you, but thank you. Rise and be happy. You have afforded me protection in my distress; and if ever I am seated again on the throne of England, my first care shall be to reward your hospitality. (*Gubba and Gandelin appear delighted.*) I am now going to protect *you.* Come, my faithful Ella, to arms! to arms! My bosom burns to face once more the haughty Dane; and here I vow to Heaven, that I will never sheathe the sword against these robbers, till either I lose my life in this just cause, or

Till dove-like peace return to England's shore,
And war and slaughter vex the land no more.

CLASS OR CONCERT SPEAKING.

The *frontispiece* exhibits a class of *seven* boys arranged for this exercise, but any number varying from *twelve* to *twenty* will be convenient, if the platform allow of their being properly placed. Even a larger number might be taught with advantage. At a recent exhibition, a class of more than *seventy* little fellows, from *six* to *twelve* years old, declaimed in this way, and their performance elicited much applause. In the first place, the piece to be spoken, should be *well committed to memory* by *every* pupil. The instructor then, standing in *front of the class,* speaks the first sentence—or as much of it as he thinks proper—giving the *appropriate gesticulation.* The pupils immediately follow him, copying his tones, look and action, as nearly as possible. Thus the whole piece is gone through with, over and over again. When the class are able to go through the whole piece properly, *by themselves,* they are heard *individually,* for the purpose of correcting such slight faults as may have escaped the instructor's notice in the *collective* training. These performances are animating, poetical, and beautiful. Having taught my pupils on this plan for more than *fourteen years,* I can assert it to be an excellent one; it produces great results with little labor.